WISDOM, INFORMATION, AND WONDER

What is knowledge for?

MARY MIDGLEY

ROUTLEDGE

London and New York

First published 1989
by Routledge
First published in paperback 1991
by Routledge
11 New Fetter Lane, London EC4P 4EE

Simultaneously published in the USA and Canada
by Routledge
29 West 35th Street, New York, NY 10001

Reprinted 1995

Transferred to Digital Printing 2004

British Library Cataloguing in Publication Data
A catalogue record for this book is available from the British Library

Library of Congress Cataloguing in Publication Data
A catalogue record for this book is available from the Library of Congress

ISBN 0–415–02830–2 (pbk)

FOR JUDY

CONTENTS

CONTENTS

PART 3 THE ROLE OF PHILOSOPHY

ACKNOWLEDGEMENTS

The ideas for this book first took shape in a course of Tennant Lectures which the University of St Andrews kindly invited me to give at their Centre for Philosophy and Public Affairs in 1984–5 on the topic 'Thought and the world'. I would like to thank everybody concerned with that course for all the help and stimulation they gave me. The book has, however, developed along a slightly different line from the lectures, attending less to current politics and more to the aims of thought, because it seemed to me that these must be discussed directly if my general point about the dangers of narrowness was to be made convincing. The only part of the lectures that recognizably remains here is part of chapter 23, still entitled 'Philosophizing out in the world'. A fuller version of this discussion had meanwhile appeared in *Social Research* (vol. 52, no. 3, autumn 1985) under the same title.

I am grateful to the editor and proprietors of that journal for permission to reprint parts of it here, and to the following for similar permission to reprint parts of other earlier articles which have also gone into this melting-pot:

1. To the editors and proprietors of *The Philosopher*, in which a version of 'Can specialization damage your health?' appeared in October 1983, and of the *International Journal of Moral and Social Studies*, in which a different version was published (vol. 2, no. 1, spring 1987). Relics of both now appear in chapters 5 and 6 of this book.
2. To the Oxford University Press, Inc., in New York, which printed 'Rival fatalisms: the hollowness of the sociobiology

debate' in *Sociobiology Examined*, edited by Ashley Montagu (© 1980 Ashley Montagu). Parts of this article now figure in chapter 7.
3. To the Royal Institute of Philosophy and the Cambridge University Press for 'The flight from blame', which appeared in *Philosophy* (no. 62, July 1987) and parts of which can now be found in chapters 14 to 16.

For help with the general theme, I have to thank very many friends and co-workers, especially, over many years, my colleagues in the admirable, small, Philosophy Department at the University of Newcastle upon Tyne, which has now been closed down, along with many other similar departments, mainly for the crime of being small. The reasons why I think that philosophy is something necessary to life, which ought to be more widely taught and studied rather than suppressed in this way, are explained in this book.

To turn to individuals: I am extremely grateful to Renford Bambrough, who has very kindly read the manuscript through, and has made some most helpful suggestions. I have also consulted, and have had most useful advice from, many others, notably Tom Baldwin, Nicholas Maxwell, Katherine Tait, Professor Maurice Wilkins, Professor Mary Clark, Jenny Teichman, Judith Hughes, Michael Bavidge, Ian Ground, and, most frequently, Geoffrey and David Midgley. Finally, I am pleased to join the growing band of writers who, instead of thanking their wives for dutifully doing the typing, can now thank their husbands for enthusiastically organizing and controlling the word processor.

Part One

CAN
SPECIALIZATION
DAMAGE YOUR
HEALTH?

Chapter One

MOON-MONSTERS AND
FREE PEOPLE

> It was indeed, said Er, a sight worth seeing, how the souls
> severally chose their lives.
>
> (Plato, *Republic*, book 10, 620)

MINDS IN JARS

In H. G. Wells's novel The First Men in the Moon, the human
explorer finds that the native lunar creatures vary greatly
among themselves in shape, size, gifts, character, and appearance. Though they all belong to a single ant-like species, each
one has been modified to fit its place in life exactly. In each,
some single organ is enlarged at the expense of all the others:

> 'Machine hands' indeed some of them are in actual
> nature – it is no figure of speech, the single tentacle of the
> mooncalf-herd is profoundly modified for clawing, lifting,
> guiding, the rest of them no more than necessary
> subordinate appendages to these more important
> parts. . . . The making of these various sorts of operative
> must be a very curious and interesting process. . . . Quite
> recently I came upon a number of young Selenites confined
> in jars from which only the forelimbs protruded, who
> were being compressed to become machine minders of a
> special sort. The extended 'hand' in this highly developed
> system of technical education is stimulated by irritants and
> nourished by injection, while the rest of the body is
> starved. . . . It is quite unreasonable, I know, but such
> glimpses of the educational methods of these beings
> affect me disagreeably. I hope, however that may pass off,

3

and I may be able to see more of this aspect of their wonderful social order. That wretched-looking hand-tentacle sticking out of its jar seemed to have a sort of limp appeal for lost possibilities; it haunts me still, although of course it is really in the end *a far more humane proceeding than our earthly method of leaving children to grow into human beings and then making machines of them.* (Emphasis mine)

The problem that Wells so sharply outlined in those last words is still with us. It is the subject of this book. All human advance needs specialization, yet this specialization conflicts with individuality. Both trends are necessary. In every growing civilization the various types of work, and the ways of life that go with them, grow ever more elaborate and diverge further and further from each other. Indeed, this constant forking is part of what we mean if we say that a civilization is growing at all, that it is not stagnant. But it forces the people involved to pursue increasingly different ideals. And there is one essential human ideal – the ideal of wholeness and balance of faculties – from which they are all constantly being driven further and further away.

Yet they are all originally whole people, and their range of personal needs does not necessarily narrow to fit this situation. The Selenite solution to this painful problem has appealed to many thinkers besides Wells and his explorer Cavor. It is the behaviourist one displayed in *Brave New World*. If only we could somehow phase out individuality – if people could be conditioned early enough in life to want nothing but what they get from their social role – then harmony would be easy. It could even be had without great spiritual sacrifice if each individual would only identify so completely with the whole as to share fully in the common experience. Each would then get all other fulfilments at second hand. Our inner lives would be actually wider and richer than they are at present – not narrower as they tend to be now for very specialized people.

THE CORPORATE DREAM

This ambitious project has tempted many large-scale theorists, from Plato to B. F. Skinner and beyond. But its unreality is clear enough when we attend to the actual difficulties of education.

Children cannot really be brought up in jars. Individuality cannot be trained out of us like a bad habit. Either it persists as the mainspring of our energies or, if it is crushed, its collapse destroys the rest of our capacities. Human beings, in fact, are not blank paper at birth and cannot be conditioned to be social insects. The selfless communal consciousness which perhaps pervades a beehive is simply not an option for us.

It is true, of course, that the nearest thing to jar-imprisonment which is possible for humans does work up to a point. People who are brought up with only one option before them will usually pursue that option, and make the best of it. Thus a firmly imposed caste system, such as the Indian one, no doubt produces many reasonably contented potters, dancers, cultivators, and the rest. But its stability is only that of a widely accepted compromise, not of a true solution. Wasteful discontent and neurosis are still likely to prevail at all levels. Discord, both between individuals and within them, is still an everyday fact of life.

For us here and now, of course, this way of resolving the dilemma by conditioning is not usually supposed even to be thinkable. Novels depicting it, such as *Brave New World*, are mostly meant as warnings, not as models. But we need to think about this unthinkable project here, because it is bound to tempt us when we begin to look at the other horn of the dilemma. Wells was not just being perverse when he cast longing glances towards collectivity and the mystic unification of human life. Nor were Plato and Hegel and the other organic theorists who had done the same before him. They were all responding to the endless wasteful discord and confusion which actually reign in human affairs. The wish for harmony which guided them is a sane and valid human wish, flowing from quite as deep a level of our being as the need for individuality. Life among social mammals and birds always seems to be carried on in this dialectical way, in very incomplete harmony arising out of conflict, rather than by the more whole-hearted self-submergence of the social insects.

If, then, we cannot cure people of being individuals, can we start at the other end of the problem and avoid dividing our labour in the way that makes so much specialization necessary? Small and simple societies do indeed do this to some extent, but it is hard to see how larger ones could manage it. For any purpose beyond the barest human subsistence, we need work which splinters us into groups. The question is simply, how can we best guard against the dangers this brings?

THE FRAGMENTATION OF KNOWLEDGE

The best-known and most obviously sinister of these dangers is indeed the condition of the 'machine hands' – people who get stuck with arduous, boring, and undervalued work, work that nobody wants to do. But this danger does not stand alone. Others as pernicious are linked to it and block our efforts to deal with the whole tangle. In particular, there is a danger at the other end of the spectrum which needs attention. It lies in the condition of people whose work is officially very highly valued indeed. It is the effect of specialization on those who pursue knowledge.

To be alarmed at this effect is not to cast doubts on the value of pursuing knowledge for its own sake. Accepting that ideal entirely, we can still ask, 'In what sense is a thing known if five hundred people each know one constituent of it and nobody knows the whole?' Or again: what if this truth has a thousand constituents and half of them are not now known to anyone, but only stored in libraries? What if all of them exist only in libraries? Is it enough that somebody knows how to look them up if they should ever be needed? Indeed, is it enough that this person has access to a system which will look them up? Does the enquirer even have to understand the questions which these truths would answer? (Knowing what the questions are is a very important element in real knowledge.) What is needed if something is to count as being known at all?

This question has long been an important one, but recent developments in the sheer quantity of academic output have made it even more pressing. It is now claimed – and claimed by some as a triumph of progress – that human knowledge is doubling itself exponentially every seven years, a process held to have begun in the late 1960s.[1] The grounds given for this are that the number of scientific papers published in the world is increasing at this rate. Does anybody suppose that the reading-time available has increased so as to allow all this stuff to be read and digested? All academic departments are now bombarded with floods of incoming articles, only a tiny proportion of which could they possibly read, even if they did nothing else – whereas in fact they must find time to do their own work as well. The main effect of this flood of paper (apart from exhausting the world's forests) must therefore be to pile up articles which, once they are published, nobody reads at all.

Those who welcome this expansion say that this difficulty will be met by increasing the number of scientists so that the supply of readers will be large enough to keep up with the flood. But, even if this could be done, the trouble is not only that these scientists too, in their turn, will also write papers. It is the one just mentioned – that, if the knowledge provided is split up among too many recipients, it no longer constitutes knowledge at all. The strange policy at present favoured for our universities, of exalting research over teaching, simply means that this unusable store will be increased still faster, while the process of educating people to think about the knowledge they have will be starved and downgraded. Since the current plan also separates research institutions from teaching ones, it entails starving the researchers too of the essential stimulus that teaching so notoriously gives. Much the quickest way to find out that you do not understand something properly is to try to explain it to somebody else, and this has traditionally been the way in which difficult knowledge has been kept alive, working, and fertile – as much in the physical sciences as elsewhere.[2]

LIVING OR DEAD?

Einstein was much concerned about this problem. He wrote, 'Knowledge exists in two forms – lifeless, stored in books, and alive, in the consciousness of men. The second form of existence is after all the essential one; the first, indispensable as it may be, occupies only an inferior position.'[3] Was Einstein right? If he was wrong, then we can stop worrying about this question and about many others as well. The libraries need then never be visited again except to fetch bits of useful information, as one goes to a shop to fetch butter, and all research not reasonably likely to be useful could be dropped. This conclusion is not a welcome one, but the other alternative is disturbing too. If Einstein was right, then our knowledge ought surely to be something alive in our consciousness. It should be working there, which means it must work as part of us. The memory-man at the fair cannot be our ideal model, however infallible his recall may be. Merely holding information as an inert piece of property, or handing it on like a dead fish to students, cannot be enough.

Academics are often aware of this problem. But they tend to speak of it resignedly as something quite insoluble. They often believe that the mere recent increase in the amount of knowledge inevitably involves its continual subdivision into smaller and smaller fractions distributed among more and more holders. 'The days of the Renaissance polymath are past,' they say; 'greater riches now demand a less unified kind of safe-keeping.'

If this gloomy conclusion were true, it would mean that we have moved into the condition of misers whose wealth has become so cumbrous that they must lock it away for safety and cannot actually use or enjoy it at all. (Perhaps indeed a miser may be defined as someone who has no idea what to do with any given resource except to store it.) As we shall see, the right use of knowledge is simply not compatible with this indefinitely continued subdivision. It involves understanding, which means treating knowledge as a whole. Without that wider outlook, the whole ideal of knowledge as it has always been understood evaporates.

But of course the wider outlook has not become impossible. What it requires is not that every scholar should master all the details of all subjects. That feat would have been impossible already in Renaissance times. What is needed is that all should have in their minds a general background map of the whole range of knowledge as a context for their own speciality, and should integrate this wider vision with their practical and emotional attitude to life. They should be able to place their own small area on the map of the world, and to move outside it freely when they need to. This is not even necessarily a particularly time-consuming business. It is a matter of a different general attitude much more than of detailed indoctrination. At an academic level, things could be dramatically improved if the first and last sections of papers, where the reasons for raising the question and the consequences of answering it are discussed, got much more attention, and the quality of reasoning shown in them was given far more weight than the mere number of papers published – a number which, considered as a measure of merit, is of little more value than the number of the writer's hairs. More widely, however, much of the change could be achieved in childhood simply by attending to the questions which children spontaneously ask, and to a range of other wide questions which link these spontaneous questions together. Once this is done, it saves a great deal of time in detailed teaching. Details make much better sense when they have a context, and what makes sense is far easier to remember. For the point is not just that different specialities need to be related to each other. It is that they all need to be related to everyday thinking, and made responsible to it. They must even acknowledge their own emotional aspect – which is invariably present – and relate that to everyday feeling. All this is of course disturbing, since remoteness from everyday thought and feeling, or even actual contempt for them, is often one of the first things that higher education seems to teach people. The reasons why I think this apparently awkward suggestion has to be made, and the ways in which it can finally come to seem less outrageous, will I hope emerge in the course of this book.

STRANGE JOURNEY, STRANGE CONCLUSION

Indefinitely increasing narrowness of specialization is not, in fact, an inevitable effect of increasing knowledge. It is largely a historical accident, helped on by various chance features of modern life, notably in the way universities are organized. It is a good deal more marked in North America than in Europe, and more so still in Britain. It has, unluckily, received a bizarre boost lately from the wide use of computer jargon, which (reasonably enough for its own purposes) treats knowledge simply as a pile of loose bits of information. The strange effect of trying to combine this notion with a traditional exaltation of knowledge can be seen in the euphoric conclusion to a recent book about the Anthropic Principle. The authors describe the grand climax of the whole cosmic process thus:

> At the instant the Omega Point is reached, life will have gained control of all matter and all forces not only in a single universe, but in all universes whose existence is

9

logically possible. Life will have spread into all spatial regions in all universes which could logically exist, *and will have stored an infinite amount of information*, including all bits of knowledge which it is logically possible to know. *And this is the end.*[4]

In case there is any doubt about the importance of this event, a footnote adds that 'A modern-day theologian might wish to say that the totality of life at the Omega Point is omnipotent, omnipresent, and omniscient.' By this storing of information, the universe has, in fact, become God.

This passage is evidently not meant to be a modest, reductive, cautious prediction. Yet it names as the end and purpose of everything the mere storing of information. To store something is to put it by for future use. There are indeed people whose only idea of what to do with information is to store it in this way. Dickens describes one of them in *Our Mutual Friend* – the gloomy schoolmaster, Bradley Headstone:

He had acquired mechanically a great store of teacher's knowledge. He could do mental arithmetic mechanically, sing at sight mechanically, blow various wind instruments mechanically, even play the great church organ mechanically. From his early childhood up, his mind had been a place of mechanical stowage. The arrangement of his wholesale warehouse, so that it might be always ready to meet the demands of retail dealers – history here, geography there, astronomy to the right, political economy to the left ... the lower mathematics, and what not, all in their several places – this care had imparted to his countenance a look of care.... There was a kind of settled trouble in his face.... He always seemed to be uneasy lest anything should be missing from his mental warehouse, and taking stock to assure himself.[5]

Mr Gradgrind in *Hard Times*, who believes that education should impart nothing but facts, is another victim of this habit of mind. And Wells's Selenites too have of course their special caste of memory-experts, who are able, since they have no skulls, to expand their brains almost indefinitely for this useful purpose. On the moon, therefore:

10

There are no books, no records of any sort, no libraries or inscriptions. All knowledge is stored in distended brains, much as the honey-ants of Texas store honey in their distended abdomens. . . . [These beings] for the most part are rapt in an impervious and apoplectic complacency, from which only a denial of their erudition can rouse them. . . . Some of the profounder scholars are altogether too great for locomotion, and are carried from place to place in a kind of sedan tub, wobbling jellies of knowledge that enlist my respectful astonishment.[6]

The picture is familiar enough. But how could it represent an ideal, how could it have any place in what is supposed to happen at the stupendous Omega Point? We are talking here about the apex of the whole cosmic process, the moment that makes it all worth while. The end has now been reached. What was the point of it all? If in any sense that point is knowledge, this knowledge will have to be something very different from an information store. To consider what it might be, we will probably do best to leave the cosmic perspective for the moment and return to more familiar ground.

Chapter Two

WISDOM AND CONTEMPLATION

A thing, then, that every soul pursues as the end of all her actions, dimly divining its existence, but perplexed and unable to grasp its nature with the same clearness and assurance as in dealing with other things, and so missing whatever value those other things might have – a thing of such supreme importance is not a matter about which those chosen Guardians of the whole future of our commonwealth can be left in the dark.

(Plato, Republic, book 6, 505)

KNOWLEDGE AT WORK

In our thinking today, what does that 'live working' of knowledge that Einstein mentioned involve? On this point, we shall need to pay special attention to the views of scientists, simply because the idea of 'science' is now much the most influential model held up for intellectual enquiry in general. This idea of science is not actually at all a clear one. It groups together a wide range of physical sciences, which vary greatly among themselves in their nature, methods, and functions, not to mention an uneasy annexe for the 'social sciences', which are visibly rather different again. All the same, as an ideal, the notion of 'science' as a single model, giving laws to all other kinds of organized thought, is today a predominant one. And it is for 'science' as so conceived that the kind of specialization we have been discussing is above all accepted and defended. Yet in this area the notion of pure knowledge as a self-justifying end in itself is also strongly proclaimed and honoured. So it becomes important for us to understand just what kind of an end contemporary scientists take knowledge to be. How do they view it?

Current scientists disagree remarkably about this from those past philosophers – such as Plato, Aristotle, and Spinoza – who called forth and established that special respect for knowledge which is such a marked characteristic of our culture. Those philosophers thought that the aim was contemplation itself – the aim not merely of all discovery but of life itself. For them, knowledge was simply an aspect of wisdom. It was part of an understanding of life as a whole, out of which a sense of what really mattered in it would become possible. Knowledge indeed had the same goal as love; contemplation was the highest human happiness. Thus Aristotle, at the end of a book devoted to the question of what the final goal of human effort is, concludes that it must be an activity of 'the best thing in us'. (Like Einstein, he said explicitly that it could not be a mere state; it had to be an active working.) He goes on:

> Whether it be reason or something else which is thought
> to be our natural ruler and guide, and to take thought of
> things noble and divine – whether it be itself also divine
> or only the most divine element in us – the activity of this
> in accordance with its proper virtue will be happiness. . . .
> The pursuit of this is thought to offer pleasures marvellous
> for their purity and their enduringness, and it is to be
> expected that those who know will pass their time more
> pleasantly than those who enquire.[1]

And again:

> (Thought) is *active* when it *possesses* its object. Therefore
> the possession rather than the receptivity is the divine
> element which thought seems to contain, and the act of
> contemplation is what is most pleasant and best.[2]

Here the idea of possession is explicitly made an active one, distinct from mere storing, and consisting in the interaction between the mind and what it contemplates. Similarly Plato, while he praises the intellectual life as central for human existence, insists that certain aspects of that life stand out as furnishing the point for the rest. Not everything is equally worth knowing, and there are some central, architectonic forms of knowledge without which others would have no value. Knowledge about what goodness means must be the centre, because it is what shows the point of all other knowledge, indeed of all other activity. At a minimal level, without touching on the religious awe that was crucial for Plato, this means that our sense of value-contrasts is needed for the very possibility of our perceiving anything else. The polarity of good and bad is an essential dimension of our world, the condition of our knowing it at all. The value of understanding the difference between good and bad cannot therefore be reduced to, and equated with, the value of any other particular thing, not even of knowledge. It has a different kind of place in the world and in our thinking. This is what makes Plato compare goodness to the sun, which is the source both of life itself and of the light which makes it possible for us to gain knowledge of life:

> This, then, which gives to the objects of knowledge their
> truth and to him who knows them his power of knowing, is
> the Form or essential nature of Goodness. It is the cause
> of knowledge and truth; and so, while you may think of it
> as an object of knowledge, you will do well to regard it as
> something beyond truth and knowledge, and, precious as
> both are, of still higher worth.[3]

Plato therefore sees all other studies as simply parts of the contemplation of goodness and stages towards its greater fullness:

> This is the right way of approaching and being initiated
> into the mysteries of love, to begin with examples of beauty
> in this world, and using them as steps to ascend
> continually with that absolute beauty as one's aim, from one
> instance of physical beauty to two and from two to all,
> then from physical beauty to moral beauty, and from moral
> beauty to the beauty of knowledge, until from knowledge
> of various kinds one arrives at the supreme knowledge
> whose sole object is that absolute beauty, and knows at
> last what absolute beauty is.[4]

Thus Plato, and it was from this base that he and Aristotle launched the whole enterprise of organized European scholarship, and convinced the world of its importance. By contrast, present- day scientists tend to say little about contemplation, and also to exalt discovery over knowledge. Their typical view is probably the one expressed by the sociobiologist Edward O. Wilson when he writes:

> Newly discovered truths, and not truth in some abstract sense alone, are the ultimate goal and yardstick of the scientific culture. Scientists do not discover in order to know; they know in order to discover. Humanists are the shamans of the intellectual tribe, wise men who interpret knowledge and transmit the folklore, rituals and sacred texts. Scientists are the scouts and hunters. No one rewards a scientist for what he knows. Nobel prizes and other trophies are bestowed for the new facts and theories he brings home to the tribe.[5]

THE FINAL FATE OF FACTS

But does the tribe receive them? These new discoveries are often barely intelligible to those outside their discoverer's field. What actually happens to these products of his bow and spear? Are they merely displayed in the tribal long-house to impress visitors? Do they just become known facts for a few, boring background furniture in which nobody is much interested and for which nobody is honoured? Does anybody really want them?

It is worth considering here a painful incident described at the end of Apsley Cherry-Garrard's book, *The Worst Journey in the World*. That book tells of the long, gruelling, winter journey undertaken during Scott's last Antarctic expedition by Cherry-Garrard, Bowers, and Dr Wilson. They risked their lives struggling through cold, dark, and inhospitable terrain in a desperate effort to bring back the first specimens ever secured of the emperor penguin's eggs. In Cherry-Garrard's opinion, the journey broke his own health and that of his two companions, contributing to their subsequent death on the main polar expedition and so to the loss of its other members. The winter journey did, however, bring back three eggs, of which two were later found to have been broken. When the one remaining egg reached England, Cherry-Garrard, as the only survivor, was left to take it to the Natural History Museum. But, when he arrived there, nobody seemed to know anything about the egg or to be in the least interested in receiving it. After waiting around for some time, he finally left it with some unconcerned official, and went his way, wondering bitterly about the purposes of science.

Who wants that egg? Where is the pay-off? Where do means in science finally give place to ends? These questions will take us deep into the framework of our whole way of thinking about value and desire. Before we have done with them, they will certainly need less crude formulations than those I have just used. All the same, crude formulations like these are not really misleading; they are needed to do justice to the urgency of the matter. The point is that objects and happenings which are not in the end ever felt and grasped in a suitable way by anybody – which never reach any sentient being at all – cannot understandably be said to have any value. Contributing to a purely abstract, imaginary entity called Science will not do instead. And to say this is not just vulgar hedonism or egoism. We do not have to suppose that the fulfilment we are looking for must always be 'pleasure'. That word is much too narrow to cover the aims involved. Hedonism has indeed altogether too narrow a notion of what an aim can be like. It conceives all aims on the 'jam tomorrow' pattern, as set products, to be manufactured by means which themselves have no value. This manufacturing pattern, which has been deeply woven into our current thinking, can only be used for the very simplest examples, such as buying a sunbed in order to bask on it, or food in order to eat it. For any more interesting activity there is no sharp division into valueless means and valued ends. Things which we desire as ends, entirely for their own sake, can be quite complex and prolonged states and activities, and can involve many others besides ourselves, extending an indefinite distance into the world around us. And this is still true in spite of the need for our own response to them which is the real point of hedonism.

Good examples of these complex wholes are the aims we set before ourselves in our personal relations, and also in the arts – in music, say, or in dancing or in mountaineering. In such matters, the fulfilment is distributed over a great spread of time and activity, much of which may be not at all pleasant. And the satisfaction seems to depend on regarding all these elements as parts of a whole, rather than as mere neutral means to a valued end. The means–end relation in time is often scarcely relevant here. The first bars of a song or a dance are not just a means to its ending, nor is the whole song just a means to the applause at the end, and certainly not just to the cheque that may follow it. The elements of the song form a whole, which again has its point as a part of various people's lives.

I think it is important to stress that the hedonistic formula is over-simple in this way, because otherwise our question about the value of the penguin's egg – that is, the value of knowledge itself – may indeed seem slick and insensitive. That question is not a demand for a simple hedonistic pay-off at a given moment. The gratification it looks for may be something much wider, slower, vaster, and more pervasive. But it still does have to touch down somewhere in the sentient lives of those who seek for it. Music recorded on tape and stored for ever unheard in the archives is music wasted. But so is music heard – or played – by people who cannot at all see the point of it. This is true of knowledge too. Crude though it may be to mention it, there does have to be a pay-off somewhere, and there really is – at least in the opinion of most of us – no supernatural being called Science to receive it. Where then does it come? We shall probably not get much help with this question by examining the Nobel prize system, which E. O. Wilson mentions. Systems of external reward are notoriously as crude and uncertain in their working as systems of punishment. The prizes, along with the dramatic discoveries they honour, may indeed form some kind of rough yardstick of scientific success, but they cannot possibly constitute what is seriously aimed at. Not surprisingly, yardstick and ultimate goal are by no means the same thing. We need to look deeper.

THE USES OF HUMANISM

Wilson makes the very interesting suggestion that the scientist is just the hunter, providing raw material for wisdom, but handing on this egg (as it were) to the actively wise humanist for opening and interpretation. This is a striking notion today. Humanists who may have got the impression that their scientific colleagues see them chiefly as frill-merchants, supplying lightweight luxur-ies for the mob and diverting the leisure of serious people, will no doubt be pleased to have Wilson's view in writing. But, if they accept this impressive role, they themselves will have some hard thinking to do. During the last century, many humanists too have become as eager as the scientists to disown even the quest for wisdom, let alone the responsibility for possessing and using it.

Thus, the great historian F. W. Maitland said that he never dealt in opinions, only in materials for the forming of opinions. Similarly, English-speaking moral philosophers spent the middle years of this century emphasizing the logical gap between facts and values, and insisting that it was none of their professional business either to make moral judgments themselves or to help other people to make them. Academic literary critics, too, have been moving steadily further and further away from their traditional function. They no longer want to be thought of as ready to help readers in using great literature to deepen and enlarge their vision of the world, a vision meant to be actively used and lived by. Instead, these critics are more and more occupied with highbrow technical battles between various theories of criticism – theories which are not even meant to concern anybody but other scholars.

There is a real change here. The point is no longer just that some parts of these studies are difficult and technical, under- standable only by those who specially study them. That has always been true, and it does not matter. What matters is the be- lief that professionals should be concerned only with these parts. On this view it is the mark of an untrained amateur to discuss – especially in public – any aspect of one's enquiry which could naturally interest what are significantly called 'lay people'. Knowledge is increasingly divorced from wisdom.

WHAT IS PROFESSIONALISM?

The notion of professional scholarship itself comes up for scrutiny here. In the last century, this notion has developed immensely, and of course has done a great deal of good. All studies have benefited from being put on a more rigorous basis – from the general acceptance that people who practise them should do it full-time, should be properly paid, and should qualify themselves by being duly tested. Ideally, these methods ought to produce ways of enquiry well-suited to the nature of each particular subject, and flowing from an understanding of its special problems. They are meant to exclude only what is irrelevant. Unfortunately, however, once a certain number of influential scholars have lost touch with the reasons why that particular study was worth pursuing in the first place, the system distorts itself. Fear of facing the large questions that are the study's central business grows acute, and begins to guide the workings of the academic machine. The cogs grind on, often more fiercely than before, but in increasingly strange directions. Now, as in the *Meistersinger*, the pedant Beckmesser grows liable, not just to exclude the unconventional young genius Walter from the Guild of Mastersingers, but to expel the real professional Hans Sachs as well. Einstein cannot get a job in physics; he is forced to go away and find himself a post in the Zurich Patent Office. Oxford philosophers ignore Collingwood, though he lives and works among them. The Scholar-Gipsy

Turns once to watch, while the thick snowflakes fall,
The line of festal light in Christ-Church hall –
– Then seeks his straw in some neglected grange.

Now this kind of ossification is an old danger, one which officially we all recognize. But in each age it takes special forms. In our own, there are peculiar features favouring it which are worth spelling out. The ancient, timeless side of the matter is indeed familiar. It is what Pope described at the end of the *Dunciad* as the Triumph of Dulness:

She comes, she comes; the sable throne behold
Of Night primeval, and of Chaos old
Before her Fancy's gilded clouds decay
And all its varying rainbows die away.
Wit shoots in vain its momentary fires,
The meteor drops, and in a flash retires.
See skulking Truth to her old cavern fled,
Mountains of casuistry heap'd o'er her head!
Philosophy, that lean'd on Heav'n before,
Shrinks to her second cause, and is no more.
Physic of Metaphysic begs defence,
And Metaphysic calls for aid on Sense!

19

See Mystery to Mathematics fly –
In vain! they gaze, turn giddy, rave and die.
Thy hand, great Anarch! lets the curtain fall,
And universal darkness buries all.

What shook Pope was not a decline of public interest in literature or learning. As he noted, in his day the quantity of both commodities around the place was increasing. So were the numbers of people employed on them. The trouble was a change in quality – an inner loss of direction which could make it all pointless. His complaint about dullness was of course not a frivolous demand for constant entertainment. It cried out simply that mental activities, unlike physical ones, cannot be carried on unless the people involved in them grasp the point of them, understand their purpose, and make that purpose their own. Since his time, that task has steadily become harder. The big, corporate, intellectual enterprises within which we all work are always expanding, so that the disproportion between each detailed project and the whole which gives it its point is always growing larger. Yet the need to grasp that point is as urgent as ever. If the citizens really stop trying to envisage their whole city, total pointlessness does indeed descend, which is what the Triumph of Dulness means. Dullness is the enemy, not of frivolity – it is easy to be both dull and frivolous – but of wisdom.

IS WISDOM FORGOTTEN?

We should note here, before going any further, the possibility that something much larger and more serious is wrong with this narrowed use of the intellect than has so far been mentioned. In an admirable book called *From Knowledge to Wisdom*, Nicholas Maxwell has argued that the radical, wasteful misdirection of our whole academic effort is actually a central cause of the sorrows and dangers of our age. Of course (he remarks) there are other things which one might naturally name as the main source of our troubles. One could, for instance, reasonably pick on 'the inertia of our institutions, which renders them, and us, incapable of responding to the crisis'. But, he adds,

the intellectual/institutional inertia of the academic
enterprise is, in a major way, responsible for the general
inertia of institutions. . . . Granted that enquiry has as its

basic aim to help enhance the quality of human life, it is actually profoundly and damagingly *irrational, unrigorous*, for enquiry to give intellectual priority to the task of improving knowledge. . . . Problems of knowledge and understanding need to be tackled as rationally subordinate to intellectually more fundamental problems of living. . . . The fundamental intellectual task of a kind of enquiry that is devoted, in a genuinely rational and rigorous way, to helping us improve the quality of human life, must be to create and make available a rich store of vividly imagined and severely criticized possible actions, so that our capacity to act intelligently and humanely in reality is thereby enhanced.[6]

The point is related to the one that Marx expressed so disastrously badly when he said that what is necessary is not to understand the world, but to change it. Marx's remark misses two vital points: first, that proper understanding is a condition of proper change, not an alternative to it, and, second, that what needs doing in the world is as often concerned with preserving it as with changing it. All the same, so far as Marx meant that what is necessary is not just to talk about the world, or to be informed about it, but to act rightly in it – 'acting' being taken to include inner as well as outer action – he was surely right. Thinking out how to live is a more basic and urgent use of the human intellect than the discovery of any fact whatsoever, and the considerations it reveals ought to guide us in our search for knowledge, as they ought in every other project we pursue. In arguing this point – which Kant would have found congenial – Maxwell proposes that we should replace the notion of aiming at knowledge by that of aiming at wisdom. I think this is basically the right proposal. I suspect, however, that there is, in a sense, even more wrong with the current notion of aiming at knowledge than Maxwell has noticed. Even on its own terms, this notion does not make sense. It presupposes a notion of knowledge that is unrealistic and self-defeating. It is not – what I think Maxwell sometimes suggests – a wrong but genuine option, it is no sort of option at all.

This book will be much occupied with trying to explore why that is so. I think we need to develop gradually the notion of wisdom which this approach involves, and to grasp better its proper

21

relation to knowledge. These are not easy problems. Perhaps the essential point for the moment is that 'knowledge' is not the name of a distinct, modern, and enlightened ideal which has superseded wisdom as the goal of all our efforts. Knowledge can indeed be an ideal, an end in itself, not merely a means to other ends. But it has then to be seen as one among other human ends, as having its own place in our priority system as a whole. If this is not done, knowledge itself is insulted, and the search for it is distorted. Moreover, I think Maxwell is surely right in saying that this distortion, because it wastes our intellectual powers, has played a serious part in distorting our lives.

Chapter Three

THE CITY OF ORGANIZED
THOUGHT AND ITS
TOWN-PLANNERS

And the king commanded, and they brought great stones,
costly stones, and hewed stones, to lay the foundation of the
house.

(First Book of Kings 5.17)

THE CLAIM TO RULE

People who draw attention to dangers like these must of course
place themselves firmly within the threatened system, not sneer
from the sidelines. I write here, not as a detached critic, but as a
committed, professional academic, and – to name my urban
district – as an English analytic or linguistic philosopher, trained
in Oxford. I am deeply concerned about certain things which
have gone wrong with my native kind of philosophy in this
century, and also about public misunderstandings of it. I shall
try in part 3 of this book to say something about what it really is,
why it is actually badly needed today, and how it can best be
used.

The main problems discussed in this book do not, however,
just concern professional philosophy, nor any other special
discipline. They are ones which visibly affect all of us who
frequent and use the city of organized thought at all – teachers,
researchers, students, writers, past students, and general con-
sumers of books and discussions. They are problems that already
worry many of us, and their effect does not stop even there. It
reaches beyond both us and our conscious involvement to the
background thinking of our age. It affects the whole value-
system, the hierarchy of ideals by which we all live.

Like other towns, the city of organized thought is not self-contained. It is shaped by and depends on a very large stretch of surrounding country – namely, the entire lives of the community which supports it and out of which it has arisen. In that territory in the last two centuries, some startling imperialistic claims have been made on behalf of our city. Attacks on traditional, God-centred value-systems have hailed it as a new, alternative centre of value – as it were, the new spiritual capital and seat of government. The kind of thought chosen for this task varies somewhat in different epochs, but of late the favoured candidate is usually named as 'science'. And, though this could be quite a wide term, it seems commonly to mean here only physical science – sometimes indeed apparently only physics itself.

These claims go far beyond the undoubted fact that modern physical science is indeed a tremendous and invaluable intellectual achievement. They put it forward as a source and model for all other thought. They have been widely made throughout most of this century, but I can only cite here a few typical examples. I take them from C. H. Waddington's book *The Scientific Attitude*, which was a somewhat euphoric best-selling manifesto, published in 1941, but no more euphoric than many others appearing before and after it. Waddington begins a challenging chapter called 'Art looks to science' thus:

> Wholehearted destruction and tentative reconstruction,
> that is how one can sum up cultural activities between the
> two wars. What I want to argue in this chapter is that the
> paramount influence behind both these phases has been
> science. . . . Scientific thought has become the pattern for
> the creative activity of our age, our only mode of transport
> through the rough seas in front of us. . . . One is justified
> in saying that science is now in a position to become the
> leader of the humanities.[1]

The idea of such a 'leader' or 'mode of transport' is slightly mysterious, but frequent references to religion make it plain that the throne to which science has succeeded is conceived as the one now left vacant by theology, which used indeed once to be referred to as 'the queen of the sciences'. Later, Waddington stakes out his claim more comprehensively:

24

Science *by itself* is able to provide mankind with a way of life which is, firstly, self-consistent and harmonious, and, secondly, free for the exercise of that objective reason on which our material progress depends. So far as I can see the scientific attitude of mind is *the only one* which is, at the present day, adequate in both these respects. There are many other worthy ideals which might supplement it; but I cannot see that any of them could take its place as the basis of a progressing and rich society.[2] (Emphasis mine)

Waddington, an evolutionary biologist, used the word 'science' in a wide sense, including under it Marxist and Freudian ideas and anything else which struck him as having the right sort of smell to be regarded as 'scientific'. Like many other people who talk in this way, he put some surprising things in this box – for instance, early twentieth-century architecture[3] and 'making the tropics fit for civilized life'.[4] This comprehensiveness enabled him – and his Marxist contemporaries such as Bernal and J. B. S. Haldane – still to regard science as a form of wisdom rather than as a rival and finally an up-to-date substitute for it. Since his day, however, in reaction against these ambitious Marxist claims, a much narrower notion of science has come to the fore – a notion whose paradigms are found in physics, and indeed centrally in highly specialized areas of physics which are quite incomprehensible to most people. When 'science' is taken in this kind of sense, the idea that it is somehow the supreme form of human thought becomes much stranger.

WHAT KIND OF ORDER?

This supremacy of science is not, of course, conceived just as a crude political rule of scientists over the rest of the population, though that ambition too was sometimes expressed. Intellectually, it is the imposition of a unified order on all thought, and thereby on all life. Waddington thought of this order simply as a general insistence on parsimony, on cutting out the unnecessary and concentrating on the essential. But decisions about what is or is not essential have to be made, and – as the examples of architecture and tropic-civilizing show – they are not automatically made rightly merely because they strike their makers as parsimonious. Such drastic decisions take sides. In tidying up the rich chaos of our life and thought, they attempt to impose a single kind of order, a standardized pattern that will completely organize the world. Is any such tidy completeness possible? Is it even a reasonable aim?

Wittgenstein later considered this question deeply in relation to various attempts that were being made to standardize the exuberant varieties of human language – an enterprise, as he noticed, not much less ambitious than that of standardizing the whole of life. He commented shrewdly:

> Ask yourself whether our language is complete; – whether it was so before the symbolism of chemistry and the notation of the infinitesimal calculus were incorporated into it; for these are, so to speak, suburbs of our language. (And how many houses or streets does it take before a town begins to be a town?) Our language can be seen as an ancient city; a maze of little streets and squares, of old and new houses, and of houses with additions of various periods; and this surrounded by a multitude of new boroughs with straight regular streets and uniform houses.[5]

Human language, and with it human life, simply does have this kind of complexity. It is an organic thing. It is capable of order – indeed in many ways it exhibits and needs order – but the kinds of order possible for it vary in various areas. These different kinds of order can be related, but they cannot be mutually reduced except by procrustean distortion. The recognition of this awkward fact tends to be staunchly resisted by people engaged in theoretical system-building. Intellectual architects who have succeeded in introducing some impressive kind of order into a particular area of thought are always tempted to extend it more widely. In this century, admirers of just those scientific suburbs that Wittgenstein names have been among those most struck with this passion for spiritual town-planning. They are not satisfied with the undoubted fact that their own habitations are wonderful – that modern physical science constitutes, by common consent, a sublime and splendid achievement. They want to place it above all other such achievements. They have conceived the ambition of knocking

26

down the rest of the city and rebuilding it in that special image – with unfailingly straight, regular streets and uniform houses.

THE DESPOTIC PATTERN

Thus arises the scientific slum-clearance model of philosophical reform. In general, it is worth noticing how influential the metaphor of building has been in our thought since the Renaissance, and how steadily that metaphor – which seems on the face of it thoroughly co-operative and constructive – has leaned towards slum-clearance, and has therefore favoured dogmatism, disputation, and destruction. Wittgenstein improved things very greatly when he moved away from this image towards a quite different range of metaphors concerned with finding one's way, with mapping and map-reading, and with generally seeing how to inhabit a piece of country or a city, rather than to create it from scratch. 'A philosophical problem has the form: "I don't know my way about." '[6] But the big change this involves has hardly yet been generally grasped; we must go back to it in part 3. Russell always remained committed to slum-clearance, while Wittgenstein (somewhat confusingly) was in his youth a drastic slum-clearer and became later a dedicated conservationist. He managed, first to produce the definitive version of the reductive, purifying enterprise (in his *Tractatus Logicophilosophicus*), and then to see its faults fully and to replace it in his maturity by the far richer, more flexible models just quoted.

Plainly, anyone who attempts the slum-clearance project has to face the dilemma just noticed about the meaning of 'science'. The terms and thought-patterns used in the physical sciences cannot be literally extended to cover all other topics. Either, then, the scientific model has to be conceived very widely, as it is in Marxism, thus losing all the rigour of its original scientific base, or it stays rigorous, and then it cannot really be extended very far. This difficulty, however, has not stopped many people today from embracing the second option, and hailing science of a highly esoteric kind, not just as the only proper form of thought, but also as the real centre and justification of human life. On this approach, all other forms of thought, such as would be needed to understand other subjects, are abandoned as

27

improper. This idea appears, for instance, very much as a matter of course at the end of the excellent popular book *The First Three Minutes* by the astrophysicist Steven Weinberg. Having dealt with the origins of the universe, Weinberg looks ahead and predicts that all earthly life will in the end become extinct. This seems to him to mean that all the values we now accept are empty and illusory. Yet he names a single exception, and ends his book thus:

> The more the universe seems comprehensible, the more it also seems pointless.
>
> But if there is no solace in the fruits of our research, there is at least some consolation in the work itself. Men and women are not content to comfort themselves with tales of gods and giants, or to confine their thoughts to the daily affairs of life; they also build telescopes and satellites and accelerators, and sit at their desks for endless hours working out the meaning of the data they gather. The effort to understand the universe is one of the very few things that lifts human life a little above the level of farce and gives it some of the grace of tragedy.[7]

Here science no longer figures as the constitutional sovereign leading the whole enterprise of human life to its proper conclusion, nor – in Waddington's other image – as a humble ship carrying it there, but as itself being the pearl of great price, the prize which gives point to all the rest of the enterprise, the solitary, set-apart bearer of pure value. How is this to be taken? Is it as if the whole city exists for the sake of the laboratories? If so, why? The phrase, 'understanding the universe' might of course mean something much wider than simply doing astro-physics. Weinberg might perhaps be willing to join us in considering what that much wider thing could be. But the obvious message of his words, and the one which most readers would naturally get from it, is that astrophysics, provided it is of the most fundamental kind, is all-sufficient. It alone (or almost alone – but we hear nothing about its possible companions) still has value, in a world from which all other value has been drained.

How could that be? This strange mixture of officially un-bounded pessimism about human values with a bold, dogmatic, exaltation of the scientific life plainly does not strike Weinberg as inconsistent or as needing any justification. It has in fact become a familiar view, widely professed among science-oriented people since Jacques Monod expressed it in *Chance and Necessity.*[8] Monod put together a seductive package of existentialist scepticism about all other human ideals and an uncriticized certainty about the value of his own professional ones. He thus unfurled a banner for unrepentant moral narrowness. His book endorsed as final a certain defensive move which people in confused times often feel driven to make temporarily – the move of withdrawing from all general thought about value-conflicts into the relative clarity of their own professional ethics.

This – to return to my image of the city – is as if townspeople responded to trouble in the countryside by withdrawing inside their walls, and to further trouble in other urban areas by retreating still further into their own well-lit suburbs. The relief is temporary, and the problem grows worse meanwhile. To apply the image: the city stands, not just for the community we all belong to, but also for the individual being of each one of us. Nobody is only a specialist. There are urgent questions to be answered about the relations between physical science and other kinds of thought, and between thought generally and the rest of life. One set of these questions – the outward ones about why society should support these enterprises at all – is beginning to get some attention again. But much less has so far been paid to the second set, arising internally for each one of us, about how the professional thinker within us relates to our various other selves – for instance, to the lover, parent, and friend, to the citizen, to the poet or mystic, and to the social being living in close and committed relations with so many other people and things. Rhetoric like Monod's, which treats the supremacy of scientific values over all others as already established, is useless for such questions.

Part Two

THE ROLE OF
SCIENCE

Chapter Four

SCEPTICISM AND PERSONAL IDENTITY

The pupils, whether or not they expected a philosophy
that should give them, as that of Green's school had given
their fathers, ideals to live for and principles to live by,
did not get it; and were told that no philosopher (except of
course a bogus philosopher) would even try to give it. The
inference which any pupil could draw for himself was that
for guidance on the problems of life, since one must not
seek it from thinkers or from thinking, from ideals or
from principles, one must look to people who were not
thinkers (but fools), to processes that were not thinking
(but passion), to aims that were not ideals (but caprices),
and to rules that were not principles (but rules of
expediency). . . . The effect on their pupils was (how
could it not have been?) to convince them that philosophy
was a silly and trifling game, and to give them a lifelong
contempt for the subject.

(R. G. Collingwood, *Autobiography*, 48)[1]

THE ESCAPE INTO SCEPTICAL DESPAIR

Can we face these questions about priorities at all? Can we really
relate the various aspects of our lives in any way that makes
moral sense? The proposal that we might try to is bound to
surprise people brought up on the idea that it simply is not
possible to think effectively at all about problems of value. One
reason why Monod's evasion caught on so readily, and why its
hollowness has not yet been fully seen, is that this somewhat
superficial, unreal kind of moral scepticism is widespread now,

33

especially for talking purposes. It is not that people have really given up trying to deal intelligently with their moral problems, and certainly not that they have stopped arguing about them. In practice, we all constantly have to make choices about priorities – about the general direction in which life ought to go – and we use our heads in dealing with these choices as we do over any others. But we tend to quail at the idea that these choices commit us to some kind of general moral reasoning about what matters. We have been trained to talk as if valid reasoning is only possible inside certain narrow professional limits, primarily those of 'science'. We therefore often use a mask of general scepticism to avoid liability for our informal thoughts. We declare moral bankruptcy in advance. Existentialism, which was an ideology adapted for justifying this declaration, probably still has quite a deep influence today, though it is officially forgotten – a fate which often attends such fashionable doctrines. Monod certainly owes a great deal of his persuasiveness to its peculiar, melodramatic style. He constantly echoes Sartre and Camus. But existentialism itself is probably best seen as just a symptom – one way among many by which people have found it possible to escape from the excessive confusions of our culture, by dividing up their inner lives.

These declarations of sceptical bankruptcy cannot be seriously intended, because they are always selective. Here, as elsewhere, no sensible person actually wants the desolating pointlessness of full-time, impartial, all-round scepticism. We just want to kill certain inconvenient opposing views. This selectivity is nicely shown when students are starting courses in moral philosophy. They often plunge in with a good will and begin to reason well about matters they have clearly thought it their business to reflect on – punishment, say, or political freedom, or the position of women, or the sanctity of life. In fact, if they had not supposed these things to be worth reasoning about, they would hardly have signed up for such a course at all. But at a certain point, where unwelcome conclusions loom or they cannot quite see their way, they suddenly remark, with the smoothest possible gear-change, that of course it is impossible to reason at all on such matters, because they are entirely a matter of everybody's own subjective opinion. Thus their reasoning faculty – which has to do public business – washes its hands of the difficult problems by passing them to an inarticulate private self which is held to be accountable to nobody.

This move is so common, and so well understood to apply only to certain selected issues, that people do not usually see any difficulty about combining it with the definite moral views which they hold at other times, or with the habit of supporting those views by argument. Monod, for instance, recommends his 'ethic of knowledge' not just by pointing out that we can choose it freely (which is the only kind of testimonial really open to him) but also by praising it as 'objective' – as though the value of objectivity had itself somehow been objectively demonstrated. He adds for good measure that 'only the ethic of knowledge could lead to socialism' – as if the value of socialism too had somehow escaped the universal acid-bath.[2]

There is no point in sniping at such convenient inconsistencies, which are found everywhere. What matters is that the project of all-round moral scepticism is an unreal one. Nobody actually thinks that morality is just a matter of everybody's subjective opinion, because human life cannot be carried on at all without a wide measure of moral agreement. (Even in the Mafia, people have to have standards that they take for granted.[3]) And a great deal of that agreement has to be made articulate, although of course much of it is inarticulate or even unconscious. This articulated agreement is essential if we are to try – as we constantly must – to live and work together and to sort out important disagreements by talking about them. In this way, too, a certain amount of controlled change becomes possible. Disagreements can sometimes be used as dialectics, to hammer out a synthesis which is deeper than both its parents and can be more widely accepted. But these outer transactions are only possible if there is also a workable degree of inner unity, achieved by reasoning. Hearts without heads cannot do business together. Indeed it is not easy to see how they could control action at all.

IS IT KNOWLEDGE?

People often find it hard to be realistic about this today because they have an impression that all talk about moral questions is only an exchange of irrational feelings, containing nothing properly called truth or knowledge. Do we actually know that it is wrong to torture people merely for amusement, or can we do no more than express our personal dislike of the proposal? Are we merely blundering about by conjecture on such matters until perhaps science comes in with real knowledge to set us right? The emotive theory of ethics, which reduced all moral thinking to pure feeling, was part of a prolonged confusion about such matters. The concept of knowledge employed was both over-ambitious and – as we have already seen – actually distorted. It has been formulated in an unrealistic way in isolation from the web of concepts that it belongs to. This has led to strange distortions also on an even more important topic – namely, the nature of the knowing subject. A strange, isolated, specialized 'I' has had to be invented to own this precious knowledge. Descartes, who instituted a quite reasonable and modest search for new standards of certainty in science, also had the vision of something much grander that might lie beyond them – of an absolute, invulnerable certainty, an ideal form of knowledge which nothing could ever shake. This unreal vision has given endless trouble. It is not only excessive; it gives priority to the wrong sort of ambition. The kind of perfection at which the Cartesian project aims is the perfection of epistemic safety. It concentrates on knowledge, not because of any special view (such as Plato held) about what we need to know and why we need to know it, but because knowledge means security from error. By assuming that the possibility of error is the evil that must above all be avoided, it distracts us (among other things) from asking about the various reasons why knowledge can be important. And, as already mentioned, it systematically directs us away from interesting and important questions that possibly cannot be completely settled, and towards less interesting ones where the risk of error seems easier to control.

All this might not matter so much if the demand for unshakable certainty could be satisfied and then put aside. But it cannot. Its ideal is unattainable, going far beyond anything the sciences have ever delivered or could deliver. In all of them, since Descartes's time, beliefs which were thought to be unshak-able have been first shaken and then abandoned. The most striking cases of this are of course non-Euclidean geometries in mathematics and the effect of relativity theory and quantum mechanics on physics, but all the sciences have had similar experiences, which we overlook only by ignoring their history. The effect is to produce today in the sciences a strange jumble of confident dogmatism with extreme relativism, subjectivism, and other forms of scepticism when these difficulties are pointed out. Sociologists of science, in particular, sometimes talk as if the whole of modern science could be treated simply as an optional local fancy, much as some anthropologists used to treat the belief-systems of the 'primitive' peoples they observed. Our rigid inherited Cartesian framework has no place for different kinds and degrees of certainty, for a system which should be adjusted to the kinds of need served by different kinds of knowledge, just as the kinds of safety that we expect in other situations are adjusted to different kinds of dangers, and to the different resources we can draw on to meet them.

Many people have noticed that we need to break out of Descartes's framework; we will come back to the question of how to do it in part 3. This is a prime and urgent business of philosophy today, and the later Wittgenstein, if we can only follow him, is a very important guide in dealing with it. But the central point for now is undoubtedly that the concept in most need of our attention at the moment is not knowledge but meaning, and this is true not only in general reflection on these concepts but also, and more obviously, in particular applications of them. Where we are now inclined to ask 'Do we know that? How do we know it? Where are our proofs?' and to find no satisfactory answer, we would usually do well to ask first 'What do we mean by that?' If we can't answer that, we are not likely to get much further with any other enquiry. The concentration on meaning will make our thinking seem more like the attempt to make a good map by which we can find our way around, and much less like the attempt to manufacture a curious unassailable final product called a piece of certain knowledge.

If all this is right, there really is no substance in the dream, which has been influential as long as Descartes's methods have been dominant, that we can split our thought into two parts – science, which securely meets these high standards of certainty, and the rest, which is mere amateur bungling. The city cannot be divided like this. There are innumerable aspects of human experience besides the scientific one that we can perfectly well

37

discuss – not, indeed, ever expecting to say anything final and infallible about them, but still successfully communicating, establishing certain things, understanding each other to some extent, and managing to alter our lives sensibly in many ways in consequence. Our moral life is among these. And in all this communication, including that on moral subjects, the notions of truth and knowledge, understood in their ordinary, modest sense, have a minor but necessary part to play. For instance, we cannot afford to lose here the everyday distinction between knowing and not knowing what we ought to do. There are cases where we do know that it would be wrong to do a particular thing, and others where we really do not know this, and these are radically different kinds of case. If there were people who did not see any difference between them, they would not be intellectual moral sceptics, but incomplete people, of the kind sometimes called psychopaths. And this kind of knowledge is as capable as any other of being conveyed, expressed, supported, and deepened by arguments.

PEARLS OF GREAT PRICE: AIMS AND PERSONAL IDENTITY

This matter of moral scepticism is unfortunately not a side-issue, but a part of our main theme. We are asking about the value of 'science' and of knowledge generally – asking where that value resides, who receives it, and what it consists in. We are asking who wants the penguin's egg and why. Sceptics like Monod seem to offer us a way of dodging this question by outlawing it, along with all other questions about value. They treat the matter as involving merely a quirk of subjective taste. And they then surprisingly claim that we – whoever 'we' may be – have simply decided to choose science as a supreme value, which is an absurdly arbitrary answer. Why should we listen to these people rather than others, why should we not choose music or poetry, sex or personal affection, chess, child-rearing, religion, or football? And it is not even an intelligible answer, because unanswered questions still arise about the form in which this supreme value is supposed to be, so to speak, delivered, reaped, and accepted. This is a question that arises about any aim; it would arise about the other activities if one of them had been elected to the supreme position instead. If science is chosen, do all scientists share in the chosen fulfilment, or only the few who really understand its findings? Does fulfilment filter through in any way to the general public? And, for those who do share, what does the sharing consist in? Does it involve the whole self, or only some favoured part, for which all the rest can properly be neglected or even sacrificed? To apply these ruminations to our original problem: does it emerge that scientists should be prepared for their work by being brought up in jars? Or is there some reason why they will do that work even better if they are allowed to become, so far as possible, whole human beings?

This question is not just about the comparative value of pure and applied science, nor is it an attack on the notion that pure science has great value. That notion is indeed under illiterate attack at present, since it has been noticed that the sciences, equally with the humanities, do not always produce a quick buck by their work. But this makes it all the more urgent to understand what kind of value is actually involved here. Simply to say that curiosity is a strong natural human urge is not enough to explain this, more especially in an age when the very existence of such natural urges has been seriously questioned. Even if the urge is natural, it is only one such urge and it plainly is not necessarily all-conquering. Most human cultures have not found that their insatiable natural curiosity drove them on to invent science as we know it; they have placed curiosity elsewhere in their hierarchies of motivation. Indeed, mere curiosity, simply on its own, is not necessarily something that deserves great exaltation, as some acute contemporary scientists have pointed out. Thus Professor Maurice Wilkins, arguing impressively for responsibility in science on the ground that the scientific goal is really a reverent understanding of the universe, remarks:

> The poet Coleridge is said to have claimed that a scientist must love the object he studies, otherwise he could not respond to its true nature. I believe Coleridge's idea of love expresses the ideal scientific attitude as well as or better than the ideal of curiosity, which has been part of the scientific tradition of objective, value-free enquiry. Love includes curiosity, but curiosity need not include love. If

39

we eulogize curiosity, we run the risk of encouraging a
scientist to be like a child who, in its intense desire to
know, tears a butterfly to pieces.[4]

Similarly Sir George Porter, defending the ideal of pure
science in his 1987 address to the Royal Society, stressed the
same point about its nature:

Let us begin at the beginning. The ultimate and the
highest purpose of science is to understand ourselves and
our place in the universe. Far from being high-flown and
remote from everyday life, this purpose is primitive; every
child asks questions of the kind that the scientist asks.

And he added, quoting from Vanevar Bush:

Science has a simple faith . . . the faith that it is the
privilege of man to understand and that is his mission. Why
does the shepherd ponder the stars? Not so that he can
better tend his sheep. Knowledge for the sake of
understanding, not merely to prevail, that is the essence
of our being.[5]

Curiosity, in fact, easily shades into the desire for power and
becomes purely exploitative, though it is just as possible for it to
move the other way and be merged with admiration and respect.
Its value depends almost wholly on which of these paths it takes,
and then on the further goals to which those motives are
themselves directed. Many different kinds of value are liable to
be in conflict here, and reflections about different *kinds* of value,
rather than merely about different intensities, are difficult; they
could do with a lot more attention today. The economic
metaphor of value, price, and exchange tends to fix our
thoughts on mere intensity of desire and divert them away from
its nature. It is of course a useful and natural metaphor, because
saying how much we would give in exchange for some thing
conveys how strongly we desire it. Thus Jesus: 'the kingdom of
heaven is like unto a merchantman, seeking goodly pearls: Who,
when he had found one pearl of great price, went and sold all he
had, and bought it.'[6] The exchange, however, has to end
somewhere. What is bought is not just stored. It is at some point
actively received and inwardly used by people who would not

have given up so much to get it if they had meant merely to put it away. In some sense, they take it into themselves, interact with it, and let it affect their own nature.

THE HUNGRY SOUL

Of late, scientists have been so anxious to exclude irrelevant, outward sorts of usefulness from the value of science that they do not easily notice this point. Yet it must surely be central. Unless the merchantman merely wants that pearl to sell again, he wants to do something with it. He wants, it seems, to enter into relation with it, to wonder at it, to contemplate its beauty. But wonder involves love. It is an essential element in wonder that we recognize what we see as something we did not make, cannot fully understand, and acknowledge as containing something greater than ourselves. This is not only true if our subject-matter is the stars; it is notoriously just as true if it is rocks or nematode worms. Those whose pearl is the kingdom of heaven, or indeed the kingdom of nature, follow it because they want to drink in its glory. Knowledge here is not just power; it is a loving union, and what is loved cannot just be the information gained; it has to be the real thing which that information tells us about. Nor can the point be only the effect on outward action, though certainly it is true that if the love is sincere action will follow. The student will learn the laws and practise the customs belonging to the kingdom of heaven or of nature, trying to become more fit to serve it. But first comes the initial gazing, the vision which conveys the point of the whole. This vision is in no way just a means to practical involvement, but itself an essential aspect of the goal. On it the seeker's spirit feeds, and without it that spirit would starve. The desire for that vision is a desire to be fulfilled by it, which means accepting that, as one is, one is imperfect and needs to be made whole.

To express this point, prophets of the great religions have deliberately used such apparently gross metaphors as starving, feeding, buying, gaining, losing, and profiting. Gross metaphors are good here because they emphasize that these needs are real ones, not casual aesthetic fancies or arbitrary projects invented just to display our creative powers. 'For what shall it profit a man, if he shall gain the whole world, and lose his own soul?'[7]

41

This question is not just an optional extra, avoidable if we choose to take a different part of the examination paper. Nor are we free to decide at our fancy what losing our souls shall consist in. This question – which is central both for the gospels and for Plato's *Republic*[8] – is also the one being asked and answered by anyone who, like Monod, claims that one single ideal or value dominates all others in the rich jungle of human life. It is a kind of question that cannot be asked and answered in isolation. It involves a 'philosophical psychology', an account of what the self or soul is, and Monod's answer to that question is that it simply is an enquiring intellect.

Supremacy-claims of this kind can of course be made on behalf of other ideals besides science or justice – music, say, or sex or exploration or poetry. They are all claims about the kind of being that we essentially are. Only if music (for instance) really is our essence, does it become reasonable to demand that everything else should be sacrificed to it. The existentialist idea that 'man has no essence' cannot be combined with such claims. And views about our general psychology are scarcely things that could appear in isolation as self-evident revelations. They are typically the sort of opinion that ought to rest on a great deal of evidence.

THE POINT OF SCIENCE

How does all this work out in the case of science? Is it actually plausible that the particular kind of curiosity that impels people to study the natural sciences is the one central demand of human nature, as Monod suggested? This would be a strange suggestion, if only because it would mean that virtually the whole human race had been wasting nearly all its time until about three centuries ago, when the practice of science in its modern sense arose in Europe, and that most of them are bound to go on doing so for the foreseeable future. Could there be reason to make this vast claim? No one who knows anything of the deluding effects of culture, by which people everywhere treat their own value-judgments as universal laws, will feel confident about projecting our science-worship in this way on to the whole human race. We could not safely project it even if, in our own culture, the dominance of science over all other valued things were established. But of course it is not established. The positions we are examining are part of a propaganda campaign to establish it, not diplomas handed out after completing that process. And, besides this competition with other aspects of life, we still have before us the difficulty raised by the penguin's egg, and by Edward O. Wilson's invocation of humanists to process the scientists' hunting-trophies for them.

At the deep level, who benefits, and how? If things go on as they increasingly seem to be going today, does anybody? Must the true prizes of human endeavour – the things which gratify the desires most central to our species – be handed over more and more to human artefacts such as libraries and machines, and belong in the end to them rather than to any human being at all? Is this the true goal of that much exalted species-specific impulse, our insatiable desire for knowledge? There are, of course, people today who apparently quite like this idea, and call on us to be well satisfied if our machines do important things for us better than we do. But just which important things? The function before us now – that of characteristically human enjoyment, of fulfilment, of receiving the highest gratifications of which humanity is capable – does not seem to be one which it would make much sense to hand over to others and to have performed for one. 'Live? Our servants can do that for us,' said Whistler. But people only say that sort of thing about aspects of living which they want to reject entirely.

Obviously, the whole idea that merely collecting vicarious, impersonal, fragmented scraps of information could be our ultimate goal only works if we take the desire for knowledge to be essentially specialized, an undiscriminating thirst for bits of information. And this notion is not impressive, especially when we remember that some bits of knowledge are universally admitted to be too trivial to form part of science. Somebody who puts in a research project for counting the sand-grains all round the United Kingdom will not get a grant, however much he or she protests that science should be pure as well as useful. But if, on the other hand, we take Steven Weinberg's wider formulation as the real model, and speak of aiming to 'understand the universe', things could look very different. The universe includes everything around us, human as well as non-human, and understanding it can start anywhere. The question about the first few seconds of the physical cosmos, currently so fascinating to physicists, is only one possible focus of interest among an infinite number of others. Scientists themselves constantly move from one focus to another, and, after each move, earlier obsession with different problems always looks unaccountable – 'why didn't they think of *x*?'

But what is characteristic of understanding, once started, is that it moves outwards. It faces every kind of problem, but it concentrates for preference on the larger ones. This does not simply mean finding wider and wider scientific laws which reveal a single kind of relation – namely, that of cause and effect. It means finding connections of the most diverse kinds, varying according to the subject-matter, which will enable us to make sense of the world. And in any normal usage, it often needs to involve a practical and emotional attitude as well as an intellectual grasp. This is specially obvious when we talk about knowing people – a kind of knowing which is fairly central to the ordinary meaning of the word. One cannot claim to know somebody merely because one has collected a pile of printed information about them. One can only claim to know them if one has dealt seriously with them at first hand, and the claim can then be justified even if one lacks much of the information. Again, to speak of understanding what somebody is trying to do involves claiming that one can, to some extent, sympathize with it, and to speak of a better understanding among nations is to speak of harmony and goodwill, not of successful mutual prying and spying. In a less obvious way, this element of bonding and commitment forms part of many other kinds of understanding. People who are quite well informed can still strike us as 'knowing nothing about' some aspect of life which they fail to experience or imagine, though their information would be relevant to it. 'Knowing France' means something much more serious and structural than just possessing batches of information. Knowledge and understanding in this wider sense – the living knowledge that Einstein spoke of – are indeed things that can reasonably be thought of as in some sense forming at least an aspect of our main aim, because they are attitudes which are rooted in own being and not just external possessions.

THE SHRINKING PROVINCE OF KNOWLEDGE

In our normal notion of knowledge and understanding, the ability to avoid what is trivial is in fact an extremely important element. To understand something – to know how it works – involves having grasped what is essential about it and seen how to ignore the irrelevant aspects. And knowing how to avoid trivial purposes such as sand-counting is a particularly important part of our general understanding of life. (The apparent absence of this kind of discrimination is surely one of the significant oddities about the notion of the ideal Omega Point we considered just now.) This power of selection – this knowledge of what matters, which is an aspect of wisdom – guards us against obsessiveness. Purposes which are in themselves natural and harmless can still be thoroughly unsuitable to rule our lives, and factual curiosity can certainly at times be one of these over-obtrusive purposes. But, in order to decide whether it is so on any given occasion, we need an inclusive mental map showing the other purposes that compete with it, and expressing the priority system on which we mean to judge between them. Hard though such maps are to draw up, we all possess them, because without them we could not deal at all with conflicts of aims. Our culture supplies each of us with the outlines of the map. But it still leaves us with many gaps and clashes which will tear our lives apart if we do not resolve them by thought.

A remarkable attempt has been made in this century to withdraw the notion of knowledge from this province of thought, indeed to cut it off radically from all the rest of life. When knowledge is secluded in this way and equated with information, understanding is pushed into the background and the notion of wisdom is quite forgotten. Our cognitive faculties are supposed to be set apart, sterilized, inhibited – in the name of a specially high development – from that large-scale operation for which we most need them. On what ground has this been done? Nobody has explicitly put out a manifesto declaring the need to abolish all large-scale thinking. Officially, the idea has usually been simply to separate that large-scale thinking from whatever brand of small-scale thinking happened to be on hand at the moment. But, as far as academics are concerned, the process has nearly always pointed only one way. The intellectual scene has been mapped into ever smaller and more discrete provinces.

Their inhabitants have usually not resisted the process much, because they have seen it as necessary for professional status, and indeed for money. If any questions did arise about who was now left to do the general thinking, philosophy and the social sciences were seen as plausible candidates. And this is reasonable, since anyone who tries to tackle these general questions does in fact find that they are doing philosophy – that is, considering the structures of large-scale forms of thought – and also doing social science – that is, trying to make well-grounded generalizations about the facts of the life around them. They will usually find, too, that they are doing history, because the present state of things can hardly ever be properly understood without some reference to how it came to be as it is. And they may well find themselves involved with other disciplines as well, for instance biology, mathematics, geography, linguistics. In trying to pick one's way among all these minefields – or treasuries, if one chooses so to consider them – it is essential to have some guiding ideas about the nature of relevance, and this too is essentially a philosophic subject. Yet professionals in all these subjects today, including philosophy, are carefully warned not to stray too widely. The whole apparatus of learned journals and of 'research' in general constantly approximates their efforts to those of the most esoteric astrophysicist or Sanskrit palaeographer. This is the confusion that I am trying to unravel.

Chapter Five

PERSONAL AND IMPERSONAL

'Do you understand', said the Thin Woman passionately, 'that it is your own children who have been kidnapped?'

'I do not,' said the Philosopher. 'Semi-tropical apes have been rumoured to kidnap children, and are reported to use them very tenderly indeed, sharing their coconuts, yams, plantains and other equatorial provender with the largest generosity, and conveying their delicate captives from tree to tree (often at a great distance from each other and from the ground) with the most guarded solicitude and benevolence.'

'Monster,' said the Thin Woman in a deep voice, 'will you listen to me?'

'I will not,' said the Philosopher.

'I am going to bed,' said the Thin Woman, 'your stirabout is on the hob.'

'Are there lumps in it, my dear?' said the Philosopher.

'I hope there are,' replied the Thin Woman, and she leapt into bed.

(James Stephens, *The Crock of Gold*, 31)[1]

TROUBLE WITH IDEOLOGY

Is it possible for us to bring our cognitive faculties back to something more like their traditional use? Or does the remedy lie in the other direction, as perhaps many people today might advise – in completing a process which is only troublesome now because it is half-finished? From this angle, a defender of current trends might well point out to us the damage which now

47

seems to be done by *under-specialization* – by intellectual cobblers who will not stick to their lasts. Half-baked ideologies, colourful pseudo-scientific myths, sensational moralistic panaceas backed by dishonestly selected data and scientific jargon are indeed as plentiful as blackberries today. They do not just waste time; they can do serious harm. Ought we indeed perhaps to put all our energies into the purely destructive work of crushing them? Would it be a good bargain to do this, even at the cost of discouraging all general speculation?

If these plagues grew from activities that ought never to have been undertaken in the first place, this would surely be the right course. The trouble is that they do not. Human life absolutely needs a conceptual framework; it needs guiding myths, and – because there will always be conflicts – it needs a morality. Our life does not come as a prepared kit, all cut up and ready to process. It comes in a flood of jumbled material that needs to be picked over and sorted out by endless imaginative work. Conceptual schemes, and the symbolism that gives them their force, must be used for this and they will grow up whatever we do. Our choice is simply between attending to this process and letting our imaginations do it while our back is turned. The cure for bad concepts lies in thinking better, not in suppressing thought. This situation is similar to the one over censorship. There the cure for the danger of dangerous facts does not usually lie in concealing them, but in supplying more and better facts to balance them, and much the same thing is true of pernicious theories. They get accepted because their faults are not seen. In order to see them, people need to be exposed to other sorts of theory, and to learn to discriminate between them.

Take the matter of images. Successful ideologies commonly make their impact by hammering at a single image, or small group of images, which expresses one side of the truth so vividly that they fill the reader's imagination, making it hard to remember that there is any other. Facts which will not fit it simply are not digested. Examples of such hypnotic images are the class war in Marxism, the conditioned rat in behaviourism, the suppressed sexual desire in psychoanalysis, and the 'selfish gene' in sociobiology. People dominated by such images are under a compulsion, which is felt as an actual obligation, to reduce everything else to these special terms. The word ideology is in general a term of abuse, and this is the particular kind of vice that I am using it to describe – a fatal combination of one-sidedness, universal pretension, and sensationalism. Thought-systems, simply as such, do not have to have this vice. Of course, some objections do arise against all sorts of systematizing; they are more complicated, and we shall have to look at them more carefully in chapter 17. But decent systematizers are not ideologues. Spinoza, Leibniz, still more Aristotle, do not have the narrow obsessiveness which gives rise to ideology.

INTELLECT AND IMAGINATION: THE PROBLEM

How are we to save ourselves from this kind of obsession? It cannot be resisted by deadening one's imagination to the point of no longer receiving any images at all. Attempts to do this are dangerously stupefying, and they cannot succeed. Imaginative work is needed even for the narrowest kind of knowledge. Instead, we need to widen our imaginative experience, to be exposed early to many colourful theories, to gain some grasp of the already existing range of charismatic ideas. This should give us a healthy immune system and save us from being knocked over by the first comer. It should put us in a position to deal with ideologies, not in a yes-or-no, black-or-white, convert-or-be-damned spirit, but discriminatingly, by taking what we need from each of them and leaving the rest. It can give us a background map on which the new insights offered can be placed, so that they do not simply blot out all our previous guiding insights.

Thus, the best inoculation against these bad ideologies is essentially the same treatment that I have been suggesting we need in order to relate academic specialities to the rest of life – namely, more and better background thinking. The point I have concentrated on so far is that this second task really does need attention – that there is something odd about our familiar resigned attitude to specialization. A cartoon I once saw seemed to bring out well the curious double vision we have about it today. It showed an astronomer's wife ushering a visitor into the observatory, where the astronomer sat crouched at the end of a huge telescope, and remarking kindly, 'My husband lives in a little world of his own.' The sense in which that remark is true and the sense in which it is not are both obvious to us today, but it is hard to know how to connect them.

This is one aspect of the old problem about how to relate the world which contains the mind with the mind which contains the world. How can we fit the art of thinking – whose subject-matter is indeed strangely universal – into place as just one aspect among others of a wider human life? We have been looking at Jacques Monod's way of doing this, which is an outspokenly imperialistic one on behalf of science. (On this view the astronomer's wife would simply vanish . . . as of course she often does.) Monod exalts, not just intellectual activity, but this one chosen form of intellectual activity, arbitrarily and without explanation, above all the other things we might value. If we find this too extreme, what alternative attitudes are on offer?

THE QUARANTINE SOLUTION

Many academic people who would not want to make Monod's bold claim for supremacy may still want to maintain that science, and the search for knowledge in general, is something set apart from the rest of life – not necessarily higher, but still quite shut off. This has an odd effect on personal identity. On this view, people with an intellectual training have two quite separate sorts of business – professional and non-professional – which should never be mixed. Uneasiness follows about the interface. There arises, for instance, a distaste for even the best popularization, and a resentment of the need to write textbooks. Indeed, the whole business of teaching becomes alarming, since it is designed to produce specialists out of alien, impure, non-specialist material. All teaching, but especially the early stages of it, is seen as a low-grade, even a corrupting activity, a chore to be avoided when possible. Inter-disciplinary discussions are similarly distrusted. Any intrusion of everyday language is seen as a pollution and a danger.

On this view, a specialized scholar is not just a divided soul, a distorted moon-monster emerging from the jar-treatment, but is rather, quite simply, two persons. In the course of education, the professional persona has to be gradually built up by pouring in suitable information, much as a pillar might be built up by pouring concrete into a mould. This process cannot fail to bore the teacher, because until quite a late stage in the proceedings the pupil does not have enough of a professional personality to discuss the subject interestingly at all. On this view, questions about 'student motivation' are concerned with providing a mechanical force, capable of holding the mould still until the pouring process is finished. They are questions about how strong that force is, not about the kind of interest that led this person into this study in the first place or what kind of notion he or she had of the subject. Such questions would be a personal matter and are therefore not relevant.

Is this account a caricature? I wish I could be sure that it was. At any rate, it is probably alarming enough to make most readers agree that this attitude will not quite do. Questions about the kind of impersonality which is actually needed will concern us repeatedly. In the end, I shall want to suggest a very different picture – to propose that none of us can study anything properly unless we do it with our whole being. A separate homunculus within, trained in the practice of an academic discipline, is not much more useful for these purposes than a performing flea.

WHO IS PART OF WHOM?

For the moment, however, let us approach the matter by looking at some other ways, apart from complete division, in which we might conceive the relations existing between the two aspects of the scholarly personality. Should we perhaps say that inside every specialist there is always an ordinary person, who can be addressed, and that, since the speciality is bound to have some connection with the rest of life – connections which may be important – we ought always at least to address that person, even if we address other aspects of the personality as well? Since, too, that person speaks everyday language, it might be important to keep using that language from time to time so as to keep him or her in the picture.

This formula seems to express something true, yet to say both too little and too much. Too little, because it surely puts things back to front. The specialist is a part of the ordinary person, not the other way round. So, when a chemist considers taking a job in the armaments industry, or a barrister thinks about the political bearings of a brief, or a metaphysician suspects that a theory has moral implications, the movement that they need to make is surely always an outward one, from part to whole. Too much, on the other hand, because the current notion of academic professionalism does demand impersonality. Our training stresses the need to keep out of our work everything subjective or emotional, indeed, everything that is individual at all. The fear of offending against this standard can seem to make a totally anonymous, colourless style and choice of topics a matter of professional honour.

Up to a point, this demand for impersonality really is a useful corrective. Beyond that point, it does something which we all see to be disastrous to the study itself. It paralyses originality. Conscientious people can come to see their legitimate stamping-ground as limited once and for all by the topics and methods already on offer. They can suppress new ideas, not just from nervousness, but on principle. The Citation Index, a device lately invented to ensure conventional thinking, helps them to do this by rewarding contributions to existing debates and penalizing unexpected suggestions, which naturally take longer to register and attract replies. Doctoral theses, too, unavoidably give training in sticking to existing lines of argument. Yet we can see, as we look back at the history of thought, that the places where the learned bees have gathered most thickly have not always been the ones where there was most honey. The life-stories of great scholars typically tell of their hard struggles to shift the focus of attention away from unprofitable places towards the problems where it was most needed. And, by a pleasing irony, defenders of orthodox methods are very often the heirs of these revolutionaries. What is called 'normal science' quite properly moves in to exploit the new insights – but the normal scientists then quite improperly proceed to damn the next set of insights when these heave above the horizon.

Can we do anything about these factors that incline us to hidebound conformism? Ought we even to try? We must, of course, start by conceding the full value of the continuous, im-personal, specialized, corporate approach. Organized western thought is an unparalleled achievement, a city within which we all live and from which we constantly benefit. Moreover, since there is nothing else quite like it, detailed ways of correcting its defects can only be worked out within it, by using its resources. Though we can draw all kinds of suggestions from outside, we cannot emigrate to a quite different system. We really do need, however, to notice the price we pay for its present complexity. It is rigid in a way which conflicts oddly with its official universality. Officially, we can enquire about anything. In fact, in any academic area, current traditions ensure that only certain quite limited topics and methods will be accepted. Officially, the reasons for these limitations are impersonal, rational, clearly statable, and ready to be changed at any time if good reason is given. Actually, they have all kinds of other sources as well as these acknowledged ones – a background web of obscure and complex historical causes, involving notably clashes of personality and feuds with neighbouring studies. They are very resistant to deliberate attempts at change. Much of this rigidity, too, is certainly not impersonal because it results from the individual temperaments of the people involved. In order to get through the appalling grind of systematic enquiry, people need to be somewhat obsessive. It also helps to be ambitious. But these qualities – which are personal ones – inevitably make it hard to change direction.

Scholars are, of course, aware of these dangers, and often make great efforts to avoid them. But this is hard, and, as the sheer quantity of information involved increases, it grows harder, not easier. It is alarmingly naïve to talk as though our aim were merely to increase that bulk of information. We already have far more facts than we can handle. What we need most is to improve our ways of sorting and relating them – to work on the concepts, to philosophize. This is necessary, not just for professional philosophers, but for every kind of enquirer whose work leads into a general problem. It is a troublesome business, and it is not surprising that people have put up rather simple conceptual screens to protect them from seeing the need to do it. But these contraptions often make things harder in the end.

Much academic conceptual apparatus is designed to insulate specialities from outside interference. For instance, the word 'anecdotal' has been much used in the physical and social sciences to stigmatize any evidence not drawn from controlled studies, or even any that is not obtained in a laboratory. (Compare the remark 'we really know nothing about *x*' meaning 'my unit has not yet been given a grant to study it by our own peculiar methods'.) Since nearly all the factual evidence for nearly all of what we know is 'anecdotal' in this wide sense, the word, so used, has no real derogatory force. And indeed, in areas like ethology, law, and anthropology, some writers have begun to point this out. They note that these other kinds of evidence have standards of their own. When these standards are satisfied – as often happens, for instance, in the lawcourts – 'anecdotal evidence' is all right; it is not inferior to any other kind.

The derogatory use of this and kindred terms has, however, been a strong propaganda weapon in the hands of people like B. F. Skinner, an excuse for rejecting, not just everyday thinking, but the entire study of history as 'unscientific', that is, unprofessional. It certainly is true that most historical events occur only once, and cannot be reproduced in the laboratory. That is why they need to be studied by their own special methods, methods which are not at all like those of physics, and are 'scientific' only in the sense that they have been systematically developed to suit their subject-matter.

Chapter Six

AUTONOMY AND ISOLATIONISM

The Principle of Sound Learning is that the noise of
vulgar fame should never trouble the cloistered calm of
academic existence. Hence, learning is called sound when
no one has ever heard of it. . . . If you should write a book
(you had better not), be sure that it is unreadable;
otherwise you will be called 'brilliant' and forfeit all respect.
(F. M. Cornford, *Microcosmographia Academica*, 11)[1]

WHAT ARE INTUITIONS?

Another term loaded in the same way to suggest that specialities
ought to be disconnected from everyday thought is 'intuition'. A
remarkable use of this word has become standard among
physical scientists, and has begun to invade other kinds of
thinking too. An intuition in this sense means any view about the
subject-matter of one's study which is held by people without
one's own training, is expressed in everyday language, and does
not require special methods to establish it.

Thus, for physics, all common-sense views on the nature of
matter are equally 'intuitions', whether they spring from the
complexities of accepted culture, from folklore, or directly from
our natural muscular perceptions. The term intuition used, till
lately, to mean always a direct perception, and would only have
allowed (at most) the last of these meanings. That sense has now
vanished, and along with it has gone the idea that an intuition is,
so far as it goes, infallible – which would have outlawed the habit
of correcting intuitions by 'counter-intuitive' discoveries, as is
constantly done today. The modern sense is a purely negative

one; to call something an intuition means simply that it is *not* a part of one's science.

Now, with cases like physics and chemistry, this does not work out too badly. These genuinely are invented and relatively isolated thought-systems, needing their own distinctive languages. They are indeed largely separate from everyday thinking, and they treat all of it, without much distinction, as a disposable starting-point. But what happens if we use this model for sociology, or for psychology, or – where it has lately reared its ugly head – for moral philosophy?

These studies are not islands, nor even peninsulas. They lie in the heartland of ordinary thought, crossed by its main traffic-routes, and they arise out of its already existing problems. The three examples which we mentioned just now show this difference sharply. Only in the first – the chemist who might work in the armaments industry – is it at all plausible that the specialist has never had to think about this problem before. The other two have no possible right to be surprised at their problems. Any barrister ought to have noticed the possible political bearing of certain kinds of lawsuit. Any metaphysician ought to know that there is such a thing as the metaphysic of morals, and that all metaphysical problems are interconnected. (People who have deliberately denied both these positions, as was done by proponents of the absolute 'fact–value gap', have not been avoiding metaphysics, but taking up a most peculiar metaphysical position, which needs a great deal of defence.) Barristers and metaphysicians who have so far failed to think about such matters have done so by chance or for bad reasons, and will now have to make up for lost time. Doing this may of course be hard, even agonizing, but it is plainly not a problem which falls outside their sphere.

THE DREAM OF SEPARATISM

Is a separate, secluded professional ethic possible? Does there exist any intellectual principle which will reliably protect specialists from these unexpected demands? Are they in some way immune from wider responsibilities, having taken out a limited scholar's licence to deal only with a prescribed area? At present, there certainly does exist an idea that there is such an immunity, an immunity that carries with it a positive duty of narrowness and compartmentalization. The autonomy of each discipline is felt to require that its citizens should not go outside it and that others should not trespass on it or ask its inhabitants to make these excursions. This idea flows, I think, from certain features peculiar to the physical sciences, and even in their case it has far less in it than is usually supposed. Let us look at their position.

The chemist's case is, indeed, genuinely different from the other two I listed. There really is a logical gap between all chemical problems and the moral one which now looms. There is a gap, not because chemistry has no neighbours, but because those neighbours are themselves somewhat remote from ethics. The question is simply, is this an infinite, unbridgeable gap, or merely rather a long and unfamiliar journey? Is there really no chain of questions and answers leading to considerations which would help to resolve the moral dilemma?

Many physical scientists today do tend to see this gap as infinite. They do not deny that each scientist may have duties as a human being, or as a citizen. But they are unwilling to bring these duties into any intelligible relation with distinctively scientific duties, for fear that the latter might go under. They see science as incorporating a private ethic of its own. They sometimes assert 'the freedom of science' as demanding that important scientific investigations should always go forward regardless of any social considerations whatever.

The effect of this is, as I have been suggesting, to crack open the unfortunate scientist's personal identity. Scientist and citizen within him are left at open war. What is our poor chemist supposed to do about this? Challenge himself to a duel? Toss up? The appeal of ideologies lies in their apparent power to resolve these dilemmas by closing the gap. They supply a universal, strident, emotional tone and pattern that seem to give unity to incoherent thinking. But this is not the only way in which specialized thought and everyday ideas can be brought together. It is reasonable to ask why the gap ever grew so wide, and why it was treated as unbridgeable in the first place. In youth, this chemist probably did not see such a gap. There was some reason why he or she chose chemistry as a profession, a reason why this study mattered, when it was weighed (even if inarticulately) against similar reasons supporting other interests and occupations. At that time, too, the appeal of chemistry was probably linked with some kind of wonder at the world, some delight at the way it is put together, which would naturally seem relevant to the project of helping to defend it, and to the danger of blowing it to pieces. It does not seem wild to suggest that, if a child or an adolescent could see this connection, a responsible adult might be able to grasp it also.

In the last few decades, scientists have indeed made a marked move in this direction. The single-minded assertion of autonomy – which was a nervously defensive position, buttressing the isolated, internal ethic of science against the rest of society – is balanced now by a steadily increasing acknowledgement of other claims which society, and indeed the rest of the biosphere, has on science. Magazines like *New Scientist* now pay very serious attention to the social, political, and humane implications of various possible scientific policies, and to the need to bring particular scientific truths to public notice. Papers and books like this are by no means just parish magazines for specialists. Certainly they still – quite rightly – lobby in the interests of pure knowledge. But they recognize the need to weigh this interest against others with which it may often compete. They treat its claim to prevail in any particular case as an arguable question, not as a matter of tribal loyalty. There have been various reasons for this change. The nuclear question has obviously played a great part in bringing it about. So have many problems over global ecology. T. H. Huxley, Einstein, and other outstanding scientists have supplied its models. Following this light, physical scientists are beginning to acknowledge, however hesitantly, that obsession is not always enough. Monomania, even when it produces Nobel prizes, is not really the ideal scientific condition.

This recognition, however, still awaits a clear and positive public formulation at a convincing level, an official conceptual adjustment, showing unmistakably that pedantic blindness is as bad a fault as vagueness. Sanctimonious obsessiveness needs to be publicly unmasked. It needs to be spelt out why an attempt to understand desertification in Africa in order to resist it is not, just as such, at some deep level academically inferior to an advance in theoretical physics. Something needs to be done here about the tendentious current use of words like 'basic' and 'fundamental' to describe any research which is not intended to be useful. Trivial questions are still trivial, even when their answers are useless. Their uselessness cannot of itself transform them into fundamental ones.

Whoever makes this adjustment – and it will need to be a scientist of stature – will have to notice an interesting paradox about the ideal of autonomy for a particular study. In some circumstances, isolating a study from outside considerations can indeed serve its peculiar value and enhance its dignity. In others, that isolation can trivialize it and brand its practitioners as the slaves of habit. It all depends on the particular connections which are being broken. But, since both possibilities exist, anyone who wants to discriminate between them has to be able to think on both sides of the line – to examine the outside scene and assess whether this time it ought to be excluded or not.

The clearest and most startling case, which we will consider more fully in chapters 14 to 16, is that of moral philosophy. Early in this century, philosophers argued that the autonomy of their discipline confined them to the study of a few, highly abstract, formal ideas such as 'right' and 'good', and sometimes invoked the supposed example of physics in an attempt to justify the enormous abstractness of their speculations, which they treated as quite distinct from the 'moral intuitions' of ordinary life. This will not work, because ordinary life contains a great deal of hard moral thinking. The business of conceptual analysis and conceptual plumbing has to start from an understanding of the systems forged in everyday experience. There are no naïve observers here. It is hard to see what the word intuition in its modern sense could possibly mean in this context, though it is still confidently used there. No tidy barrier can enclose moral philosophy. Its proper autonomy is not a matter of detachment from other ways of thinking, or of restriction to a few special abstract areas. Instead, like other enquiries, it gains its individuality from a special kind of interest, which dictates its own suitable methods – a peculiar determination to take conflicts seriously and try to resolve them by putting them in their wider context and considering (as Plato put it) 'how we ought to live' as a whole. The more narrowly philosophical question, 'how we ought to think about how we ought to live', is only an aspect of the first question, since thought is an aspect of life. The question as a whole is one for everybody, even though many parts of its philosophical segment need hard and specialized attention. Moral philosophers have, of course, been terrified of being taken for Victorian sages, who might actually be prepared to say that something in the real world was right or wrong. As none of us can help committing ourselves all the time to judgments of this kind, this particular fear seems misplaced. But the wider fear of looking disreputable if we acknowledge the relevance of everyday thinking, or of other studies, to our own enquiries is no more sensible.

PROFESSIONALISM AND PERSONALITY

Academics do not need to be condemned to a Jekyll-and-Hyde existence, dividing their inner life between a specialist who is a standard robot and a private person who is an idiot. To frame a more usable notion of the kind of impersonality we need for scholarship, we have somehow to sketch a wider map of the enclosing personality within which this and other enterprises find their place. There is a vital distinction here between two elements in professionalism, one of which needs to be impersonal while the other needs not to be.[2] The first element involves a set of skills and attitudes which are genuinely anonymous, in the sense that they ought to be the same for every member of a given profession. These are the qualifications we have in mind when we say things like 'Is there a doctor in the house?' or 'What he really needs is a good lawyer.' The other element is the contribution of the individual personality, which is most obviously central in the arts. Nobody is likely to doubt that a musician, for instance, needs individual qualities as well as the anonymous reliability, training, industry, and so forth which make up a professional approach to music. But this individual element is just as vital in many other contexts, some of which arise in almost every profession once we get beyond the basic general demands just mentioned. We do not always simply want 'a doctor' or 'a lawyer', any more than we just want 'a musician'. We may want our own doctor, or we may say (as someone is reported to have said of Conrad), 'I wish I had ever had the chance to serve under a captain like him.' The relative weight attached to these two sides of professionalism naturally varies a great deal from one kind of work to another. Face-to-face situations are among those that give a special importance to the individual element. The character of a surgeon or an engineer usually matters much less to their clients than does that of a doctor, a nurse, or a teacher. But in the arts it is still a vital matter, even where there is no meeting face to face. The personal impact conveyed through poetry, music, and the rest is a most potent influence on our lives, and it would be hard to form an idea of professionalism in the arts which left no room for it.

What, then, is the proper place of academic work on this spectrum? Unquestionably, its teaching aspect is work of the kind where individuality makes most difference. It does so in all teaching. Although good teachers should in one way be self-effacing – should be capable of subordinating personal ambition to the subject to be taught – yet, for almost every kind of work, the example of their personal attitude forms a crucial part of what is learnt. Truly professional teachers are not just ones who know their subject properly and have studied teaching methods. They are ones who are there for the right reasons – who themselves love their subject and want to share progress in it with their pupils, ones in whose lives teaching has been an organic growth. Moreover, teaching has a vital part to play in the development of new ideas themselves. The more original those ideas are, the more essential it usually is that their inventor should have to keep trying to express them clearly, and taking note of various responses. New ideas, indeed, are mostly developed communally by co-operative groups, among whom pupils – including obstructive pupils – are an invaluable element.

This fact is well-known. But many academics seem now to draw from it the strange conclusion we have noticed, namely, that teaching cannot be any part of their real business, simply because the personal element in it is so important. This strange attitude is expressed in a wild attempt – currently under discussion as I write – to divide off the teaching from the research element in British universities, and to seclude it in inferior institutions. Even, however, if academics do manage to get rid of teaching in this or other ways, a similar difficulty crops up again about the activity to which they would most naturally withdraw, namely, writing. Writing is an art, a form of personal communication, and the writing of scholars has in the past been seen as a form of teaching. Its personal aspect has often been no less central a part of it than it is for many other forms of writing.

Great scholars, from Plato to Darwin and Huxley, Einstein and Haldane, have accepted the responsibility of writing in a way that they well knew would influence the world around them. They have done this even though they knew what risks they ran of being misrepresented and misunderstood, because they also knew that such work was necessary to forward the general understanding of the matters that most concerned them. Had they not done this, our city of organized thought could never have been built.

Was all this work really just some sort of unprofessional mistake? Ought they to have kept silent? Were their efforts misdirected, a mere embarrassing consequence of their ignorance, or their immaturity, or their irresponsible exhibitionism? If not – if they were indeed justified in what they did – has the world really changed in some way which makes it impossible for us to follow their example? If this had happened, it would be peculiarly awkward, since the ideas that they gave us are still active in our culture, and, unless the work of bringing those ideas up to date and supplementing them with new ones is duly carried on, we shall be imprisoned in their limitations.

Chapter Seven

RIGOUR AND THE NATURAL HISTORY OF CONTROVERSY

He saith among the trumpets, Ha ha; and he smelleth the
battle afar off, the thunder of the captains, and the
shouting.

(Book of Job, 39.25)

COCKPITS AND CRICKET MATCHES

It may be sensible to ask here, are the points I have been making
already conceded? Is it perhaps already widely agreed that the
entire personalities of scholars are involved in their work, that
they are not mere honeypot-ants or robots programmed for the
gathering and storing of information, but professional under-
standers? Is it accordingly already accepted that, for all but the
most recondite aspects of their work, they ought to be able to explain what they are doing to outsiders? Traditionally, I think
much of this has been admitted in practice. But in recent
decades we have not taken the trouble to think out the theory
behind it carefully enough, nor to declare it plainly to the public.
This omission has now trapped us, leaving us little room to resist
corrupt and distorted ideas about it which have now actually
been put into current practice. Outside the profession, the idea
now reigns that scholars exist solely to supply a product called
'research'. At present, anyone writing a reference for a person
applying for an academic post is warned to concentrate their
attention solely on the applicant's 'research record', that is, on
the sheer number and technicality of learned books and papers
they have managed to publish, quite regardless of their teaching
and pastoral work among students, of the quality of their

63

original ideas, and of the need there is, with any difficult problem, to think long and carefully before ever starting to write. Except in the few areas where visibly useful information does quickly emerge, this bizarre flood of paper can surely serve only to discredit further the whole enterprise of learning.

In this alarming situation, I have suggested that we – meaning not just academics, but everyone who cares that thinking should be done properly – need to look again with a fresh eye at how we want it done. Of late, the current notion of professionalism has been mainly a negative one – an insistence on the need *not* to wander beyond one's province. I have suggested that something more positive is needed, that learning must be seen as part of a general understanding of the world which is continuous with active and constructive attitudes towards it. In saying this, I am not denying that much bad thinking now goes on upon this wider stage – that the world is full of crude ideologies – but I want to say that this is because the thinking is bad, not because it is done on large issues. The remedy is not to turn one's back on these important topics, but to see to it that they are handled better, not to exclude feeling from one's discussions, but to insist that it should be the right feeling.

This is, of course, an unfamiliar suggestion. Many professionals have at present a strong impression that the only possible effect of attending to large questions, or of allowing interplay between thought and feeling, must be to produce crude ideologies. The mere existence of these ideologies shows, in their view, that feeling should never have been allowed near systematic thought. The dams against feeling should have been higher, and the proper remedy is to make sure that they always are so. This may possibly strike us as a fairly desperate proposal, since the feelings involved are not only strong and natural, but also necessary aspects of large-scale enquiry. But there is another consideration which may bring home to us still more sharply that this project of shutting out feeling from scholarship is an unrealistic one. There is at least one kind of feeling which is already present inside it, and plays a great part in shaping its institutions – namely pugnacity, a tendency to engage in feuds and controversies for their own sake. Of course some of these do turn out really profitable; they are fertile dialectics producing valuable insights. (We will look at these more fully in chapter 9.)

But, as every scholar knows, some of our colleagues – at least our opponents – like opposition just for the sake of it.

Is this a serious matter? History suggests that it may be. Historians in the future (if there are any) will of course study our age as we study ages already past, seeing what we ought to have done and wondering how we came to make the mistakes that we did. As usual, they will find it hard to see how we can have missed the clues which will be plain to them – clues which are undoubtedly already staring us in the face. So far, this story is a common one, a normal historical predicament. But in one way the present age is rather exceptional. There are at work today an unparalleled number of highly trained and capable scholars, with a wealth of information in their hands quite unthinkable in earlier times. I am not being cynical, nor underestimating our immense actual achievement when I ask, with this really splendid array of academic resources, could we, both on practical and theoretical questions, do a bit better? Is there an element of chronic waste in the system? And might the proliferation of disputes be one of the things that is stopping us?

Again, it is worth while to consider here the lessons of the past. If we ask what was occupying the trained minds of any past epoch – what prevented most of them from seeing the problems they really ought to have been tackling – we usually find that they were divided into warring tribes by some vigorous but unprofitable dispute. Sometimes it was unprofitable because it was about something really trivial, like the biblical prophecies that occupied Newton. Sometimes, more distressingly still, it was on a serious topic but was carried on as a fight between two half-truths, like the long dispute between justification by works and justification by faith, and the still-thriving free-will controversy. I use these examples from matters of general interest because they are more convenient for general discussion, but the same kind of disputatiousness is found in every branch of learning.

Now, of course, it will not do to condemn controversial pugnacity altogether. To do that would be to take sides once more, to commit one more blunder of the kind just mentioned. We do indeed need to be sharp and critical, sometimes we need to be intolerant. There are limits to the value of tolerance. But it needs saying that there are limits to the value of intolerance too. Truth, even on small subjects and still more on large ones, is rarely pure and never simple. As John Milton said, the truth is never found in one piece, ready-made. Instead it has been cut into a thousand fragments and scattered to the four winds. 'And ever since that time', Milton went on, 'the sad friends of truth, such as durst appear, imitating the careful search that Isis made for. . . Osiris, went up and down gathering up limb by limb still as they could find them. We have not yet found them all, Lords and Commons, nor ever shall do till her Master's second coming.'[1] Milton was writing for a limited purpose – simply to defend freedom of speech. He was attacking the Puritan Commonwealth for its censorship of books. But censorship is only one expression of the intolerant blindness that surrounds controversy. If intellect is to be properly used, we intellectuals in all ages need constantly to bear in mind the plea that Cromwell made to those same stiff-necked and confident Puritan sectarians: 'I beseech ye my brethren in the bowels of Christ, think it possible that ye may be mistaken.'

Why are we so drawn to controversy, and why does that controversy so often prove unprofitable? It seems important here to ask a large question. Is the point of academic enquiry to get right answers, or to avoid getting wrong ones? At a glance, these two enterprises look rather alike, but actually they diverge surprisingly. And there are many features in academic life that tend to direct us to the second aim rather than the first. In our professional work, we are usually addressing an audience of fellow-experts who, in spite of their disagreements, do agree on a wide range of basic assumptions. If this audience is small, we can often find strength to resist them, and this is also easy if it is already divided and we have only to join one party. But, where it is monolithic, at a certain point the mass goes critical. We become incessantly conscious of their eyes on our backs. Unless we are exceptionally tough, their tacit expectations will dominate us. It is hard for us even to think of taking a quite different line.

WHAT IS RIGOUR?

So how is any mistake that these experts are all making ever to be corrected? (Anyone who doubts that they could all be making such a mistake might do well to look at the back numbers of journals in their own subject for ten, twenty, forty years ago.) This difficulty is serious, because what restrains us here is not just our faults – laziness, timidity, and so on – but our professional virtues. It is our business to be fair-minded and humble – to avoid hasty bias, to bring evidence for all our opinions and evidence for that evidence, and to be prepared with further evidence for every bit of it. We are trained to fear rashness. The upshot is that we tend to think of rigour as meaning simply the careful practice of these defensive and negative techniques. It is really surprising how freely we use military metaphors of attack and defence. We come to expect the information we gather to be used in consolidating a defensible position rather than in improving existing conditions or making a new move possible. Even when we turn to the apparently more co-operative image of *building*, we often do not use it to call for co-operation but rather for bulldozers to clear the site – a matter that has already been mentioned[2] and will have to be mentioned again later. Talk of a *journey*, of *advancing* towards the solution of a large problem, or *exploring* a country-side has now been usefully introduced, and can undoubtedly help us. The advantages of this image over the slum-clearance form of the building metaphor may be seen if we consider the proposal that we ought to start our journey by burning all existing maps, compasses, travel-books, and binoculars, in order to be sure of incorporating no previous errors. But there is yet another metaphor that could be useful, which I cannot recollect having seen used, namely the idea of coming into a stretch of country or a garden in order to cultivate it and look after it. The hospitable, conserving approach which this would suggest is in effect very near to Aristotle's method of 'saving the appearances' – that is, of finding out first what is believed about a subject already and seeing whether any of it actually needs to be removed, before deciding what new moves are called for. But I do not know that Aristotle ever used the image.

As things are, however, we mostly proceed dialectically, by conflict and contradiction. This is why, in the small hours, it can begin to seem as if the worst thing that could happen to us in our professional lives would be to make a mistake, and to have it found out. There is not much to remind us of how much worse it would be to have entirely wasted those lives, and a great part of other people's too, in saying nothing. Among critics within our own discipline, we are only too conscious of Cromwell's warning; each of us continually suspects that he may be mistaken. But the thought that those critics, whose ideas we have accepted, might all be mistaken becomes almost unbearable. Because individually we are so diffident, tribally we grow dogmatic. In this way, the mere increased numbers of enquirers is counterproductive. It prolongs the lifetime of mistakes, because the sheer inertia that keeps them circulating through the larger mass is much stronger. Academic isolationism sets in. We use compasses that orient us to our own ship rather than to the ocean on which we are all sailing. We grow dedicated to security from error, as locally defined. This is fairly tragic, since of course that security is never attainable. We are all fallible. With enough exposers around, all of us are certain to get caught in the end. The only place completely safe from exposure is the tomb. The only truly successful defensive rigour is *rigor mortis.*

PROPHETS

Is this account something of a caricature? Certainly we do all know in principle that we ought to say something positive, and if possible something big. But it is really hard to do so, and most of us do tend to expect that new thing to lie within the framework of assumptions at present in use in our discipline. There are occasional very interesting exceptions to this rule – academics who simply move out on their own and start a new line of argument without giving a damn what anybody says about it. Somebody like Wittgenstein, G. E. Moore, F. R. Leavis occasionally heaves over the horizon. (The procedure in the sciences is slightly different, with a little more lip-service paid to argument, but the key move is the same; a new starting point is tacitly adopted. The wide range of possibilities may be hinted at by picking out a few names – Einstein, J. B. S. Haldane, Jacques Monod, Edward O. Wilson, Richard Dawkins, Fred Hoyle.) To become such an initiator, you do not necessarily have to have originality of mind – though that helps – but what you must have is a hide like a rhinoceros for controversy. Those otherwise very diverse men Wittgenstein, Moore, and Leavis all had that advantage. Whatever their sensibilities on other matters, it simply never crossed any of their minds to suspect seriously that critics of their whole approach might be right. The result is rather odd. People like this are accepted as licensed prophets, and are quoted as authorities, but nobody ever thinks of imitating this feature of their method. At present, no philosophical article is complete without its quotation from Wittgenstein – 'for what saith Wittgenstein?' This quotation is often brief, isolated, extreme, rhetorical, dogmatic, and obscure. The quoters, however, do not usually complain about this. Nor do they argue that, since Wittgenstein didn't bother to bring any support for his opinions, they need bring none for their own, that the readers can work it out for themselves and be damned to them. No indeed; *they* give their references. The prophets don't influence current practice.

This means that the virtue of controversial courage does not get cultivated – except in the passive form of enduring criticism patiently. Most of us still continue to work within the local conventions. We do not expect to have to defend them, and we are not trained to do so. Consequently, quite advanced specialists, including prophets, when confronted by unexpected criticism of their general assumptions, tend to flounder helplessly, like deep-sea fish brought suddenly to the surface. In the physical sciences, their indignation is usually silent, because they expect people outside their own subject to be fools anyway. In the social sciences and humanities, however, they are apt to explode in cries of inarticulate outrage, and to accuse their critics of unspeakable political motivations. Plainly, neither party fully understood the assumptions on which its own methods were based. And it is not easy to do this. But that is a difficulty for which there is no remedy but practice.

All such deep assumptions lead beyond a single discipline, and are connected with those used for other studies and other forms of thought. Scholars ought never to be surprised to find that somebody outside their own speciality is in a position to criticize their assumptions, and can see relevant points about them which they themselves had never noticed. To think about these general assumptions is to see that they do have these outside connections, and to gain some idea of the directions from which trouble may come. Someone who has considered this will be partly prepared for criticism, and, when it comes, can soon set about seeing what it amounts to. It is even possible to have thought it over already for oneself. It can then be got in focus as a limited problem, rather than as a major tribal threat needing to be met by war.

That is the skill which real academic rigour requires of us. Unless we have some idea where our own province stands on the wider map of knowledge, we cannot grasp properly the principles which apply within it. The supposed rigour of isolationism is a fraud. Rigour itself demands some skill in general controversy, and in distinguishing the methods needed for each part of that controversy. As Aristotle put it:

> it is the mark of an educated man to look for precision in each class of things just so far as the nature of the subject admits. It is evidently equally foolish to accept probable reasoning from a mathematician and to demand scientific proofs from a literary critic.[3]

That sort of education is endless, and nobody is going to achieve it completely. People engaged on specialized work cannot be blamed if their first reaction to disturbance is irritation and confusion. But, when we have had time to recover from our first shock, we ought to be able to accept the wider issue put before us as a proper demand for attention to the wider map, to the communal road and water system, the set of assumptions which unites and serves us all. Instead of hardening our first mindless irritation into a feud, we need to set about overhauling the assumptions we have so far taken for granted. Hard? Of course it's hard. Real interdisciplinary work includes some of the hardest thinking in the trade, though the substitute kind that sometimes passes under its name includes some of the easiest. People manufacturing the substitute have only got to follow the well-known recipe for becoming an expert on Chinese metaphysics: always talk Chinese to metaphysicians and metaphysics to the Chinese, avoid short words, and never answer questions. People attempting the real thing may have to rethink their ideas from scratch.

USING PROPHETS RIGHTLY

This process is made much harder when the prophets are seen – as they are at present – as sharply separated in function from the everyday academics who are their followers. The process of properly digesting and absorbing new ideas calls for many collaborators, who ought to be close to the original proposer in presuppositions, background, and intelligence, and yet not be mere interpreters, but of a standing to take responsibility for serious parts of the work. Indeed, it is misleading to speak merely of digestion; the initial framing of useful new concepts is itself co-operative work that needs many minds. And, though these helpers must in one way stand close to the originator, in other ways they should vary widely, because it is characteristic of important new ideas to have widely varied and unexpected consequences, leading right outside the boundaries of existing disciplines. If the right kind of active, creative helpers are not present, the penalty is that the biases and weaknesses of the original proposer go uncorrected; indeed, they tend to be steadily amplified as the ideas pass through the heads of more and more submissive and uncritical interpreters. The disaster is not – as some people think today – the occurrence and success of a prophet as such. It is the lack of a public properly educated to stand up to prophets, to take their ideas to pieces and to get them into perspective, to compare different conceptual schemes together and see what each is good for.

THE NEED FOR PHILOSOPHY

Until quite lately, exactly this kind of work was seen as central philosophical business. Philosophy has had its place in western culture, not just as one prestigious and esoteric speciality among others, but as the general clearing-house for resolving obstinate disputes by relating different kinds of thought. It arose in the first place out of Socrates' attempt to bring together some very different ways of practical everyday thinking, and then out of Plato's more ambitious effort to relate all these ways of thinking to the emerging certainties of mathematics. (This immense task still gives trouble today and, as we shall see, it plays an important part in our current problems.) Philosophy became influential just because it often managed to suggest ways of dealing with these painful clashes and filling awkward gaps in that thought. It has managed to do this even though, right from the start, it has had to contain some very difficult and specialized areas. Some of these have remained difficult, but some have seemed so only at

71

first, because they were unfamiliar, and have become common-place later, when their basic problems of method had been solved. Once that is done, they have often set up on their own as independent disciplines. A wide range of studies, from astronomy to psychology, began their life in this way, by being hived off from parts of philosophy. This is not because philosophy consists of vague speculations, which are then superseded by the certainties of science. It is because building the conceptual framework for any study is a philosophical task, and that framework, once it is well built, can often be taken for granted in the later factual enquiries.

This peculiar method-sorting function of philosophy explains why people often find it so hard to see what its subject-matter is, and also why they easily get the impression that it has never made any progress. Once problems of method have been solved, it becomes hard to see that they were ever there. Thus biology still walks comfortably on many of the floorboards laid down by Aristotle – on the idea of organ and organism; on the notion of classifying organisms by genus and differentia; on the distinction between explanation by cause and explanation by function; above all, on the general realization that understanding the living world is a distinct enterprise needing its own set of concepts, not – as Plato thought – an incurably confused branch of applied mathematics. Similarly, in political and moral matters, we all take many of Kant's and Rousseau's ideas about freedom for granted as if they were a natural part of the air. Other areas, however, have remained arcane, and the public is right to suppose that philosophy is, on the whole, rather a difficult study. The difficulty lies in keeping one's attention on the way in which one is thinking, rather than on what one would like to be thinking about. This is a somewhat unnatural posture for our minds, and it actually is very hard to do it for long enough to work out new ways of thinking, even where the old ones are plainly unsatisfactory. And it is still harder to state the new ones clearly once one has found them, because changed concepts call for new ways of talking, which at first get misunderstood. Until these new ways have been established and the new language has grown familiar, these attempts are liable to sound like shocking nonsense.

72

At any given time, therefore, the parts of philosophy that have succeeded tend to be invisible, and the visible parts tend to look extremely odd. That is why the subject has such a public relations problem, a problem made worse by the way in which the subject-matter seems to be constantly shifting, because new conceptual difficulties are continually cropping up over different topics. Thus, many people still expect philosophy to be concerned mainly with religion, and are uneasy when they find that it seems to be dealing with science. But, in an age when much of the current thinking is actually involved with science, this is to be expected. Though the philosophy of religion is still important, it cannot stand alone. Philosophers must go where the work is.

In trying to re-map the intellectual world as a coherent whole, rather than an arbitrary jumble of loose specialities, the cases of science and philosophy seem to call with particular urgency for new thinking. In part 3 we will move on to deal directly with the case of philosophy. But first there is something more to be said about the nature of science – about the sense in which it is, or is not, entirely separate from our ordinary thinking.

Chapter Eight

THE SECLUSION OF SCIENCE

There is a great gulf fixed.

(St Luke's Gospel 16.26)

FREEDOM, AUTONOMY, AND IRRESPONSIBILITY

In what sense is science cut off from the rest of human thought, even from the rest of human life? That it is so is something that has been repeatedly and strongly claimed by eminent scientists. But what they say is often strangely vague, and needs a lot of care to interpret. Thus, Professor Sir Ernest Chain, co-discoverer of penicillin, wrote in 1970, in an article called 'Social responsibility and the scientist':

Science, as long as it limits itself to the descriptive study of Nature, has no moral or ethical quality, and this applies to the physical as well as the biological sciences. No quality of good or evil is attached to results of research aimed at determining natural constants, such as that of gravity or the velocity of light, or measuring the movements of stars, describing the kinetic properties of an enzyme, or describing the behaviour of animals (whatever our emotional attitude towards it may be) or studying the metabolic activity of a microbe, whether harmful or beneficial to mankind, or studying physiological function or pharmacological and toxic action.
No quality of good or evil can be ascribed to studies aimed at the elucidation (of such questions).[1]

74

What does it mean to say that 'no quality of good or evil is attached to results of research', or 'can be ascribed to' these studies? The first formulation sounds like a claim that the effects of these studies are always value-neutral, neither bad nor good. The second sounds more like a claim that there is never any reason for or against pursuing them – that the studies are themselves neither bad nor good. The first claim is clearly false, the second is certainly not what Chain intends. Again, here is a similar, though at first rather clearer, passage from Einstein himself:

> The scientific way of thinking has a further characteristic. The concepts which it uses to build up its coherent systems do not express emotions. For the scientist there is only 'being' but no wishing, no valuing. No good, no evil – in short, no goal. As long as we remain within the realm of science proper, we can never encounter a sentence of the type 'Thou shalt not lie'. There is something like a Puritan's restraint in the scientist who seeks truth: he keeps away from anything voluntaristic or emotional.
> Incidentally, this trait is the result of a slow development peculiar to modern Western thought.[2]

Again, there is something very strange about this. Is it not the business of the scientist, simply as scientist, not to lie? Does not this business arise 'within the realm of science proper'? What would it mean to claim that he is not encountering this rule in the course of his work, at least when he is tempted to break it? Where does the boundary of 'his work' lie? Again, if he is tempted to break that rule, or any other rule directly applying to his work, can he 'keep away from anything voluntaristic' in the process of resisting these temptations? Can the puritanical attitude operate in some way independent of the usual processes of volition? Need it involve no appropriate emotion? Normally, puritanism seems to be primarily a particular emotional and voluntaristic response to the world around one. Is it perhaps the duty of a scientist, if he is attacked by temptation, to suppress his emotional revulsion to lying and put aside the voluntaristic habit of acting on such emotions, so that in the end he will simply lie as the temptation inclines him?

TWO VIEWS

(1) Chain

If we are to understand remarks as oddly expressed as these, we need to grasp what is actually being claimed, and, in Chain's case, this is not doubtful. The whole point of his article is to justify scientists in working without hesitation on every kind of modern armament, including thermonuclear bombs, and also chemical and biological weapons in so far as these can be made effective. A scientist, says Chain, is in no way responsible for the destructive effects of any weapons that he helps to develop, because

> the responsibility is not his, but society's. *He has no choice* but to assist his nation by developing the most effective defence techniques, and also the most effective, and therefore the most destructive, aggressive war weapons, but the decision to use the weapons and the responsibility for its destructive effects rests not with him but with society.[3] (Emphasis mine)

We might perhaps ask: has not the scientist then at least some special part to play in the discussions by which 'society' takes these decisions? No, says Chain, because:

> There is no reason for believing that scientists are better qualified than others to give advice in political matters.... Their professional skill does not automatically confer on them wisdom, and wisdom is required when dealing with human relations.... There is no evidence that scientists *per se* have any greater claim to wisdom than other members of society; there is, in fact, a good deal of evidence to the contrary. *They are just as prejudiced and emotional as any other group of people, certainly in relation to matters outside their professional competence....* The views of the scientists, therefore, carry no greater authority in major political issues than those of non-scientists.[4] (Emphasis Chain's)

Chain does concede that scientists have an urgent duty to warn the public about dangers of which they have special knowledge, both over warfare and over other threats to the environment. Here, however, he adds, 'the role of the scientist must be largely educational', which plainly means that he must not go into politics, and certainly he must not betray any official secrets. 'The scientist working in a laboratory concerned with war technology who gives away secrets is a traitor.' Will all then go well, provided that these rules are observed? This is not too clear. Observing with regret that 'since the times when I studied, science has been falling increasingly into disrepute', and that many people now regard it as fairly noxious, Chain remarks vaguely that 'maybe there is something in these people's thoughts, and self-destruction of mankind is its ultimate destiny decreed by the unfathomable laws of those forces which brought us into being'. He concludes, however, that this cheerful speculation is not a sufficient reason for halting all scientific research.

Throughout this discussion, Chain displays a quite extra-ordinary view of personal identity, a total refusal to notice that scientist and citizen are one and the same person. He speaks of 'society' as if it were a separate entity, giving orders that must be obeyed without question. He rules that the scientist has to obey those orders because 'he has no choice'. So it is not being denied that this person is in fact a citizen. (Chain is not, for instance, writing an individualistic tract to say that scientists stand outside society.) But this scientist's trained intellect and expertise are treated as belonging to him only in his scientific capacity. He is not licensed to bring them into his civic thinking, and it is even held, with a remarkable insolence thinly disguised as modesty, that his scientific background makes him downright bad at doing so. As we try to grasp this strange viewpoint, questions naturally arise about the standing that Chain himself wants to claim in writing his article. Does he speak here as a citizen or as a scientist? The main question about the situation of scientists concerns both. Moreover, quite a lot of Chain's argument is devoted to directly political themes such as the cold war, the overriding need for every society to defend itself, and the effectiveness of deterrence by threat. This discussion is needed, because unless his special views on these matters are accepted his ideas about the proper role of scientists are not likely to look very plausible. Again, other parts of the article deal with psychological matters such as the human race's supposedly uncontrollable thirst for knowledge. If a biochemist like Chain can expect to be listened to on these general topics, what possible reason could there be for silencing other scientists who hold different views from his about them? Is it only his opponents who lack wisdom? Chain has not in fact barred political questions out of science; he has only made the familiar move of settling them arbitrarily in advance of argument on lines that happen to suit him. This unfortunate habit, once noticed, tends to discredit those who practise it. And, in fact, the absurdity of this kind of attempt to stifle controversy has luckily been becoming clearer in the last few decades. It would scarcely be possible to find a scientist of anything like Chain's eminence taking up this sort of naïve position today.

(2) Einstein

What, however, was Einstein saying? In view of his whole life-history, it evidently has to be something different from Chain. (What makes these two pronouncements so interesting is just their superficial likeness, together with the great difference in their real meaning.) Einstein, as we know, not only devoted himself steadily throughout his life to various political campaigns for peace and justice, but also constantly called on other scholars, especially scientists, to join in this work as a natural part of their intellectual vocation. The full force of his political activity was first aroused by the notorious Berlin 'Manifesto to the Civilized World' put out in October 1914, justifying the German invasion of Belgium and claiming total righteousness for the war-effort behind it. This document was signed by ninety-three eminent German intellectuals from every field of art and thought, many of them scientists, including such major figures as Ernst Häckel, Wilhelm Röntgen, Paul Ehrlich, and Max Planck.[5]

Einstein at once came forward among the very few major scholars calling for a completely opposite line, and trying to organize intellectual influences from all the combatant nations to urge negotiations for an early peace. Like Bertrand Russell, who took just the same vigorous line in England, Einstein did not only object to war as such. He thought that this particular war was a pointless one, resulting largely from misguided intrigues and blundering diplomacy, a war that could benefit no one – an opinion which has on the whole been that of later historians. Einstein therefore, like Russell, began a lifetime's work of campaigning to bring the causes of such disasters under control. When we think about this effort now, we have an obvious temptation, because that control has not materialized, to see the whole project as a failure. And many people do think in this way, though they punctiliously add that of course Einstein was a saint. It is worth while, however, to ask how things would have gone if these people had not done what they did. In particular, when one thinks about that manifesto, and tries to imagine an equally scandalous document getting this range of signatures today, it becomes clear what a difference Einstein and Russell and their few courageous co-workers made. There is a strong natural temptation for intellectuals to take Chain's line, to assume vaguely that these things are not really their business, and then to be panicked or blandished by politicians into lending their prestige to whatever proposal is suddenly put before them. (Planck, for instance, apparently did not even read the text of the manifesto.) Einstein, who never forgot this experience, therefore continually reminded his colleagues of the heavy responsibility that this prestige unavoidably brings with it. More deeply, too, he saw the powers of a trained mind not just as constituting a useful information-machine, but as an aspect of a whole person, an apparatus adapted to make good thinking possible on large general subjects as well as on small ones. It certainly did not occur to him to treat wisdom as a dispensable part of a scientist's equipment.

What then did Einstein actually mean by the rather mysterious disclaimers just quoted? They appear as a concession at the start of a very brief article, whose main point is that reasoning, of a kind familiar to scientists, actually does have its place in ethics, so that there is more continuity between ethics and science than might at first be supposed. In the passage quoted, Einstein explains that this is still true even though science itself does not contain any commands or expressions of emotion. But he certainly puts this conceded point with an emphasis which shows that he wants to stress it as well, which must mean that he thinks it is needed to oppose some current belief. I think it is clear that what he is opposing is simply the excessive claim that science can itself furnish the first principles for ethics, as for all other forms of thought – the kind of claim widely made at the time, for instance by Waddington in the remarks we looked at earlier, and implied also in Russell's hope of substituting scientific for ethical discussion. The need to renounce this ambition is surely what Einstein had in mind when he wrote of 'something like a Puritan's restraint' being required to help scientists to avoid this particular entanglement. But there is no visible link at all between this advice to scientists to refrain from overweening intellectual imperialism and Chain's call on them to collapse into abject political submission. Einstein was telling his colleagues not to suppose that their work entitled them to take over society. Chain was telling them not to criticize in any way the role that society, in the form of the current government, happened to allot to that work.

POSSIBLE FORMS OF AUTONOMY

The great difference that emerges between the real meanings of these apparently very similar passages makes it worth our while to look a little further at the variety of ways in which such claims may be understood, more especially since rather obscure re-marks of this kind are widespread in all sorts of writings, and are often not fully explained. Starting from the more plausible, we might list them roughly like this:

1. In their enquiries, scientists must be guided always by the evidence, never by their wishes.
2. Purely factual propositions can never have practical or evaluative consequences.
3. In selecting subjects to enquire about, scientists must be guided only by relevance, never (a) by their wishes or outside pressures, or (b) by consideration of the good or harm that will result from the enquiries to any human being whatever or indeed to any other form of life.
4. Scientists need not concern themselves about the use that will be made of their discoveries. They are not responsible for the consequences of this use, even when they could have predicted them.
5. Scientists need not concern themselves about the conditions

which make their enquiries possible. They are not responsible for anything objectionable about the sources of their funds, even when they know about it.

6. Scientists may use in their work any methods which that work seems to demand, including actions which in any other context would be wrong. Moral objections do not apply to these activities at all.

7. No non-scientific considerations will ever be relevant to the scientific enquiries themselves. If (for instance) philosophical, historical, or theological questions seem to arise in the course of this work, these can either be ignored or settled in whatever way seems proper to the scientist. There can never be any need for scientists to learn alien methods.

8. The value of science itself is self-contained and self-evident in a way which makes it unnecessary ever to spell out what it consists in, or to weigh it against any other kind of value.

9. Scientific education is entirely a matter for educators and is no concern of scientists.

Glancing through this list, many people will be inclined to sign up readily for items 1–3a, but to reject 3b, and finally to regard most of the others as at best dangerous half-truths, needing careful thought and qualification, while some are simply indefensible. As we shall see – except for 1, which applies to everybody and not only to scientists – even these first relatively decent formulations are by no means as solid as they may look. But in any case they will not cover anything like the controversial ground needed. All these positions, even the most extraordinary, are from time to time implied and acted on in controversy, though they are seldom clearly discussed and spelt out.

Can they be phrased in a way that does justice to the half-truths in them without allowing their various disturbing implications? One attractive way of trying to disinfect some of them might be to add some such words as '*qua* scientists' or 'in their role as scientists', with the hope that these will sort out the dubious cases. How far will this take us?

Unfortunately, this move only blurs the real trouble, which concerns the nature of professions and of professional roles themselves. Membership of any profession involves a great mass of essential concerns outside the special work which the profession exists to perform. The case of music is a good parallel. Is it no business of musicians – *qua* musicians – to worry about how music is funded? Or about the persecution and oppression of musicians in other countries, or indeed in their own? Does the state of musical education not concern them? Would it not matter to them – as musicians – if music were being put to sinister uses, for instance to induce docility in political prisoners? And, on the theoretical side, should they not take an interest in the history of their art, in the principles and methods by which it is criticized, in the relation of music to acoustics, to mathematics, to other arts like dancing and poetry, and in general to life? Of course not all these matters will concern all musicians. But, for those that do, their interest will surely form part of their professional roles – their lives *qua* musicians. If these things were held not to be the business of musicians, then whose business (one feels inclined to ask) would they possibly be?

Yet it is true that these things are not part of the actual work of composing or performing music. That work does have its own internal rules, which cannot be displaced by rules governing the background activities. It could be as necessary to point this out over music as it is over science. And the existence of those internal rules means that music is indeed an autonomous art. But this autonomy cannot possibly mean that the only kind of business which arises for musicians – *qua* musicians – is the keeping of those internal rules.

What is autonomy? The word means independence of a special kind, namely, being governed by one's own laws. It was a word invented by the Greeks primarily for colonies that had made themselves independent of the states which founded them. For a state, however, this kind of independence is a very limited matter. It does not make it independent of all links with the rest of the human race. Self-governing states are still subject to international law, and to all the other, less formal, accountabilities which bind all states to their neighbours. All it lacks is a 'mother-country' that would make some of its major decisions for it. The point of this parallel between states and professions is to stress that each is always a body within a larger body. Independence is only relative, applying to matters which either do not much concern the larger body, or which it has consented to have dealt with separately. Absolute independence is not possible for such a group, any more, indeed, than it is for an individual living among others. And a profession is, of course, an even less likely candidate for absolute independence than a nation is, since it is not even geographically isolated. A profession exists because the community it belongs to needs it. Its members live among fellow-citizens, and its work often affects the life around it profoundly.

This is what makes all the bolder isolationist claims given above so surprising. Their strangeness has, I think, been somewhat obscured till lately because they have not been clearly distinguished from a quite different set of claims – claims that science is actually so useful, so advantageous to society, that its instrumental value exceeds that of all possible rivals, activities. On this view, science, far from falling outside the value-system, has already been brought within it, weighed, and found supreme. Far from needing no justification, it has already been completely justified.

SCIENCE AS SUPREMELY USEFUL

From the seventeenth century on, this praise of modern science as a means to other human ends has been as much stressed as the exaltation of it as an end in itself, and the two have not always been clearly distinguished. Ever since those early days, however, some people have been sceptical about the instrumental claim, not being confident that all the promised benefits would be delivered. They have given warnings that science was in itself a neutral instrument which could be used for bad purposes as well as for good ones, and that, unless the nature of mankind changed radically, the bad ones might very well prevail. It is only in the last half-century, however, that this kind of warning has begun to have any wide influence. It does so today because the dangerous effects of technology have become so obvious that many scientists are now among those who are most eager to warn us about them. These warnings are obviously now not a proof of an anti-science attitude, but an aspect of science itself. At this point, accordingly, it becomes necessary to stop making enormous, wholesale claims about the usefulness of science as such, and to attend instead to many detailed problems about the comparative usefulness of different ways of doing science. Many points that I have been making, notably those concerned with the need to alter our whole conception of knowledge, are intended to form part of this discussion.

THE MENACE OF IDEOLOGICAL IMPERIALISM

It is important, however, to be sure that we grasp the bearings of this argument. What were the people who proclaimed these rather obscure forms of purdah for science actually demanding? and in particular what were they denying? The special combination of fervour and ambiguity which they often show indicates (here as usual) quite a large range of targets. Sometimes these proclamations are aimed, as Einstein's was, against theoretical and ideological excesses, against attempts to extend scientific doctrines to provide a guide to life, a solution to all vast and difficult human problems – attempts sometimes made by scientists themselves, but sometimes also by non-scientists who wanted to hijack the prestige of science for their schemes. These attempts have been made as long as modern science has existed. In the seventeenth century they produced mechanism, whether religious (as with Newton) or atheistical (as with Hobbes and La Mettrie). Mechanism made the role of science dramatic enough, but in the nineteenth century Herbert Spencer and others added the even more exciting notion of 'evolutionary ethics', the picture of a cosmic process, not just ordered, but thoroughly beneficent, providing – through science, which could interpret it – an unfailing guide for all human conduct and a guarantee for the whole human future.

This was not only a more colourful and ambitious doctrine than mechanism, able to reach a wider public, but also one much more obviously at odds with its supposed scientific base. The notions on which it rests, notions of perpetual progress and of the human race as the centre of the cosmic drama, were no part of official Darwinian biology at all. Darwin himself rejected this Spencerian story, and T. H. Huxley denounced it roundly. Such rejections, however, have had little effect on the force of this myth, which still has great influence today, even among scientists. It is important to notice that, in general, dramas like this

84

cannot be destroyed merely by official disclaimers. They have their life in the imagination, not just in the intellect, and they have to be dealt with at their own level and on their own ground. As I have already suggested, it is no use merely ordering the imagination to keep out of science. Science cannot do its work without it. What is wrong with the distortions is not that they connect science with some influential picture of the world, but that they have chosen a bad picture. They have to be dealt with, not by cutting science off from all such pictures, but by thinking harder about the rest of life.

The simpler policy of disgusted silence has, however, naturally had great appeal for scientists who have suddenly found their subject being dramatized in this way. Rather than be drawn into disputes which seem alien to their methods and training, they often prefer simply to rewrite the by-laws and prosecute ideologists for trespass. This has been the main method used against the two scientifically oriented doctrines which cropped up next – the Marxist and the Freudian. It is interesting to notice how, in the first half of this century, many scientific writers who were not propagandists at all simply took it for granted that at least one of these ideologies was indeed 'scientific'. They seem often even to have managed to pay this tribute to both of them at once, which, considering the radical conflicts between these thought-systems, is a striking testimony of faith. In Britain, an impressive constellation of polymathic Marxist scientists – J. D. Bernal, Joseph Needham, J. B. S. Haldane, and (less deeply committed) Conrad Waddington – lent high status to this position, and only the excesses of Stalinism finally made it untenable. If no officially Marxist nation had existed, or even none so undeniably obnoxious, it might well have lasted much longer. Yet sooner or later it would certainly have had to be opposed. The trouble with these ideologies is not that they contain no truth, but that they are too simple, too one-sided, too dogmatic in claiming universal empire for limited insights.

Attempts to extend these methods far beyond the subject-matter that actually suits them naturally produce weaker and weaker results. In particular, *a priori* applications of Marxist principles to physical science have been notoriously unlucky. Sometimes, as in the case of Lysenko, they have ended in real disaster. At the level of theory, their emptiness is well seen in several passages which Jacques Monod quotes from Engels, notably the one on the dialectical development of a grain of barley:

> Let us take a grain of barley . . . if [it] meets with conditions which for it are normal . . . a specific change takes place, it germinates; the grain as such ceases to exist, it is negated and in its place appears the plant which has arisen from it, the negation of the grain. But what is the normal life-process of this plant? It grows, flowers, is fertilized, and finally once more produces grains of barley, and as soon as these have ripened the stalk dies, is in its turn negated. As a result of the negation of this negation we have once again the original grain of barley, but not as a single unit, but ten, twenty or thirty-fold.[6]

And again: 'It is the same', Engels adds later,

> in mathematics. Let us take any algebraical magnitude whatever; for example, a. If this is negated, we get $-a$ (minus a). If we negate that negation, by multiplying $-a$ by $-a$, we get $+a$ (squared), i.e. the original positive magnitude, but at a higher degree, raised to its second power.

These determined efforts by Engels to round Marx's social theory out into a full-scale metaphysical system, grounded on physical science, have had a really unfortunate effect. Such systems have been discredited, not least because it has been seen how quite different ones can be constructed with equal ease and convincingness. They no longer command any confidence.

Altogether, it is no wonder that the claims to scientific standing put forward by Marxists and Freudians led to a Popperian retribution. Physical scientists closed their gates against all such thought-systems wholesale, without the trouble of examining them separately, on the simple ground that they were 'not science'. The word science, formerly a very wide one, was given a far narrower definition, limited to the recognized physical sciences, indeed to such parts of them as were strictly verifiable – or, as Popper soon insisted, falsifiable – preferably by laboratory methods. What fell outside this circle was now dismissed as unscientific, sometimes as meaningless, often as 'metaphysical' – a term which many followers of Popper apparently took to be a synonym for vacuous.

Some alarm followed, when it was noticed that on this view the theory of evolution itself, in its currently accepted Darwinian form, fell outside science and into this waste-paper basket. Some of those present were prepared to wrap themselves in their puritanical principles and leave it there. Others were not. Popper himself finally obliged by conceding that the boundary need not be so simply conceived or so strictly defended. Borderlines might be more subtly redrawn, to allow Darwinian thinking still to count as part of science. Those involved seem, however, not to have been struck, as they certainly should have been at this point, by the question of what this concession meant. Indeed, what was the significance of the whole insistence on the boundary of 'science'?

SCIENCE AND PSEUDO-SCIENCE

What does it mean to say that some enquiry is or is not 'a science'? In this context, the central meaning of the term was evidently honorific. The only contrast dwelt on was that between science and pseudo-science – between real enquiry about the physical world and bad imitations of such enquiry. There was no mention of other sorts of enquiry – of the relation between science and (for instance) logic, law, history, archaeology, linguistics, or mathematics. This was an extraordinary lapse, because what fell outside the newly defined borders of science might obviously fall into some one of these provinces, and it might be very important to notice that it did so. This was indeed true in the case of evolutionary theory. That theory is a historical one, as well as being an essential part of biology, and it can be very important for biologists to notice that their subject has an essential historical aspect. So has cosmology. The story of the universe too is a unique sequence, just as the story of life on earth is, and both need to be studied by historical methods.

What then was Marx actually doing? Obviously, he was chiefly doing political theory, history, and economics, and his claim to ground his views about these matters on physical science was an outlying, largely unnecessary, part of his work. The subjects he

was studying can, of course, be studied more or less 'scientifically' in the sense of critically and methodically. But their aims
and methods are not those provided by any of the physical
sciences, so it is perverse to dismiss him for not having used
those methods. On top of these studies, Marx was plainly also
trying to do something metaphysical, and apparently making
some striking and instructive mistakes in the process. But
neither in his case nor in Freud's is 'talking metaphysics'
equivalent to talking nonsense. With Freud, the essential subject-matter is the psychology of motivation. Since none of the
physical sciences has anything directly to say about this, it is not
at all surprising or wrong that he did not commonly use their
methods. Freud's claims to be 'scientific' about it may well often
be unjustified, but the main trouble about them is that they are
obscure. Their interpretation depends on the very questions we
are now raising about the meaning of all such claims. But these,
like many others that have been gathering around us, are
primarily philosophical questions.

What does it mean when we start to do philosophy? The part
that philosophical work must play in our thinking is itself
something that has to be considered if we want to ask the
questions that have occupied us so far about the autonomy of
other subjects. I want to say that the state of philosophy is never
just a local issue. It matters vitally to any culture how its central
concepts are being handled. People have to think somehow,
and, where they do not do it consciously and critically, they are
more or less helpless passengers in the vehicles bequeathed to
them by earlier ages, so that to refuse to think about philosophy
is to bind oneself a prisoner to the philosophy of the past.
Today, certain groups of obsolete philosophical notions are very
influential, and because the world is changing so fast they are
particularly dangerous. Among those ideas are the ones which
chiefly fuelled the drive towards academic specialization,
particularly towards the specialization of philosophy itself. The
ideas that caused philosophy to shut itself away from its publicly
useful functions have now been shown to be mistakes –
philosophical mistakes, as well as just ordinary blunders. To say
this, however, necessarily involves us in looking at those ideas
themselves, and tracing briefly the history of their rise and fall.

This, therefore, I shall try to do in part 3. I am as well aware as any critic can be that this account must be painfully sketchy, but I think its main outlines matter so much to our central theme that the story must be told somehow. The invention of linguistic philosophy and the difficulty it has had in usefully reaching most of the people who needed it are not just private matters. They concern all of us who are trying to think today.

Part Three

THE ROLE OF
PHILOSOPHY

Chapter Nine

CAN PHILOSOPHY
BE NEUTRAL?

Only the learned read old books and we have now so
dealt with the learned that they are of all men the least
likely to acquire wisdom by doing so. We have done this
by inculcating the Historical Point of View. . . . When a
learned man is presented with any statement in an
ancient author, the one question he never asks is whether it
is true. He asks who influenced the ancient writer, and
how far the statement is consistent with what he said in
other books, and what phase in the writer's development,
or in the general history of thought, it illustrates, and how
it affected later writers, and how often it has been
misunderstood (specially by the learned man's own
colleagues) and what the general course of criticism on it
has been for the last ten years, and what is the 'present
state of the question'. To regard the ancient writer as a
possible source of knowledge – to anticipate that what he
said could possibly modify your thoughts or your
behaviour – this would be rejected as unutterably simple-
minded. And since we cannot deceive the whole human
race all the time, it is most important thus to cut every
generation off from all others; for where learning makes
a free commerce between the ages there is always the
danger that the characteristic errors of one may be
corrected by the characteristic truths of another.
(The Devil in *The Screwtape Letters* by C. S. Lewis,
letter xxvii)[1]

THE PROBLEM OF MISCELLANEOUS QUESTIONS

To look back briefly on our journey so far: The difficulty from which we started was the one raised by the general conflict between specialization and human wholeness. And, among the areas of life in which this conflict makes trouble, we have dwelt chiefly on its effect on the quest for knowledge, because knowledge is now one of the ideals which our culture honours most highly – for many people, indeed, perhaps actually the highest ideal of all. If, therefore, that ideal is indeed disintegrating – if our methods of pursuing it are increasingly ill-adapted for their aim – this is a very serious matter, not just for professional intellectuals directly involved in the quest, but for all those who own and value and contribute to the culture in which this quest is central.

For rather similar reasons, I have concentrated so far mainly on one special area of that general quest for knowledge – the area known somewhat loosely as 'science'. Specialization undoubtedly raises many similar problems elsewhere, all over the field of learning. But the notion of science has, as already mentioned, a unique importance today, being widely regarded, both by its own practitioners and by outsiders, as the pattern for all other enquiries. The name 'science' does not denote just one set of methods among many, but is a title of honour, taken to mark the only set that is really legitimate at all. That is why the attack launched against certain kinds of thinking, such as the Marxist or the Freudian one, by saying that they are 'not science', is not just a redescription, but is meant as a blow that should finally exclude them from serious professional attention. The effect is to inhibit widely ranging enquiries that fall outside the 'scientific' field by banishing them from the academic scene altogether.

As already mentioned, if we once begin to ask the meaning of this kind of procedure, we move at once into what might look like a quite different field of enquiry, namely, philosophy. Questions about how to classify investigations which do not fit easily into existing classes are bound to be philosophical business, because the whole enterprise of classifying them is philosophical in the first place. Whoever does it, this work is not a part of the other detailed enquiries, but an exercise in sorting out the basic framework of concepts that they all share. It demands an understanding of the logic of different ways of thinking, a skill in finding how to fit different kinds of idea together. A main reason why philosophy arose originally among the Greeks was that a number of different ways of thinking had already arisen, and the relations between them were beginning to prove puzzling. This was happening both over practical thinking, where moral ideas clashed, and in purely theoretical enquiry, where different studies – especially mathematical ones – were also beginning to collide. Such puzzles have formed a prominent element in philosophical work ever since.

What is strange today, however, and what must be our next concern, is that in this century philosophers too, especially in Britain, have begun to narrow their frontiers and to erect barriers of their own. They are no longer willing to take responsibility for the mass of miscellaneous business which might seem to be theirs precisely because nobody else is equipped to classify or cope with it. They too may now be heard dismissing large problems on the ground that they are 'not philosophy' or (still more surprisingly) are 'nothing to do with philosophy'. Enquirers who are thus sent away empty-handed are liable to become rather indignant. This is not just because they have not been given a solution. They may recognize that this would be hard. It is because they have been refused any help or attention at all, indeed have sometimes been told that their questions are meaningless. Philosophers have appeared only to want to talk to other philosophers, and in a dialect that other people do not understand. Along with this goes an evident change in what is implied in being 'a philosopher'. Just as literary critics do not expect to have to write poetry, so these philosophers seem to see themselves chiefly as critics of special argumentative skills in other philosophers, not as heirs to the whole task of those who have borne that name before them.[2] If philosophy were a newly invented study, this might not surprise the public, but it is not. It has justly gained enormous prestige in the past by being willing to deal with similar large problems, and having some success in doing so. As Wittgenstein rightly said, 'a philosophical problem has the form "I don't know my way about" ',[3] and philosophers used to help people who had such problems. The prestige remains and philosophers have not renounced it. But now (says the public) they seem only interested in taking in each other's washing. What is going on here?[4]

THE SOCRATIC PATTERN

Now this difficulty is in part an old problem. Right from Socrates' time, worried enquirers have expressed irritation at the apparent evasiveness of the professional philosophical approach. They have protested that they are sure the fellow could do much better if he would only go straight at the problem, but he insists on dodging this task by logic-chopping – in particular, he insists on wasting time in defining all sorts of terms. The suspicion is that *either* he knows the answer and won't tell it to us – which is mean – *or* he doesn't know it, in which case he should be unmasked as a fraud.

This is probably the kind of situation which gave rise to the word philosophy in the first place. It is said to have been invented by Pythagoras, who forbade people to call him *sophos*, wise, explaining that he was only *philosophos*, a lover of wisdom. Wisdom which is loved and truly valued is seen to be something difficult, which it will take time to search for. Accordingly, when philosophy is being properly used, the bystanders have to curb their impatience, much like hasty customers who cannot see why the skilled mechanic insists on doing things so slowly. And today's philosophical specialists certainly feel that they are only following Socrates' example in resisting impatience in that way. I want to suggest that in this century a good many of them have actually moved far beyond that example into a quite different and much less defensible line of business, though some of them have now seen the danger and are moving back again. But, if we are to get this point clear, we need to look carefully first at the original Socratic situation.

What disturbed people about Socrates was an apparent discrepancy between his obvious authority, stemming from a genuine, long-standing dedication to facing the large questions, and his refusal to produce ready-made answers. At his trial, he explained how he came to be charged with corrupting the young and introducing new gods, by describing his habit of continually asking everybody just what they meant, instead of saying

96

anything positive himself. This policy, he said, was due to his awareness of his own ignorance, and his only claim to be considered wise at all rested on that awareness – an awareness which other people unfortunately often lacked.

Plainly, his method was a reaction against the over-confidence of his contemporaries the sophists, sages who took high pay for answering all kinds of questions, and some of whom indeed declared themselves able to answer absolutely any question that could be asked. Instead of this, Socrates worked by asking people what they meant in a way which drew their attention to the confusions in their own thinking, and showed how those confusions had been expressed in the questions they had asked. In this way he could sometimes make it possible for them to think out those questions afresh, and with good luck to do better than answering them, by dealing directly with the rather different questions which lay underneath. But the kind of end this provided was never quite what the questioner had hoped for in the first place, and many people were not at all willing to take the trouble to reach it.

THE PROBLEM OF NEUTRALITY

This is the method that the European philosophical tradition – which takes its rise from Plato's interpretation of Socrates – has since then always followed. It raises, however, an important difficulty about neutrality, which arises at once over the remarks just mentioned, reported by Plato from Socrates' speech at his trial. Literally taken, what he says there implies that he – and anyone else who follows his example – is simply a detached intellectual therapist, sorting out other people's logic. This therapist need not himself have any views about the questions being disputed, only about the logical clarity of the terms used in them. Socrates strengthens this impression of neutrality, too, by using the famous image of the gadfly. His mission (he says) has been that of a stinging fly sent by God to wake up that noble but lazy horse, Athens, and to give it some healthy exercise.[5]

What could be more neutral than that? All the same, this literal interpretation is certainly wrong. Socratic irony and understatement set us many famous puzzles, but we do not have to solve all of them in order to see that the idea of total neutrality is an impossible one. This is plain at once, not just from his tone but from what he says about the charge of corrupting the young. He explains that what has happened here is that young men who have enjoyed hearing him catch their elders out in ignorance and confusion have sometimes picked up this skill, and have caused general resentment by practising it indiscriminately.

Now it is surely a very important question in what way, if at all, these imitative gadflies differ from their model. If all that was needed were really the sting – the provocative effect of criticism – they would not differ significantly at all. Any moderately clever person can go about forcing people to define their terms and pointing out that they cannot do it consistently. If this were all, Socrates could contentedly acknowledge these lads as his successors. Actually, however, he speaks of their activities, rather in passing, just as an unlucky accidental side-effect of his mission and one which has discredited its central business.

The reason for this is so obvious that I have to apologize for mentioning it, but sometimes obvious things need to be said. Socrates' primary concern was not to teach logic. His central interest is not logical at all. He is certainly attacking ignorance and confusion, but not for their own sakes. He is doing it because they are being used to protect and justify iniquity. From the endless mass of confusions and pretensions that surrounds him, he has picked out only the ones that have this special iniquity-preserving function – the special lies that people tell themselves and each other in order to justify doing unjustifiable things. And the way in which he exposes them is always angled to reveal certain particular awkward moral truths which these lies are being used to conceal. In spite of his real interest in logical methods, this selective emphasis is striking throughout all that we know of him. It comes out particularly strongly when, in his last words to the hostile jurors, he mentions the question of who will succeed him:

> Having said so much, I feel moved to prophesy to you
> who have given your vote against me. . . . You have brought
> about my death in the belief that through it you will be
> delivered from submitting your conduct to criticism; but I
> say that the result will be just the opposite. You will have
> more critics, whom up till now I have restrained without

your knowing it, and being younger they will be harsher to you and will cause you more annoyance. *If you expect to stop denunciation of your wrong way of life by putting people to death, there is something amiss with your reasoning.*[6] (Emphasis mine)

Certainly there is something amiss with their reasoning – a familiar logical fault which continually afflicts unjust and tyrannical governments. But what primarily interested Socrates about it was not that it showed bad logic.

THE SUPPOSEDLY IMPARTIAL ENQUIRER

Plato and the other philosophers who followed him in the central European tradition did not usually continue to cultivate the kind of Socratic irony that would have made them claim neutrality about the large topics they were discussing. They guarded themselves against undue bias in other ways, notably by making their own presuppositions as explicit as possible, and trying to be fair and comprehensive in citing the views that they opposed. In this century, however, some philosophers have begun to be a good deal influenced by the ideal of pure neutrality, and indeed to see it as the mark of a proper professional approach. In particular, they have suggested that the point of a philosophical education is simply that it provides an impartial training in mental skills. This claim was well expressed by R. M. Hare, when he was discussing the peculiar qualities of Oxford philosophy in the course of an interview with the sympathetic journalist Ved Mehta:

> 'The thing wrong with the Existentialists and the other continental philosophers', Hare said, 'is that they haven't had their noses rubbed in the necessity of saying exactly what they mean. I sometimes think it's because they don't have a tutorial system. You see, if you learn philosophy here you read a thing to your tutor and he says to you, "What do you mean by that?" and then you have to tell him. I think what makes us good philosophers is, ultimately, the method of teaching.'[7]

No doubt this method does often succeed in sharpening the pupil's faculties. But the interesting thing about Hare's claim is what it leaves out – namely (again) the choice of questions, the tutor's principles of selection. How does this tutor decide just which parts of the student's essay to question and which to let pass? And what determines whether the student's answer shall count as satisfactory or not? Inevitably, the tutor's own views, and those popular in the relevant Oxbridge circles, will have a great effect on these choices. The impression of universality and impartiality is a flattering illusion. The result will not be just to train the student's faculties, but to train them in whatever direction is locally and currently favoured. Having worked myself at both ends of this Oxbridge system, I would agree that it can have great merits and can often really help the student. But I think the price of this help – the amount of unconscious indoctrination going on – is not usually fully grasped by either party. In the past, when wider, positive doctrines were visibly attached to their tutor's attitude, it must have been much easier to detect what was happening. But now, when the main message often is the narrowing itself, this has become much harder.

There is something particularly strange, too, about its effect on the tutor. It is not a normal social situation to be licensed to keep on asking somebody else what they mean, without being liable oneself to answer the same question in one's turn – without ever having to come off the fence. Wittgenstein is said to have found the proper defence against this practice by suddenly roaring 'WHAT DO YOU MEAN WHAT DO I MEAN?' at his interrogators. This is not just a wily counter-move; it is a relevant enquiry. Normally, when we ask somebody what they mean, we are not just complaining about their obscurity. We have some particular ambiguity in mind, some real substantial question about the matter under discussion. Where this is not happening, or where that more serious question never emerges, language has indeed gone on holiday.[8] Student and tutor are then engaged in a different kind of game[9] – one that has much less to do with serious education and more to do with fashion and the dominance hierarchy. In so far as this happens, there is beginning to be corruption. Even if Hare is right to suspect that continental philosophers risk corruption from the presence of enthusiastic audiences for their ideas in cafés and of a general public which takes them seriously, it does not follow, unfortunately, that there is nothing corrupting about the methods pursued at Oxbridge too.

Corruption is not, of course, a necessary part of the method Hare describes, that of asking students what they mean. People who use that method can perfectly well use other methods also. Tutors can, if they choose, both point out which main issues they have chosen to concentrate on and explain why they have chosen these rather than others which might seem to the student as important or more so. But, unless they are specially reminded to do this, they will find it much easier simply to follow up the topics which are currently being most discussed among their friends and colleagues. This bias is indeed in itself harmless and natural. Up to a point, as a temporary measure, it is even necessary, since one cannot explain everything at once. But when it is not recognized as a bias – when it is unconscious and hidden by complacency – it becomes a serious menace. Its victims then identify what are actually local and temporary interests as constituting the only real professional approach. Tutors inevitably see it as their business to cure students of unprofessional ways of thinking – that is, of asking unfamiliar questions.

If they attempt this cure openly and explicitly, students can of course detect it, oppose it with the natural contrariness of youth, and be converted – if they finally are – by rational means. But, if it is never made explicit, this is very hard. Probably few philosophers – or indeed other academics – ever realize how much of their influence is conveyed through expression and tone of voice, rather than through argument. Certain nuances of disappointment and contempt can often do more to direct a student than a ton of good arguments. The change in philosophical methods that we are now discussing has unfortunately owed a lot to them. A mere contemptuous tone of voice, conveying shudder-quotes, has often borne the main burden of persuasion. It has proved fatally easy to pick up some of Wittgenstein's or J. L. Austin's gestures or expressions of disgust, where it would have been quite hard to state their arguments, and much harder still to grasp their reasons for using them.

CLEAR TO ME BUT NOT TO YOU

Against these weapons, the only armour a student can use at all effectively is a well-informed previous commitment to some

101

distinctive ideology, such as Marxism or fundamentalist Christianity. Where this is loudly present, tutors are forced to show their hand, and so to become more conscious of it themselves. This kind of armour, however, has of course its own drawbacks. Where it is not present, no such open comparison of positions is likely to arise. The tutor then does not have the feeling of opposing one actual doctrine by another, but merely of confronting something confusing and socially unsuitable – a solecism, a failure to act properly, something which it would on the whole be embarrassing to comment on. Reticent non-attention seems the most suitable response. But only the most thick-skinned of students can withstand the suggestion that their remark has been in bad taste because it was amateurish and confused. The tutor, meanwhile, has a quite genuine impression that the remarks actually *were* confused, and of course they may really have been so. But it is an awkward fact, often overlooked in this concentration on clarity, that familiar, accepted ideas always tend to seem clearer than unfamiliar ones, whether they actually are so or not. The clarity of an argument depends on its relation to the relevant premisses. But in real life (as opposed to mathematics) most of the premisses of an argument are unstated, and many of them have never even been made explicit. The real need is somehow to become conscious of this mass of hidden premisses, and to pick out for attention the ones that matter most. But this process takes time, during which things seem to become more confused. If clarity is one's sole aim, it can be reached much faster by refusing to consider any premisses except those that have already occurred to one as leading to one's own chosen conclusions. This simplifying of the premisses is what many people think of as a 'rational' approach, and it is just what gives the notion of rationality such a bad name that people are quite happy to say that they prefer to be irrational. In philosophy teaching, it leads to a flat, dogmatic insistence on the current fashionable approach as the only possible professional path. This insistence is sometimes made even more deadly by withdrawing traditional philosophical writings from the syllabus, and replacing them by this year's crop of articles from the journals. Where Kant and Hume and Descartes are at least being read, the student stands some chance of catching their doctrines, even in spite of the tutor. Where they are not read, tutor and student alike get only the latest fashion. This can easily mean that those who ask for bread are given only a plastic credit card, more or less warranted to ensure status until it is made obsolete by next year's issues of the journals. For the only thing certain about fashion is that it is never going to last for long.

THE PROBLEM OF CHANGE

This distressing fact is usually invisible, but it becomes obvious even to the participants themselves when – as must frequently happen – intellectual fashions do change. The ideas that one generation has held up as vital for a professional approach are then shown up as confused and inadequate by their successors. Unfortunately, common though this event is, nobody ever finds it easy to believe that it will happen again till they have lived through it repeatedly. Sages usually go on talking as if they were the definitive, ultimate occupants of their particular chairs of honour, very much as the Neapolitans have repeatedly moved back to till the fields around Vesuvius. This incredulity does not, however, arise from any lack of evidence. C. S. Lewis, remarking on changing attitudes to the Bible, mentioned some instructive parallels:

> I have learnt in other fields of study how transitory the
> 'assured results of modern scholarship' may be. . . . When I
> was a boy one would have been laughed at for supposing
> that there had been a real Homer; the disintegrators
> seemed to have triumphed for ever. But Homer seems to
> be creeping back. . . . Nor can a man of my age ever forget
> how suddenly and completely the idealist philosophy of
> his youth fell. McTaggart, Green, Bosanquet, Bradley
> seemed enthroned for ever; they went down as suddenly
> as the Bastille. And the interesting thing is that while I
> lived under that dynasty I felt various difficulties and
> objections which I never dared to express. They were so
> frightfully obvious that I felt sure they must be mere
> misunderstandings; the great men could not have made
> such very elementary mistakes as those which my
> objections implied. But very similar objections – though
> put, no doubt, far more cogently than I could have put
> them – were among the criticisms which finally prevailed.

103

They would now be the stock answers to English Hegelianism.[10]

It is worth noting here that Lewis was by no means a specially timid man. He was, moreover, a highly intelligent one, independent-minded and intensely interested in intellectual matters. He had certainly read and reflected far more in his youth than most students have. He was, too, a mature ex-service undergraduate, reading philosophy in the somewhat disturbed epoch just after the First World War. And he was studying it at Oxford, where the idealist tradition was not a deep-rooted, native growth but quite a recent import. If he, with all these advantages, found that he could not question an accepted way of thinking which the next generation of British philosophers saw reason to root out entirely, does it not seem that we are dealing here with a powerful social and psychological force, liable to distort our ideas about the nature of the academic enterprise?

CORRUPTING THE YOUNG

There is, I think, something genuinely corrupting about supposedly neutral, 'Socratic' methods of training in argument if they are used, as Socrates himself did not use them, in the air, without commitment to any particular point of view. Of course, this commitment does not have to arise instantly. Casual debating can be harmless enough. But, if debates go on for long without any commitment emerging, then other and much worse motives for continuing them will infallibly begin to take over.

By this commitment I mean open recognition that one is responsible for making it clear why one picks out certain questions for attention rather than others, and why it is important that certain views rather than others about them should prevail. This responsibility involves being ready, in the long run, to account for why one is choosing this whole approach. The long run can of course be quite long. There is nothing wrong with strange and unexpected starting-points; indeed, it is an essential part of a student's training to accept these. A questioning tutor – or a book – can often rightly begin work, as Socrates often did, by raising topics which may strike the student or reader as wild, perverse, and irrelevant. It is quite proper to ask for patience while the point of this move gradually reveals itself. And this patience is itself an important piece of professional equipment.

But patience ought not to have to be endless. In the end, it should be rewarded. The problem of whether and why this particular issue was so important ought finally to surface and to be dealt with, so that other competing problems can have their say. If this is never done, the larger curiosity which is repeatedly starved of satisfaction will finally die and can no longer be the sustaining force in the enquiry. Then all those other possible motives which Plato noted so shrewdly – ambition, vanity, competitiveness, obstinacy, obsessiveness, and sheer force of habit – will tend to take it over.

That is what I am describing as the danger of corruption. Of course it is not confined to academic work, still less to philosophy. It is the endemic danger which, as we noted at the outset, hangs over all specializations and becomes graver in proportion as they build round themselves the protective shell of a profession. But there is something specially destructive about its working in academic enquiries, and above all in philosophy. Activities like these lie in particular danger of losing their point, because that point ranges so far beyond the obviously useful. Like the fine arts, they do not often get the salutary check which comes from outside customers knocking on the door with clear and legitimate demands. The public does want something from academic enquiries, and particularly from philosophy, but its demands are often not at all clear, and when they are they are not always legitimate. So a certain reserve about meeting them easily grows up, and can harden into a refusal to admit that they have any force at all. Pundits may then firmly declare that their speciality is too complex and technical to explain to outsiders at all.

Now there are of course indeed detailed areas of thought where this is true – many of them in the physical sciences and mathematics, much fewer in the humanities. But to inhabit such an area ought surely not to be a matter of pride – a coveted position to which all real academics aspire. It should, one would suppose, rather be the business of all concerned to keep down the size and number of such areas to the minimum, and to ensure that those who must live in these stressful climates spend some of their time outside them and are kept in touch with their neighbours. Of course it is not our business to refuse to make difficult enquiries. But it surely is our business to be constantly improving the techniques of mutual explanation, so as to make them easier. Psychological continuity, the bridge that connects enquiries with each other and with our personal lives, is not an optional luxury or a guilty indulgence. For the reasons already mentioned, it is a vital lifeline for us all. It is the condition of human wholeness. Even for areas of thought which are genuinely exotic, this lifeline is necessary. But it is of course much more obviously so for ones which arise out of everyday life and can bear on it directly, such as psychology. It is very remarkable that such studies can have become sealed off from it. But they have. The notion of neutrality in philosophy which we have just been considering has arisen out of just such a narrowing and sealing-off of that enquiry. To look a little into how this has happened must be our next business.

Chapter Ten

THE WORK OF
PURIFICATION

And I saw a new heaven and a new earth.

(Book of Revelation 21.1)

DESTRUCTIVE ZEAL

The process by which English-speaking philosophy contracted itself self-suppressingly into a corner of its former field, in the plaintive hope that this would make it look more like science, was made possible, like most such changes, by controversial zeal. Feuds lead to divisions, and divisions lead to attempts to exile the adversary. And the kind of controversial zeal that rose to revolutionary fervour in this case was in itself nothing new. Repeatedly, earlier philosophers had been so appalled by the particular confusions of their times that they had called for a wholly fresh start. In their day Kant, Hobbes, Spinoza, and many others had claimed, just as their successors did at the beginning of this century, to be introducing true method for the first time into philosophy. And, since the seventeenth century, these innovators had usually given the name 'science' to their newly introduced method – something which the usage of their day fully justified, since until lately 'science' just meant 'methodical study'. Notoriously, however, the pioneer and chief exponent of this scorched-earth or slum-clearance approach to philosophy was Descartes:

As for the opinions which up to that time I had
embraced, I thought that I could not do better than resolve
at once to sweep them wholly away.[1]

> I thought that . . . I ought to reject as absolutely false all
> opinions in regard to which I could suppose the least
> grounds for doubt.[2]

In all these cases the claims have turned out to have some solid
grounds; these have indeed been great and valuable changes of
method. But in all of them the claims have been hugely
exaggerated. The break with the past has been nothing like as
drastic as it seemed at the time, and the new methods, though
genuinely useful, have not proved to give the universal clarifi-
cation that had been expected. In fact, innovations in thinking,
like other valuable human projects, cannot be dispassionately
assessed by the people who are bringing them about. It is almost
inevitable that these people should overestimate the importance
of what they are doing. They are also peculiarly liable to the
phenomenon that hill-walkers call the *false crest* – the impression
that the summit is already in sight, so that, provided their
methods are used, only a little more work and research money
will be needed to reach it.

If, therefore, one insisted on judging these philosophic
advances by how they match up to these claims, one would think
them disappointing. But of course that would be an absurd way
to judge them. The claims are froth on the surface of thought.
The illusion of finality and completeness is just a natural illusion
like any other, and any claims to primacy in dispute that are
based on it are part of the pathology or the politics of learning,
not part of its substance. If, then, we turn to the latest in this
series of claims – to the declarations of total change which were
made at the beginning of this century by people like Russell,
Moore, and Wittgenstein – is there any reason to treat them
differently, to accept them as genuinely marking an entirely new
epoch, a departure which has made nearly all previous philosophy out of date?

I want to say that there was indeed an important change made
at that time, one which was vitally needed in order to make
effective large-scale thinking possible in an age as confusing as
our own. But it is nothing like as simple or drastic a change as
most of its more vocal exponents have supposed, and moreover
it is still incomplete. It probably needs as many more large new
ideas to complete it as were contributed by Moore, Russell, and

Wittgenstein early in this century. It has also been exceptionally badly put forward to the general public, largely because it has become entangled with the quite different general change to increased academic specialization in a way that has confused nearly everybody concerned in it, and persuaded many of them that they need make no effort at all to explain themselves. It has therefore been widely and thoroughly misunderstood.

THE SURFACE REVOLUTION

The best way to deal with this discouraging position is, I believe, to start by looking here at the simple, popularly accepted account of the new kind of philosophy, so as to get its cruder version out of the way before moving on to the real thing, and this is all I shall try to do in this chapter. I take this simple account from one of its most widely read, clearest, and most influential spokesmen, Bertrand Russell. Though he did not finally grasp or follow through what (in my view) turned out to be the movement's central contribution, he certainly set it going. Russell made his way, so to speak, to a hilltop from which the general direction of the necessary journey could be seen, and he showed immense helpfulness and generosity in bringing others up there to see it with him. It was he who persuaded Moore to study philosophy, it was he who told the world about Frege, it was he who first received the impact of Wittgenstein, arriving unannounced on his doorstep stuttering of strangely original ideas, and who made it possible for both the man and the ideas to develop and be received in England. Moreover, Russell's beautifully clear writings introduced the new philosophy to a wide public. He was not a prophet, in the sense that I discussed before, because he always tried to explain what was happening. But there is another reason why he is a key figure in the changes of attitude involved. He is important also because of his very limitations. The divisions within Russell's own personality were typical of his age and typical of those that shaped the new approach, so that he is a symbolic as well as an influential figure in its whole formation. Russell's work for peace and political justice occupied as much of his enormous energies as did his philosophical work. Yet, though he longed to connect these two projects, he could see no honest way of doing so. The projects

109

themselves remained for him radically divided, and the different sides of his personality that responded to them – his feelings and his intellect – were, in spite of his efforts, also separated and often at war. He therefore came to reject entirely the wide areas of philosophy that might have made an intelligible connection between them – areas that cover most of its traditional terrain.

Russell states this rejection forcibly at the end of his *History of Western Philosophy*,[3] a book which, it is worth noting, soon became a best-seller and has long remained so. It concludes his last chapter, which is called 'The philosophy of logical analysis', and it thus supplies a kind of happy ending to the whole book.[4] Russell explains here that, unfortunately, philosophy has so far consisted of two quite distinct elements, which ought never to have been combined, and have now at last been separated. Only the first of these is real philosophy; it is an attempt to discover the truth about the world. The second is 'an ethical and political doctrine as to the best way of living'. Contamination by this doctrine has not only distorted the search for truth but has constantly turned it from its proper purpose towards an irrelevant one – namely, the improvement of morals. 'Philosophers', says Russell, 'from Plato to William James, have allowed their opinions about the constitution of the universe to be influenced by their desire for edification.' They have assumed therefore, 'in advance of enquiry, that certain beliefs, whether true or false, are such as to promote good behaviour', and have accordingly taught those beliefs without regard for their truth. In particular, these philosophers have concentrated their energies on inventing proofs of the existence of God and the immortality of the soul – proofs which they must have known were bogus. 'Knowing, as they supposed, what beliefs would make men virtuous, they have invented arguments, often very sophistical, to prove that these beliefs are true.' (Among those accused of this fraudulence, he particularly names Kant.)

Russell rules, therefore, that most philosophy up to the present has been dishonest, but explains that logical analysts have at last managed to cure this vice:

> In the welter of conflicting fanaticisms, one of the few unifying forces is scientific truthfulness. . . . To have insisted upon the *introduction* of this virtue into

110

philosophy, and to have invented a powerful method by which it can be made fruitful, are the chief merits of the philosophical school of which I am a member.

This school, he says, 'is thus able, in regard to certain problems, to achieve definite answers, *which have the quality of science rather than of philosophy*'. This notion remained central with him, and it has done so with many influential philosophers ever since. Thus Quine writes, 'Philosophy, or what appeals to me under that head, is continuous with science. It is a wing of science where aspects of method are examined more deeply or in a wider perspective than elsewhere.'[5]

These favoured problems, he says, include questions such as 'What is number?' 'What are space and time?' 'What is mind and what is matter?' He concedes that of course to confine philosophy henceforward to questions like these will very much narrow its apparent scope, but explains that this will be no real loss. It is not important that

> there remains a vast field, traditionally included in philosophy, where scientific methods are inadequate. This field includes ultimate questions of value; science alone, for example, cannot prove that it is bad to enjoy the infliction of cruelty. *Whatever can be known can be known by means of science*; but things which are legitimately matters of feeling lie outside its province. (All emphases mine)

We need to look with a fresh eye at this strange picture of the scope of thought, which has now become so familiar that it is hard for us to take in its extreme oddness. He divides the whole field of human interests – the whole range of the questions we can ask and think about – into two sections: (1) science, which is co-extensive with real knowledge, and (2) pure feeling, which falls right outside it. All enquiry that aims at knowledge must therefore from now on qualify as science.

How could this simple-minded division possibly work? Even Russell's hasty pen would perhaps have faltered at this bizarre formulation, this strange outcome of his earlier moves, if the picture had not already become official doctrine. (It is, for instance, very close to the Logical Positivist one that A. J. Ayer had presented in *Language, Truth and Logic* in 1936.) Russell is saying that outside 'science' there is, not just no knowledge, but no disciplined thought at all, no concepts that could need the attention of philosophers. Anybody who seems to be thinking in a systematic way about anything other than science – thinking, for instance, about history or about what to do and how to live – is really only experiencing emotion. And, if people in this situation try to clear up their thoughts by articulating them in the form of arguments, they can only be illicitly trying to influence those around them.

THE SHRINKING OF KNOWLEDGE

We can perhaps best sort out this notion by beginning with its less startling element – the equation of science with knowledge. Could these two really be co-extensive? How could science ever have got started at all without presupposing an enormous amount of pre-existing knowledge? Through our senses, through our memory and the testimony of others, and through informal calculation, we all lay in a great mass of information and skills that are necessary if science is ever to start. If this whole background were dismissed as not 'knowledge', it is hard to see how the science that rests on it could be knowledge either. When people start to study science, they are not then beginning for the first time in their lives to know something. What they do then is to get a certain sort of explanation for some of the things they already know. And this informal background is not confined to the past. Working scientists would not get far if they could not go on taking the deliverances of their senses, their memories, and the reports of their colleagues as knowledge. And, if they do take these as knowledge, then they can also trust the discoveries made, through these same means, by others who are not scientists at all. They can and do, for instance, trust well-qualified explorers and geographers, linguists, mathematicians, and historians, as well as their own technicians. In any ordinary sense, all this material is knowledge, and only if we treat it as such does it become possible to do science. Science, in fact, like other learned studies, is quite a small and recent branch on the tree of human knowledge. And of course, incidentally, if this great background of knowledge outside science could not be trusted, we could scarcely be expected to take seriously a history-book such as the *History of Western Philosophy*.

Why is Russell writing as if all facts were included in science, when, if we use the word 'science' in its modern sense, they so visibly are not? He clearly is not using the word in its more modest, older Latin sense, merely to mean 'knowledge', since that is not his usage elsewhere in the book. For instance, in his closely related remarks at the beginning, he speaks of non-scientific questions as ones that cannot be answered 'in the laboratory' (p. 13). And of course, if the word merely meant knowledge in general, what he says would be trivial, which it certainly is not meant to be.

THE HYPNOTIC EFFECTS OF GLORY

The difficulty here is of course not just about an eccentricity of Russell's. It concerns the whole thinking of our age. In proportion as the notion of science has begun to loom larger for us, it has become woollier and more ambiguous. About the beginning of this century, the meaning of the word was narrowed from 'methodical study' in general to 'methodical study of the physical world, as carried on in laboratories' in particular. But the wider, honorific meaning did not vanish, and the adjective 'scientific' remains firmly pegged to it. To be 'unscientific' still ranks as a disgrace for any study. Thus both meanings persist together, generating untold confusion.

It therefore easily seems to us as if the only possible method-ical study were that of the physical world as carried on in laboratories, all other ways of thinking being by definition casual and inexact. What changed the word's meaning in the first place was a well-justified public admiration for the success of the physical sciences, causing them to be accepted as the central case of methodical study. That same strong light of admiration has also oddly simplified the accepted notion of physical science itself, making this new and splendid study seem far more homogeneous than it actually is. The deep differences of method between the various physical sciences easily become blurred and forgotten. An abstract amalgam called 'the scien-tific method' is credited with the whole brilliant range of achievements. People often forget, for instance, that there are physical sciences in which experiments done in laboratories play little part – sciences such as astronomy, geology, ethology, and palaeontology. Mathematics, of course, does not use experiment at all, yet it is often thought of as a science. All branches of science require, too, some general thinking to form their peculiar concepts, thinking which cannot be reduced to any single general method, let alone a regular laboratory drill. In fact, within physical 'science' as well as outside it, many different methods of investigation have to be used, including different methods of thought, and the first skill needed is the one that Aristotle named – that of discovering the right method for a particular enquiry.

However, the idea of breaking up the concept of science in this more critical way seems usually not to have struck those many people outside physical science who felt threatened by its rising prestige. Instead, in order to avoid being dismissed as amateurs, these people tended to welcome the idea of a single, highly abstract, 'scientific method' which could in principle be extended to fit all other respectable studies. This annexe seemed to provide a way into the castle. If they could prove that they too shared this method, they might be able to claim that their enquiries had (as Russell plaintively put it) 'the quality of science'. These claims therefore began to be widely made in the social sciences and humanities. There is a certain pathos about them, because they never really impress physical scientists; they are never going to qualify outsiders to join the club. All the same, they have seemed, and still do seem, vitally important to many of those who make them. The idea that 'scientific' thinking is the only reputable kind of thinking is still very compelling. Those gripped by it naturally attach great import-ance to slum-clearance – to getting rid of all parts of their own study that cannot easily be made to look like experimental physical science. And in philosophy, as in other parts of the humanities, that means most of it.

Chapter Eleven

THE PROBLEM OF
THE UNKNOWN

Intelligent practice is not a step-child of theory. On the contrary, theorising is one practice amongst others and is itself intelligently or stupidly conducted.

(Gilbert Ryle, *The Concept of Mind*, 26)[1]

WIDER HORIZONS

Russell himself had pointed out this very dilemma at the outset of his *History of Western Philosophy*. He wrote there that

Almost all the questions of most interest to speculative minds are such as science cannot answer. . . . Science tells us what we can know, but what we can know is little, and if we forget how much we cannot know we become insensitive to many things of great importance.[2]

He then listed a wide range of vast, familiar traditional philosophic questions as still urgently needing our study, including among them a number of moral questions. And the kind of thing that, in this mood, he thought could be expected of philosophy becomes clear in a later passage where, summing up the achievements of the past, he writes, 'The problem of a durable and satisfactory social order can only be solved by combining the solidity of the Roman Empire with the idealism of St Augustine's City of God. To achieve this, *a new philosophy will be needed*' (emphasis mine).[3]

Some of the moral problems Russell names in his opening passage are ones which he certainly did himself think worth discussing, since he had actually written about them movingly

115

elsewhere. Notably, he mentions the question, 'Must the good be eternal in order to be valued, or is it worth seeking even if the universe is moving inexorably towards death?' – a topic which he had dealt with very seriously in essays such as 'Mysticism and logic' and 'A free man's worship'. And, still in this passage at the beginning of the *History*, he did not at all dismiss these moral questions from philosophy as merely matters of feeling. He simply said of them, along with the other big questions, that they are probably insoluble, yet still so important that it is part of our human business to wrestle with them, even if we have no real hope of a final answer. 'To teach how to live without certainty, and yet without being paralysed by hesitation, is perhaps the chief thing that philosophy, in our age, can still do for those who study it.'

This was the constructive, bold, and generous spirit in which Russell began his *History of Western Philosophy*. He could then assure his readers in good faith that the big questions deserved their attention, and that the study of this history would therefore not be a waste of their time. Yet, if what he wrote at the end had been true, it surely would have been a waste of time. Why investigate a load of pious fraud?

ON KNOWING HOW TO DO THINGS

It is worth looking a little more carefully here at what Russell says in this constructive, inclusive mood, at the outset of his enterprise. He there describes philosophy as able to teach us 'how to live without certainty'. The big problems raised by the last two words of this promise are ones that we must return to later – how and in what sense have we to live 'without certainty'? But the point that matters for the moment is that this lesson is essentially a practical one. It is a lesson in *how to live*. Now 'how to live' is not a fact, and it could scarcely be any part of a science. Yet knowing in some degree how to live surely is a necessary part of knowledge. It even looks like a precondition of all other valuable knowing. Indeed, as both Kant[4] and Ryle[5] have suggested, practical knowledge, 'knowing how', is at least as fundamental a skill as 'knowing that', since – as we have noticed before – the mere possession of knowledge is empty unless it can be actively used. Among the many problems that we have about 'how to live', there is, then, certainly one particularly awkward squad of difficulties which are concerned with how to think. They are problems about the way in which we should use the rest of our knowledge, about how we should relate its various parts, and how we had better view knowledge itself. As Wittgenstein later put it, 'a philosophical problem has the form "I don't know my way about" '.[6] And as Russell reasonably remarks here, if one has ambitious ideas about what certainty is, learning 'how to live without certainty and yet without being paralysed by hesitation' is indeed a most necessary skill for our lives. And this skill gets more crucial as more and more information is continually being flung at us.

PROBLEMS OF EXPLORATION

Accordingly, Russell at the outset of his book seemed to have left plenty of room for large philosophical questions of this kind. Yet there was still something very odd about the conception that he had of them – something which I think accounts for the later revulsion which made him throw them all out of the window. Even in his inclusive mood, he was not seeing them as questions of a peculiar *form* – practical questions about how best to live and think. He writes as if they were ordinary factual questions which could in principle be finally settled, but which just happen to be specially hard to answer – questions perhaps rather like 'What is at the centre of the earth?' or 'What is beyond the farthest star that we can see?' Similarly, when in his exclusive mood he chooses a few philosophical questions as answerable after all, he makes them look like factual, physical ones. The questions he mentions ('What is number? What are space and time? What is mind and what is matter?') look superficially like 'What is water?' where the answer expected is H_2O. Really, however, these questions are quite different. They are asking something more like 'How is it best to think of time, space, number, matter or the like, for the purposes we need and in the context of the data we have got?' These questions are indeed relevant to science, but they are relevant to its philosophical part. Their expected answers are not meant to state a fact, still less to prove one. They are meant to give guidance on how we need to think – guidance which is in an important way of the same kind as the guidance we get from clarifying crucial moral concepts, like that of honesty or freedom.

117

This notion of guidance was of the first importance to Wittgenstein, who suggested that we should regard the problem to be studied as a rough tract of unknown country, which we are not asking about only for theoretical purposes, such as passing exams, but because we shall need to live in it and therefore to move about in it confidently and freely.[7] This problem therefore has to be tackled, not just by learning a list of facts about it, but by personally finding one's way around it. And this piece of rough ground is not some artificial, fenced-off adventure-playground, it is an integral part of the world we live in. Thus, as Renford Bambrough remarks, 'The short answer to the question "What made you decide to become a philosopher?" might be "What made *you* decide to become a human being?" '[8] Russell, however, never considered this quite different approach to conceptual questions. That is why he found it so hard to see any proper way of dealing with large issues, though he was, all the same, never really willing to abandon them. For instance in 1917, when he was in prison for his opposition to the war, he wrote a letter outlining an ambitious scheme for a long series of books on problems in epistemology and related areas of metaphysics, and then added, 'When too old for serious work, I should like to write a book like Santayana's "Life of Reason", on how to behave reasonably in this preposterous world. I hope by then I shall know.'[9] The idea that this would not be serious work, and that old age alone would sufficiently qualify him for it, sounds typical of the sardonic, defensive, sceptical Russell who wrote the end of the *History.* Yet, at about the same time, he wrote very differently in another letter:

I must, I *must* before I die find *some* way to say the essential thing that is in me, that I have never said yet – a thing that is not love or hate or pity or scorn but the very breath of life. . . . I want to bring back into the world of men some little bit of new wisdom. There is a little wisdom in the world; Heraclitus, Spinoza, and a saying here and there. I want to add to it, even if ever so little.[10]

THE PLACE OF MORAL PHILOSOPHY

If he had not done this in *Mysticism and Logic,* then he never did do it. But is there any reason to think he was wrong to want to? If there is not, if we are not compelled to turn our backs deliberately on all the large questions, but can tackle them by using the approach which has just been suggested, then the existence of moral philosophy, which so deeply shocked the later Russell, is not sinister at all. This matter must be dealt with more fully in chapter 12, but a word is needed about it here. Moral philosophy is not just moralizing or propaganda. It is indeed a mapping enterprise, an attempt to sort out the difficult concepts which we must use if we are to think about how we should live. We have to use philosophy wherever we need to think more carefully, wherever confused concepts are causing trouble. And that happens at least as often over moral questions as over any other kind. The fact that feeling comes into morality does not mean that there is no thought in it. For instance, if – to use Russell's own example – we object to somebody's enjoying the infliction of cruelty, we are certainly not just pouring forth an isolated, inexplicable feeling, like somebody screaming because they have an instinctive horror of cats. We are – or should be – expressing quite a complex, considered attitude, which has wider implications and is shaped by how we see the world. We commit ourselves to a great deal that other people can question and discuss. If somebody starts to defend jubilant cruelty, we do not just have to scream or knock him down. We can deploy this attitude, if necessary, to explain why we disagree.

This is not such a remote speculation as it might seem. The question is not at all typical of the moral questions that normally need discussion, because people do not often defend such attitudes. This is no doubt why Russell got the impression that the thing could not be done. But it so happens that Nietzsche did defend the enjoyment of cruelty, arguing that it was a deep, universal human feeling, bound up with many reactions that everybody values, so that condemnation of it was hypocritical.[11] And again, from a quite different angle, some modern moral philosophers inclined to behaviourism have argued that only *actions* can be considered right or wrong, all states of mind being more or less uncontrollable and anyway morally irrelevant. This would mean that it was not *wrong* to enjoy cruelty, though it might of course still be called bad in some other sense, like the weather.[12]

Now these two positions may be wrong but they are certainly not just inarticulate, undiscussable feelings. Both of them in fact grow out of much wider theoretical approaches to other questions, approaches that can be, and often are, stated and defended. Relevant reasons can be brought for and against these views about the enjoyment of cruelty. This possibility of argument may, however, not be the main point to stress here, because our first business in dealing with such ideas is not to take sides for or against them, but to understand them, to discover more clearly what they are intended to mean. When Russell calls this kind of question an 'ultimate question of value', he is talking as if we already fully understood it. He is making the very common suggestion that it brings us at once to the limits of our thinking. But it plainly does not. It only seems to do so because it often stops us *talking*.

Paradoxical and startling contentions like Nietzsche's are liable to bewilder us, and this bewilderment may make us unable to start answering them. People often use these paradoxes deliberately to do just this. But bewilderment is only a psychological break in the discussion, not an intellectual frontier. After bewilderment, what is needed is that both sides should try to state their positions more clearly so as to discover what the issue actually is that divides them. And to bring this about has been the main business of moral philosophy. People who make this effort can become able to change their moral views, not just impulsively or by infection, but by a deeper understanding of what is at issue. Since this has been what serious moral philosophers, and metaphysicians dealing with concepts related to morals, were trying to bring about, there is no need to suspect them of dishonest motives. Because Russell was convinced that they could not really be doing conceptual work on moral problems, he accused them of pretending to do it. But, if there is no such impossibility, there is no pretence. His claim that they had spent a disproportionate time faking up proofs of God's existence is especially bizarre. Among the huge number of problems that philosophers have dealt with, this one is by no means uniquely prominent, and, when it is dealt with, this is often (notably for Descartes) partly because of the very important logical and metaphysical problems it raises. But, since Kant's time at least, philosophers have generally accepted that such proofs are in any case not primarily mechanisms for conversion, but ways of explaining what the notion of God involves for those who do hold it – something which, of course, is often also true of mathematical proofs. This notion of God is in any case one among the many that are potent in the world, serving to shape people's lives and thoughts. But so is the notion of science. And all notions of this kind can constitute proper business for philosophy.

THE GENERATION DRAMA

These matters must be looked at more fully later, when we come to discuss the present dilemmas of philosophy itself. All I want to do in this chapter is to show how the dramatic narrowing of its tradition came to seem so natural, so necessary and urgent, to those who brought it about – notably to Moore and Russell when they launched the process. Because the current general drive for specialization chimed in with their own controversial zeal, they were fully convinced that the particular kind of philosophy they wanted to do was indeed the only kind that ought to be done. The special controversy that focused this zeal should now be named. It was the struggle of British empiricism to throw off its brief and uncharacteristic enthralment to German metaphysics, particularly to the metaphysics of Hegel. Hegelian thought had been an uncommonly ambitious attempt to unify and organize the whole of philosophy into a single system. Indeed, this system aimed to give laws, not only to the whole of philosophy, but to all areas of thought. Russell, like many others brought up to accept it, later revolted and denounced it hotly, although (as often happens) elements from it remained with him and continued to shape some aspects of his thought. Moreover, he merged his sense of this particular revolt with his other, earlier, indignant revulsion against puritanical Christianity. And – again like many others – he saw this dual revolt against religion and metaphysics as part of a generation-battle to be fought out by the young and clear-headed against powerful, superstitious, and oppressive elders, with weapons drawn from the early Enlightenment, notably from Voltaire and Hume.

This strong and simple drama was of course only the local, philosophical form of a wider warfare conceived early in this century as raging between a 'Victorian' and a 'modern' attitude

121

to life. In its day this drama made quite good historical sense, and contributed to some remarkable achievements, especially in the arts. But as time went on – as the 'moderns' grew greyer and the problems of the world changed – this orientation became less and less helpful. The original enemies had largely been replaced by others, and obsession with the earlier model proved a bad guide to present dilemmas. In philosophy, the attempt to hold together the diverse themes brought together by various aspects of the original feud became increasingly strained. By 1946, when the *History of Western Philosophy* came out, Russell was already much more at odds with his juniors than with his seniors. More than a decade later, he contributed an approving foreword to a savage book which bitterly and comprehensively attacked the whole 'linguistic' or 'analytic' movement in philosophy – Ernest Gellner's *Words and Things*.[13] I mention this rather melancholy sequel merely to show how misleading these dramatic, pugnacious representations of contemporary issues often are. We need to keep separating the various different issues that get tangled together by the dramas.

It is a vital part of a philosophical approach to be constantly aware of this need to make distinctions. Russell himself mentions this in the exclusivist manifesto from which I have been quoting, in a brief passage which really does point forward towards the distinctive contribution of the new philosophy. He writes that linguistic analysis 'has the merit, as compared with the philosophies of the system-builders, of being able to tackle its problems one at a time, instead of having to invent at a stroke a block theory of the whole universe'. Now this idea too is in itself plainly not new. It is the main theme of Descartes's *Discourse on Method*, and Descartes himself, as well as many later writers, had already used that advice to tremendous effect. All the same, this familiar project gains a quite new importance in the post-Hegelian context. The unifying enterprises of Hegel and his followers (particularly Marx) had made this separation of different kinds of question both much harder and much more necessary. Because the intellectual territory to be covered was itself now so immensely larger, system-building had gone into a new phase, with ambitions beyond what orthodox Thomism could ever have conceived. For the first time, it really was being expressed in what could fairly be called 'block theories of the whole universe'. There was a real inflation of philosophical pretensions far beyond what philosophy could actually deliver, a real imperialistic attempt to unify all thought in a way that defied its actual pluralities. The effort to grapple with this problem – to cut back the excessive claims without dropping into mere chaos and confusion – has been the real root of modern analytic philosophy. Wittgenstein's method, indicated by his metaphor of finding one's way through difficult country, was designed to meet this need. But Russell never really grasped how large were the changes that it would entail.

Chapter Twelve

THE QUESTION OF CERTAINTY AND THE REAL PHILOSOPHICAL REVOLUTION

I was convinced of the necessity of undertaking once in my life to rid myself of all the opinions I had adopted, and of commencing anew the work of building from the foundation, if I desired to establish a firm and abiding superstructure in the sciences.

(Descartes, Meditation 1, opening passage)

BREAKING THE CARTESIAN PATTERN

In chapter 14 we shall turn to the case where this reductive, Russellian conception of linguistic or analytic philosophy did most harm – the case of moral philosophy. But, before turning to this lunar landscape, we need, for the sake of balance and the general point of our enquiry, to say something, however brief, of what its true and valuable function has been. Since I said that this kind of philosophy does have such a function, that it meets a real and crucial need, I have been attending largely to its defects, because these are widely known already and they would distract us from its real work if they were not got out of the way. But what that real work is – what the true contribution of linguistic philosophy has been – is a very central matter.

Briefly, then, and with the usual disadvantages of brevity, the point is this. European thought, about the end of the nineteenth century, felt itself to be in the situation of a hermit crab that has grown too large for its shell. The crab feels cramped on all sides, and desperately wants a new house, but it does not know how to get it, and it is terrified of scuttling about naked. The shell is, of course, a conceptual scheme. The outgrown shell in this case was the one that had been supplied by Descartes to fit the science of his day, and had been used to excellent effect during the succeeding three centuries, but was now becoming painfully inadequate. To complete this picture, it is important to add that perhaps the animal occupying this shell is not really a hermit crab at all. It may be some other, much less helpless form of creature, which has in its infancy occupied a shell and has so far supposed that it needs one, but which in its mature form will find houses and activities of quite other kinds.

This Cartesian framework of ideas has three crucial characteristics:

1. It starts from a systematic scepticism, making everything turn on the question, 'What can we truly know?'
2. It answers this question by ruling that the only thing each of us directly knows is our own self – the knowing subject or soul; 'I think, therefore I am.' This subject's next problem is then how to link the self it knows to the other objects in the world in a way that will allow them to become known too.
3. In order to forge the links which will make this knowledge of the world possible, it calls for a powerful, universal thought-system, a device grounded in the reason of the knowing subject itself, and reaching out to grapple to it all the objects that are to be known. This Descartes hoped could be provided by a special sort of disciplined clear thinking, framed on the model of mathematics.

In the succeeding three centuries, therefore, philosophies based on this model made great efforts to supply this reliable thought-system – one which could be used to justify the whole of science, and whatever else we needed to know as well. Though they succeeded well enough for many limited local purposes, they ran into very great difficulties about the general architecture of the scheme. It did not prove possible to reduce all acceptable thinking to a single unifying pattern. Moreover, the notion of the original isolated soul gave increasing trouble. Thought-systems of the most varied kinds were devised, but none seemed able to bridge the strange gap that still yawned between the thinker and the world he needed to think about. The sceptical solvents that had been used in setting up the problem always tended to prove stronger than the various answers that were proposed for it. Solipsism – the incurable isolation of a single self – continued to loom. How closely it affected our present topic is clear in the following typical passage from a letter of Russell's:

> In my lecture yesterday [he wrote in March 1912] I changed my mind in the middle. I had gone to prove that there probably is an external world, but the argument seemed to me fallacious when I began to give it, so I proved to my class that there was no reason to think anything existed except myself – at least no *good* reason – no such reason as would justify a man in investing money, for instance. That was very sad, but it doesn't matter much. It made a better lecture than if it had been more pat.[1]

CERTAINTY AND SOLITUDE

Evidently this may have been a lively lecture, but how much sense did Russell's position really make? And – to take up his own comment – how much did it actually matter what answer he gave? That it did matter to him personally is something that he often made plain with his usual lucidity and openness. Thus, describing his conversion from Hegelian idealism in 1902, he wrote, 'It was an intense excitement, after having supposed the sensible world unreal, to be able to believe again that there really were such things as tables and chairs.'[2] And, if tables and chairs are serious matters, other people (who would all vanish from a solipsist world) are certainly not less so. On the question of other people's reality, it is surely not irrelevant to think here about the inner loneliness of which Russell so often complained, and which was also visible to those around him. As he wrote to Ottoline Morell:

> I have a kind of physical loneliness, which almost anybody can more or less relieve. . . . Beyond that, I have a very intense and terrible spiritual loneliness. . . . Most people, even when I am very fond of them, remain external to me.[3]

One might compare Hume's comments on the loneliness that his scepticism induced at the end of the first volume of his *Treatise of Human Nature*. These things are not (I repeat) irrelevant, nor is it mere gossip-hunting to mention them here.

All thoughts belong to somebody. Russell's immense communicativeness has of course made him a natural subject for gossip, and the great buzz of journalistic blowflies that gather round Bloomsbury has intensified it, so that his real greatness tends to get submerged beneath a jumble of caricatures. Nevertheless, his remarkable powers of communication were themselves an aspect of that greatness, and we ought to attend to what they enable him to tell us. Of course, it would be monstrous to put quotations like these together as if they could be used to sum up Russell's character. What they do legitimately do, however, is to point out a special cluster of his difficulties and defects, one of which he was himself well aware of, which was typical of his age, and was also relevant to his work. It therefore, through his enormous influence, affected intellectual history. He himself tried to deal with it in various ways. But one thing that he never considered doing was to question the Cartesian paradigm. His perspective remained always the one that he revealed in the significant title of his little book *The Problems of Philosophy* – a book that deals only with epistemological matters, and centrally with the relation between sense-data and physics. His view was always that

> There is one great question. Can human beings *know*
> anything, and if so what and how?. . . . Ultimately one has
> to come down to a sheer assertion that one does know
> this or that – e.g. one's own existence – and then one can
> ask why one knows it, and *whether anything else fulfils the
> same conditions*.[4] (Emphasis mine)

This was, of course, Descartes's recommended method. But how, one might ask, could anything else possibly fulfil exactly the same conditions as *that* particular piece of information? The search is doomed from the start. Russell's faith in this approach never faltered, however, and he regarded philosophers who moved away from it with a certain mystified disgust. As usually happens when people claim to question everything, he sat very firmly on a particular set of assumptions which dictated just what he was and was not going to question, and which determined also the form of the questions. The nature of these assumptions closed off any effective approach to the big questions that he named at the outset of the *History of Western*

Philosophy. There, and at intervals throughout his other writings, he said that it was the business of philosophy to teach us 'how to live without certainty'. 'But that', as his daughter remarked thoughtfully, 'was what he never managed to do.'[5]

THE QUEST FOR SAFETY

What kind of certainty was it that Russell and the other followers of Descartes demanded? Why did they think it so important? What longed-for guarantee do we not have that we ought to have, and what form would that guarantee take if we could get it? In what sense is this guarantee actually missing from the world as we know it? These were the questions to which Wittgenstein later turned, and they are undoubtedly the key to the whole problem. For the moment, I want just to note again the strange fact, already mentioned in chapter 4, that, since Descartes began to make these moves, the idea of the quest for knowledge has gradually become transformed, concentrating more and more on safety rather than on substance. The search is increasingly conceived, not as the effort to understand something which is itself of great importance, but rather as the accumulating of information which is guaranteed to be correct, almost regardless of its content. Although everybody knows that some information actually is trivial[6] – for instance, information about how many sand-grains there are on the beach – and although good scientists make great efforts to pick out questions which do help understanding, the idea of indiscriminate accumulation is still very powerful. As we saw from the prophecies of physicists interpreting the Anthropic Principle, it can even lead distinguished scholars to suggest the aim of the whole process is simply to store that information securely.

Obviously, there is scope here for richly ludicrous Marxist interpretations. Does bourgeois society really see the life of the mind merely as one more way of acquiring property, a process in which security of title matters far more than the nature of what is acquired, since the acquired objects are in any case only meant to be stowed away in cellars for purposes of future trading? Or is their secure possession aggressively intended, as a form of conspicuous waste, a display of surplus power calculated to overawe the workers by its very futility? Again, from a psychoanalytic angle, might it not seem reasonable to suspect that an insatiable demand for more security than can ever be found on the intellectual side of life could flow from a neglected sense of inadequacy on the emotional one? I take both these suggestions rather seriously, and we will come back to them in a moment. But of course they are no substitutes for direct attention to the official business in hand, namely, questions about the nature of certainty itself.

Descartes's quest was a perfectly serious one, not arising merely out of paranoia. The reasons that he gave for it are excellent; they concern the confusion of standards which has (he says) emerged from his education, and which he finds to be pervasive throughout the thought of his day.[7] The Renaissance predicament of unrelated disciplines that was emerging prefigured our own. Descartes describes how he has been brought up to use a number of partial thought-systems that do not fit together, and how scholastic philosophy has failed to give him any general map on which to relate them. He has learnt mathematics, and has himself made advances in it which raise large questions about its nature and significance. And he now hears of various scientific discoveries – notably those of Galileo and Harvey – which seem hard to relate to any of these other areas. Galileo's conflict with the church is of course a central problem for him, but it does not by any means stand alone. Conflicts arise at many points, both within these different partial thought-systems themselves and between them, and also between some of them and everyday thinking. There are also confusions within everyday thinking itself, for instance, in the way that we conceive our own souls and bodies.

MAKING SENSE OF CERTAINTY

Descartes was simply looking for a realistic way to arbitrate these conflicts and confusions. What went wrong was something that he could not have been expected to foresee. He assumed that he could solve his problem by finding a single tribunal qualified to judge between these contending parties. As it has turned out, there does not seem to be such a thing. What did not occur to him was that there does not have to be one, any more than there has to be a single absolute and infallible ruler if any order is to be introduced into human affairs. Moving away from Cartesianism, we may suggest that theoretical disputes as well as practical ones are best settled, not from on high, but by peaceful negotiation between the parties involved, with background help and advice from outside observers. When clashes arise, such for instance as those between the findings of different branches of science over questions about the workings of evolution, the proper procedure is not for each party to try to knock the other down with a proof that its own view is wholly correct, but for both parties, and anyone else involved, to work harder to understand each other, and to reformulate what they are saying in a way that does justice to other contributions. In this way, countless disputes have in fact been so completely resolved that they are now forgotten. There are also many of which traces still remain, but in a changed form and without the venom that marked them when they looked like simple yes-or-no issues. Examples are the disputes surrounding phlogiston chemistry, which led into wider questions about the meaning of conservation laws, and the quarrels about 'uniformitarianism' among early nineteenth-century geologists, which led to useful thoughts about what it means to say that 'the same force' is still operating in very different times and circumstances. In an important, everyday sense, these controversies have been settled and the answers to them are certain. Science does *not* require the positing of phlogiston, nor of repeated sudden, total changes in natural forces producing 'catastrophes' that are in principle unintelligible. Of course, this does not mean that the thinking of another age might not change in a way that made these suppositions look more intelligible. But – as Wittgenstein's analogy of the river-bed brings out[8] – certainty always belongs within a context. Until such a general change has actually occurred, whatever is deeply linked with the whole mass of an age's presuppositions is certain, and – since we all live at one time rather than timelessly – the contrast between such things and the looser, floating elements that really are uncertain is of the first importance to us.

In this way, then, certainty in the ordinary, human sense can indeed be found. It is not true that we have to 'live without certainty', any more than it is true that we have to 'live without safety'. Indeed, these two cases are quite closely parallel. There is a real sense in which we do have to live without safety, because our life is unsafe in many particular ways, exposed to many dangers, some of them very serious, some inescapable, but some quite easy to avoid. Yet in this mixed, typically human, situation, we can and do make ourselves and others safe against many of these particular dangers. And in doing this we very much need to use the concept of safety, as well as that of danger, even though (as with many other concepts) we never find any pure and absolute instances of it. But what is true of danger is also true of doubt; indeed, doubt is itself only a species of danger. Given any particular doubt, any particular question that really arises, we can set about looking for an answer, and will usually be able to find suitable material to build and support it. But the idea of a guarantee that would make us safe against all doubts – that would have an answer ready against all questions, whether we can now even conceive of them or not – is as vacuous as the idea of total safety, an all-purpose precaution that would protect us against all possible kinds of danger.

THE QUESTION OF IMMORTAL LONGINGS

This approach is surely the right one to the problem of certainty. But we should perhaps pause a moment here to see where it takes us. If certainty is indeed only a form of safety, we might still want to ask how far the demand for total, unconditional safety is itself actually a proper one? This demand is not an immediately practical one, but might it not all the same have its own spiritual and emotional reality?[9] Notoriously, human beings do find it hard to accept the essentially precarious situation that they seem to occupy. In endless different ways, they feel the need to affirm somehow that, in spite of terrible appearances, 'all shall be well and all manner of thing shall be well'. In suggesting just now that we ought to take seriously psychoanalytic and Marxist ideas about the symbolism of the search for knowledge, I had in mind this larger range of motives. I do not want to suggest that either of these thought-systems can deal with it adequately; it is something much larger than either of them. But I do want to say that they are telling us important truths about the range of motivation involved, and that without attending to that range we shall not be able to understand its purpose.

131

It should not be at all surprising if the baser and more ludicrous motives that Marx and Freud might suggest do find an influential place here. Any activity that commands widespread awe and respect is bound to be pursued from base motives, and is also bound to appeal to people's weaknesses as well as to their strengths. That, no doubt, is why so many crimes have been committed in the name of religion. Yet all the same, we still need to understand what are the proper and relevant motives. Here it is important to notice that the quest for ultimate security is not necessarily a debased one in itself, that it may well be an essential part of our nature, and that it has in fact constantly been linked with the highest aspirations of which humanity is capable. The question is simply, how is it to be understood? What kind of security is being sought? What is to be preserved, and against what dangers? What, in short, does this particular search for eternal life signify? And the first point to insist on here seems to be that we must not use this search as a vehicle for debased aims. When rich old gentlemen in the United States leave directions that their bodies are to be preserved in cold storage while their fortunes are spent on research with a view to eventually reviving them and restoring them to health, they seem to me to provide an example of the wrong sort of idea of eternal life – as indeed Aldous Huxley pointed out in his novel *After Many a Summer*. And I am not at all sure that the 'Anthropic Principle' theorists' vision is much better. Certainly the idea of aiming at the mere endless perpetuation of human life, whether by planet-hopping or by transforming ourselves into some peculiar inorganic form, is an empty and contemptible project. Readers unaccustomed to such literature may be interested to know that otherwise competent physicists have seriously advised us to turn ourselves either into light (J. D. Bernal[10]) or into patterns of cosmic dust (Freeman Dyson[11]), with a view to outliving everything else in the cosmos. These are schemes that leave all the real problems of human life untouched. What would be the point of producing an endlessly perpetuated society of cosmic-dust patterns that still knew no better than we now do how to live and how to treat each other?[12]

The trouble with ideas like this is that they treat the symbolism of the search for eternal life literally. When, on the other hand, St Augustine accounts for human restlessness and dissatisfaction by saying, 'Thou hast made us for thyself, and our heart is unquiet until it rests in thee',[13] or when Julian of Norwich says that 'all manner of thing shall be well', they strike me as following out that symbolism in the right kind of direction, however mysterious things remain, and however much I may be puzzled by many other things about the Christian religion. I do not think it makes much sense to try to get rid of the idea of eternal life. But it does make a great deal of sense to insist that the particular idea of it that we form is not an idiotic one. This is a matter of understanding our own ideals, and our own motives. And it is at this point that the reductive interpretations of Marx and Freud reach their limitations, and more profound and positive ones, such as those of Jung, begin in my view to be needed.

Chapter Thirteen

WHAT FOUNDATIONS ARE

A man that could look no way but downwards, with a
muckrake in his hand.

(John Bunyan, *Pilgrim's Progress*, pt. ii)

TROUBLE WITH GRAVITATION

These brief remarks about the general search for security seem
needed as a background for the particular case of it now in hand
– namely, the unrealistic Cartesian demand for an all-purpose
guarantee of knowledge. Here again, some kind of unsuitable
literalism seems to be at work. If we ask what knowledge means
to us – why it matters to us – it is not easy to see how the answer
could really be 'it matters because it is so safe, and that is the
quality always to be sought in it'. I have already suggested that
earlier, more contemplative conceptions of knowledge can
suggest more fertile answers to this question. But these are
exactly the views that we are moving away from. In Russell's way
of thinking, which is still extremely common, the demand for an
absolute, transcendent, non-terrestrial guarantee of certainty
has been combined with an extremely reductive, down-to-earth
notion of the kind of knowledge actually to be sought. The
confused, paradoxical situation that results goes far beyond the
mere, ordinary confusions that are the normal human lot.

Descartes, however, did envisage the possibility of this kind of
guarantee, and it brings into his enquiry a kind of unreal
ambition which has to some degree infected the whole later
history of science. It is reflected vividly in the images he uses. In
his modest phase, he talks merely of rebuilding his own house,

his private mental dwelling which has grown up without a proper design owing to the defects of his education.[1] But very quickly, in a remarkable passage that stands at the head of chapter 17 and will be discussed there, he is talking of pulling down and rebuilding whole cities. Soon, there appears a still more startling image:

> I will continue always in this track until I shall find something that is certain, or at least, if I can do nothing more, until I shall know with certainty that there is nothing certain. *Archimedes, that he might transport the entire globe from the place that it occupied to another, demanded only a point that was firm and immovable*; so also, I shall be entitled to entertain the highest expectations, if I am fortunate enough to discover only one thing that is certain certain and indubitable.[2] (Emphasis mine)

Who had asked Descartes to shift the whole terrestrial globe? And, even if he did manage to find a new point to rest it on, might not somebody else find a further point from which to shift that point, and so on? The metaphor of foundations has got quite out of hand here. It expresses the notion that the items we can know can be arranged in a single, one-dimensional series in order of their certainty. In this case, what we would have to do would be to get them piled up in that order, resting the less certain always upon the more certain to make the whole set form a pyramid. In order to manage this, we would have first to find something intrinsically undoubtable to put at the bottom, something both immovable and large enough to support the whole pyramid. Philosophers have long noticed that Descartes's *Cogito* cannot really fill this place, and no other likely candidate has ever been found. Indeed, it seems implicit in the gravitational metaphor that none ever can be found, since there is no end to the progress that is possible downwards. Thus Russell, when explaining his original motive for studying philosophy, wrote, 'What I most desired was to find some reason for supposing mathematics true'.[3] His search in fact resolved itself into a far more profitable attempt to find out what mathematics means. But even if it had not done so, if he had somehow found those reasons, why should they in their turn have been supposed true? The whole linear arrangement which gave rise to that metaphor is doomed. The evidence that makes any proposition certain is seldom, if ever, supplied by one single, more certain, item. It always consists in a great mass of connections that can be made on every side between it and the rest of our experience. The propositions that are most certain are those nearest to the centre of the pattern. Normally, no reason to doubt these truths emerges at all. But when we do try to find such reasons – as Descartes strenuously did – then the reasons for doubt have themselves to be weighed, not just against the isolated proposition under threat, but against the whole mass of experience of which it forms a part. There is a solid structure that would need to be torn apart in all directions for effective doubting, not a vertical pile that might be toppled by shaking a single item.[4]

This mistake of Descartes's is today often called *foundationalism*. The name is quite a good one, but it is important to notice what the criticism actually says. It does not say that our knowledge is, in the ordinary sense, a building without foundations, that our houses may fall down at any moment, that we might as well believe anything as anything else, that there are no standards of evidence, that truths change all the time and are different for every person or every society, that we must do all our reasoning in existential leaps and live 'without certainty' in the ordinary sense of that word.[5] It does indeed say that we cannot get a special kind of transcendent, cosmic guarantee that will underwrite that normal certainty. But this refusal to give us what we do not need is only a part of the criticism. The more important part is that the linear, gravitational metaphor suggested by talk of 'foundations' is, for most purposes, a bad picture of our thought. That picture had indeed a use for Descartes, when he was trying to make room for that large and important item, modern physics, on a cramped and crowded intellectual scene that did not leave a place for it. He made his point effectively about that by his vivid drama of slum-clearance and planned rebuilding. But that does not mean at all that we have to think of thought in this way in other contexts.

HOW IMPERSONAL IS METAPHYSICS?

I have just been suggesting that this dedication to the Cartesian model was not just an intellectual matter, in Russell or in anyone else. It flowed from and reinforced many wider personal attitudes, emotional, imaginative, moral, and practical. It belonged with a world-picture. The idea that this suggestion is illicit, that such theoretical questions are altogether impersonal, would rule out this kind of connection. But that idea is itself a part of the Cartesian paradigm that is now under scrutiny; it belongs with the notion of the self as an isolated intellect, connected only contingently with a body and a set of emotions. It has no sacred status. Its potential for misdirecting people may be well seen in the behaviourist educational theories which fascinated Russell – for instance, when he explains how necessary it is to train small children not to call for their parents when they are left alone and are frightened, since they can have no good reason for doing so if there is nothing physically wrong with them. This notion – which was of course widely accepted at the time – only makes sense if babies are supposed to be naturally solitary beings, who do not really need any society, and will not ask for it unless they have been somehow corrupted.[6]

Obviously, we must not make such connections at a trivial level, but to fail to make them at all is to miss the point of the whole enquiry. When we read the great philosophers and historians, they speak to us, not as anonymous robots, but as whole people, each in their own distinctive voices. If we listen seriously to them at all, we hear a person speaking, not just a flow of ticker-tape information emitted by a knowledge-machine. In fact, the great philosophers all *sing*. This fact may be easier to notice in some cases than in others – easier in the case of (say) Plato or Hume or Hobbes than in that of Kant or Spinoza. But this is merely because these latter songs are rather like those of the humpbacked whale – harder to pick up because they are deeper and slower. Our response to these writings is as personal as it is to what our friends say, and often much more so than the response with which we listen to a public speech. That response can change our lives.

In the case of novels and plays, most people would perhaps readily admit this. And in the eighteenth century people unhesitatingly put all these things together in the category of 'literature', expecting readers to pick up Thucydides or Epictetus for the same kind of reasons as Cervantes or Shakespeare, and with the same kind of positive, committed attention. They were right. It is quite unrealistic to split these approaches apart in an attempt to purify scholarship. It is, I think, oddly complacent of metaphysicians in particular to tell us, as they sometimes do, that we need not be afraid of their bizarre doctrines, because they will not affect us personally; metaphysics makes no difference to our lives. This is simply false. For good or ill, metaphysics flows out of and acts directly on the imagination, which shapes our lives. It is for instance often clear that conversion to or from a particular philosophical standpoint makes people view life itself quite differently. This is as true of modern philosophers as of older ones – as true when the standpoint belongs to Wittgenstein or Russell or Ayer as when it belongs to Plato or Berkeley or Hume or Nietzsche. This change is not just some chance psychological side-effect, or the result of naïve errors in the philosopher or the convert. It is conceptually necessary. Metaphysics works directly on the imagination. The business of metaphysicians is not to prevent this happening. They cannot do that, and if they try to they will only make the convert's position more confusing. What they need to do is to make sure that the change is the right one, and this is a responsibility they cannot avoid. That is why the ideal of philosophy as a neutral, wholly impersonal, discipline cannot work.

CHOOSING AN ESCAPE-ROUTE

In the nineteenth century, then, the Cartesian world-picture was running into serious and increasing trouble. The saving system which it called for to bind the self to the world, and to include within itself all the ways of understanding that world, had not yet been found. Either, therefore, that saving system would have to be of a quite new, different, and more rigorous kind, or the gap ought never have been allowed to open up in the first place, in which case a quite different approach to the whole problem was going to be needed. Descartes could guide us no longer.

What makes modern linguistic philosophy so confusing is that it tried first one of these escape-routes and then the other. It looks like a wave that first goes right out and then comes in again to a point never reached before. It began with a vigorous, very sophisticated attempt at the first enterprise – traditional system-building – in Wittgenstein's *Tractatus Logico-philosophicus*, which, though it was meant as revolutionary, and in some ways really was so, still held to some central lines of the old position.

138

When this failed, it seemed to go into reverse and apply itself, with equal vigour and much more success, to getting rid of such systems altogether. There is in fact more continuity here than meets the eye, and the second, more successful phase is in some ways a continuation of the first. But this continuity must emerge gradually. It is best first to consider the two movements separately.

The first phase was 'logical atomism' – Russell's and the young Wittgenstein's attempt at the classic task of finding a single, universal, philosophical structure linking human thought to the world, an underlying pattern which would bring the two together at a deep level entirely remote from ordinary experience. It was hoped that this could be done by exploiting Frege's recent developments in logic so as to show that both thought and the world had ultimate logical constituents – not, of course, literal physical atoms, but elementary parts – which corresponded, one to one, in a pattern that could constitute secure knowledge.

In what sense was this project 'linguistic'? The part played by language in this whole way of thinking is very complex, but a little can be said about it here. The point was not just that philosophers queried the meaning of particular key words. They had been doing that since the days of Socrates. It was that they now began to concentrate on the nature of language as a whole, indeed on the nature of signs generally, and on their relation to thought. The centre of the stage was now occupied, not by the concept of knowledge, but by that of meaning. Logical atomism aimed to build language into its explanatory structure to an extent unknown in previous metaphysical systems, and the ways in which it proposed to do this were very complex. They were, however, popularized in a greatly simplified form by the logical positivists in the drastic, reductive formula that 'the meaning of a statement is the method of its verification', the only acceptable kind of verification being to establish a fact by sense-experience. All sentences that could not be verified in this way were to be dismissed as nonsense. In its simplest form (for instance in A. J. Ayer's *Language, Truth and Logic*) the rule was taken to show that words could only have meaning if they either directly reported sense-experience of the physical world or were 'logical constructions' out of such reports. Mathematics and logic itself, which

139

could scarcely be treated as verifiable by the senses, got an honorary status as tautologies. Psychology became wholly behaviouristic; ethics and theology were dismissed as merely emotive noises, and no attention at all was paid to such humble manifestations of language as 'Help!' 'Hullo', 'Goodbye', or 'Could you pass me the adjustable spanner, please?'[7] It also remained obscure in what way, if any, the sentences in books like *Language, Truth and Logic* could themselves have meaning. This somewhat wild theory, which caught on quite widely for destructive purposes, is a prime example of a confused idea that achieved popularity by claiming to be scientific.

When Ernest Gellner, in his book *Words and Things*, accused linguistic philosophers of talking about words rather than about the things that words stand for, he expressed a quite widespread popular view, which is entirely understandable in the light of aberrations like logical positivism. But, even apart from the aberrations, there were some grounds for the charge. To prefer to talk about words rather than about things is indeed a common vice, not just of philosophers, nor even of academics, but of intellectuals in general. More generally still, everybody likes to have some screen of symbols between themselves and difficult or alarming subjects, a trait which does much to account for the enormous popularity of computers today. This tendency does become a vice when it gets out of control, which it was doing with special vigour in the fifties because of the expansion of universities, and because of certain aspects of the drive towards increasing specialization. Some features of this particular philosophical movement did moreover specially encourage it. It naturally attracted people who were particularly fascinated by words, and moreover (as Gellner reasonably pointed out) the peculiar place of Oxford and Cambridge in the English class system did not help. The impression that it was 'bad form' to say anything interesting could be propagated in these places with particular ease.

All the same, the basic idea that language was important and vitally needed attention was not a part of this vice but a vital signpost; it pointed the right way out of the Cartesian trap. Gellner's book unluckily suffered, in spite of its shrewd and observant criticisms, from a total lack of any constructive

140

suggestions about the right way to go forward. He simply was not interested in what philosophers ought to be doing, or in what difficulties they were trying to get out of, only in the wrongness of what they were doing at the time. If any positive proposal emerged, it was that everybody should go away and do sociology instead – a remedy popular at that time, but one that does not help with the problem. The social sciences have their own quite separate work to do. They must certainly take a great interest in concepts. But, if they become primarily interested in conceptual questions, then they simply turn themselves into branches of philosophy, and they then inherit the questions which currently bother existing philosophers.

BRINGING BACK THE WORLD

Granted, then, for the moment that there was reason to investigate the role of language, how ought that to be done? Logical Positivism was not much help here because it was primarily an ideology; its theory of meaning was too confused to be held for long except strictly for party reasons. For one thing, it entirely overlooked that very large part of language which is perfectly meaningful, but does not aim at truth and falsehood – language used (as Wittgenstein later put it) for things like 'asking, thanking, cursing, greeting, praying'.[8] For it was Wittgenstein who found the new direction.

Having carried his first enterprise about as far as it could go in his *Tractatus Logico-philosophicus*, he saw reason to drop this whole approach completely – indeed, he denounced its errors steadily for the rest of his life. He abandoned all three interdependent Cartesian starting-points. He no longer isolated the group of concepts that centres on knowledge and meaning for separate treatment. He asked why any such particular group should be expected to make sense on its own, apart from the web of others that surround it in a language – and, more widely still, in a form of life? He no longer isolated the self as a privileged and peculiar first object of knowledge. He pointed out, rather, that we could never have known ourselves, nor had this concept of a self at all, if we did not already think of it as part of a world of others. Certainly, too, we would have no language to speak of

141

it in if we did not conceive those others as able to communicate like ourselves, and living in a public world which could be communicated about. Thus, the insight which Descartes took as basic – 'I think, therefore I am' – is not basic at all. It could not be, because it is expressed in language, and a language implies a society. Self-knowledge presupposes a knowledge of how to use that language. And this practical knowledge too would make no sense if it were not itself part of a familiar form of life. As for sceptical doubt, it too is a socially developed concept with its own limited use. It would make no sense except against the background of a prior, publicly established concept of knowledge. It presupposes standards of what can and what can't count as satisfactory evidence – standards which (again) can only be located as elements in an existing form of life. The demand for certainty, like the wider demand for safety, is only understandable as a response to particular kinds of threat and danger. If either of these demands is indefinitely expanded into a call for unconditional protection from whatever evil might turn up, it becomes senseless.

Accordingly, the unmeetable demand of Descartes's third point no longer arises. We do not have to build a universal super-system, a ponderous intellectual machine in order to connect our lonely minds safely to an alien world. We are parts of that world in the first place. That is the kind of beings that we originally are. Our language and the form of life of which it is part supply the web within which we can find our way around in it. And, if we want to ask what is the meaning of the words and sentences in this language, we no longer have to say – as we did on the first model – that each of them corresponds mysteriously to a set of distant atomic facts far below in the remote, metaphysical substructure. Instead we concentrate first on their lateral connections in the web; we ask first what they do, how they connect with other words and with life. In general, 'the meaning is the use'.[9]

We must return to this new approach in chapter 18. For the moment, the sad point to notice is that for a long time moral philosophy never got the benefit of it, but was pushed aside in a briskly reductive way in order to fit it in somehow to the cramping Cartesian paradigm. This had extremely strange effects. The bible of this reductive campaign was G. E. Moore's book *Principia Ethica*. And Moore, though later in life he did a great deal to develop the attitude of respect for our existing language and thought-patterns which guided the mature Wittgenstein, began life, like Russell, as a confident reformer devoted to slum-clearance, with results that we must look at in the next chapter.

Chapter Fourteen

MOORE AND THE WITHDRAWAL OF MORAL PHILOSOPHY

BONES. And murder?

GEORGE. And murder too, yes.

BONES. He thinks there's nothing *wrong* with killing people?

GEORGE. Well, put like that of course. . . . But, *philosophically*, he doesn't think it's actually, inherently wrong in itself, no.

BONES [*amazed*]. What sort of philosophy is that?

GEORGE. Mainstream, I'd call it. Orthodox mainstream. . . . In the circumstances I was lucky to get the Chair of Moral Philosophy. Only the Chair of Divinity lies further below the salt.

(Tom Stoppard, *Jumpers*)

THE IDEA OF THE MODERN

G. E. Moore's first book *Principia Ethica*, which came out in 1903, changed the face of English-speaking moral philosophy for more than half a century, extending the surface revolution we have already noticed to ethics, and justifying the total retreat of the learned from this central area of everyday human thought. The personality of its author was very important here. In this book, the young Moore emerged at once as a prophet, already displaying his extraordinary personal force, though he scarcely yet showed his real greatness. This greatness was expressed later, when Moore supplied the central and deepest new insight for linguistic philosophy, an insight concerned with the dependence of all intellectual systems on common sense, with its vehicle common language. Moore then began to explore a deep sense in which common thought and language have to be primary, because they flow from and express the way in which people actually live, while intellectual systems, however important and however influential, grow like branches out of this living thought. The systems therefore cannot simply displace or ignore it, as Russell tended to assume they could; they cannot treat it as a mere vulgar error. They have to find their place somewhere within it, as the parts of the city that Wittgenstein later described all find their place within that city and go to make it a whole. Though this basic respect for common sense had often been hinted at earlier in the British empiricist tradition – notably by Reid, Locke, and Butler – it had never before been fully developed. Nor is it at all easy to develop it without falling into a slick relativism, a readiness to exalt as 'common sense' whatever ideas happen temporarily to prevail. All the same, Moore in articles such as 'The defence of common sense' and Wittgenstein in all his later work did make progress towards that development. I take this progress to have been the real achievement of the linguistic or analytic movement.

Principia Ethica, however, contained very little of this spirit. It did indeed in some sense exalt ordinary thought on moral matters, or at least what Moore took to be ordinary thought. But it did so by treating it as something which was not really thought at all but pure intuition, unrelated to the main system of other existing ideas. Moore declared that all the reasoning used to support moral judgments was empty because it was vitiated by a 'naturalistic fallacy'. The whole mass of argument by which ordinary people – as well as philosophers – normally test and compare these judgments was useless. Thus the book painted in strong colours the irrationalist, anti-cognitive picture of morals that Russell later reproduced at the end of his *History*.

It is of great interest that this message was so eagerly welcomed. One thing this shows is that the times were ripe for it. Both within and without the academic field, many people were exhausted by the confusion of existing moral argument and were ready for a short cut. But in order to enforce this particular short cut so effectively, something more was needed. Much of the book's force was due to its philosophical style, which was exceedingly prophetic. With the enviable confidence of youth,

Moore dismissed virtually all earlier moral philosophers as simply incompetent. He explained that – barring a partial exception for Sidgwick – these people had been mere bunglers, incapable of seeing a vast fallacy – a fallacy so gross and central that it made their whole work, not just inadequate, but quite useless as argument. Before 1903, therefore, there had in effect been no relevant argument about ethics at all:

> The offering of irrelevant evidence generally indicates that the philosopher who offers it has had before his mind, not the question which he professes to answer, but some entirely different one. Ethical discussion, hitherto, has perhaps consisted chiefly in reasoning of this totally irrelevant kind.[1]

> [The naturalistic fallacy] is to be met with in almost every book on ethics. . . . It is a very simple fallacy indeed. In general, ethical philosophers have attempted to define good, without recognizing what such an attempt must mean. . . . We are, therefore, justified in concluding that the attempt to define good is chiefly due to want of clearness as to the possible nature of definition.[2]

Words like 'almost', 'perhaps', and 'chiefly' which might seem to soften these bizarre claims actually do not, because they are promises that are never kept. It should have been very important to Moore to examine any exceptions there might be to his ukase, even partial ones, but he never did. These qualifications therefore are just a stylistic trick, fully deserving Bernard Williams's remark, 'Moore's philosophy is marked by an affectation of modest caution, which clogged his prose with qualifications but rarely restrained him from wild error.'[3]

At this time of day, naturally, there would be no point in criticizing Moore himself for this, but the response of his successors is still important. Moral philosophers did not in fact give up teaching traditional ethics, as one might have thought they ought to if they believed Moore. Yet, as we noticed in discussing prophets in chapter 7, they gave to Moore's own teaching on the subject an awe-struck reverence very different from his own parricidal attitude. It is not suprising that readers enjoyed his sweeping approach, but what made them take it so seriously? One might have expected *Principia Ethica* to be treated as philosophers treated Ayer's *Language, Truth and Logic* – as a clever squib from a promising young man who would have something useful to say one day. Why – far from this – did it take people so long to see the weaknesses in the idea of a single, all-pervading 'naturalistic fallacy' or 'gap between facts and values' and the total transformation of ethics which was supposed to follow from exposing it?

What made this possible was, I think, the power of two linked ideas that were very influential at the time and still are so today – the ideas of modernness (or modernity) and of professionalism. The notion of modernness painted a single, benign change as taking place throughout all aspects of civilization. In this change (as Mr Slope put it in *Barchester Towers*) the rubbish of past ages was everywhere being carted away, and there was no difficulty at all in identifying that rubbish. The slums to be cleared were already marked, and they were known to cover most of the main areas of existing thought. There was therefore nothing surprising about finding that all one's predecessors had been mistaken. A uniformly dark past was giving way to a uniformly bright present and future.

The trouble with this idea has always been, not just that it lumps together a huge rag-bag of quite different changes, but that it cannot cope with continuing change at all. The single revolution can have no successors. There is no indication at all of what is supposed to happen after it – for instance, twenty, forty, or eighty years later; for instance, today. In all areas of life where the word 'modern' was used like this as a sufficient, self-explanatory ideal, and above all in the arts, this idea has made endless trouble, leaving its pious proponents to flounder strangely now in talk about 'post-modernism' and similar strange entities. But, in its day, the concept was strong and liberating, and Moore's title appeals to a deep faith in it, which his public shared. In his time, Newton's *Principia* was still seen as founding modern science once for all – a science differing from all its predecessors as day from night, a definitive science which would never need to be altered for the future. That is the claim which the title *Principia Ethica* – equally with the title *Principia Mathematica* chosen by Russell and Whitehead – is meant to echo. No rumours about relativity or quantum mechanics had yet disturbed the peace. The perspective was Pope's:

Nature and Nature's laws lay hid in night:
God said, *Let Newton be!* and all was light.

Later, of course, as J.C. Squire sadly added,

It did not last: the Devil howling 'Ho!
Let Einstein be!' restored the status quo.[4]

But, in the opening years of the century, *Principia* still meant permanence. The modern was the final.

WHAT IS IT TO BE PROFESSIONAL?

This notion of once-for-all modern enlightenment was linked with that of professionalism, because a number of occupations were at this time being raised to the status of professions – a matter of special delicacy in this country because of its entanglement with social class. New standards for these professions formed part of the luminous 'modern' conceptual framework. Occupations ranging from architecture to nursing and midwifery went through this change, many of them with lastingly traumatic results. But, for reasons already touched on, the case that most concerns us here is probably that of scientists. The very word scientist came into use at this time, as a name for a paid, specialized, qualified, organized, full-time practitioner, replacing the free-lance amateurs – mainly country gentlemen and clergymen – who had chiefly staffed the profession before. Darwin and Lyell usually spoke of themselves as naturalists. The invention of the new status owed much to T. H. Huxley – not only a stern enough thinker to ask for more discipline, but also a poor man, who knew by experience how hard it was for unprivileged people to study science under the old system. His situation contains a paradox which well lights up the nature of the change he took part in, and the unforeseen price that would later be paid for it.[5] Huxley himself remained a sage, a man of the widest possible interests and capacities, well-read in metaphysics, taking part in controversy on every subject of public importance and relating it all to his scientific reasonings. But the specialization he fought for ran quite contrary to this role. The

148

more that specialization was demanded as a mark of professionalism, the more were scientists called on to drop their wider
interests. It was not just that they now had no time for them. It
was that such interests began to be looked on as downright
frivolous and unprofessional.

As we have seen, other academic enquiries were narrowing in
the same sort of way and for similar reasons. Everywhere there
was increasing stress on the negative, defensive criterion of not
doing the things that fell outside one's newly raised professional
barrier, rather than on a clear, positive standard of what ought
to be contained within it – something which was always much
harder to provide. In all cases, probably, the place where the
barrier was actually raised was partly a chance matter. It
depended to some extent on who happened to hold the
controversial field at the time and to exploit the notion of
professionalism most effectively. In many fields, later controversy has shifted the accolade, but it always has trouble in doing
so. The first raiser of a professional barrier enjoys a lasting
advantage. The position of F. R. Leavis in literary criticism is an
interesting case, which may have some useful parallels with
Moore's. But the instance that seems most worth pursuing now
is still T. H. Huxley's, because there the parallel is very striking.
Moore's situation was divided in a way very like Huxley's. Like
Huxley, Moore too seems to have been a key figure in making
his successors feel it a positive professional duty to lock
themselves inside a narrow academic field. But, like Huxley, he
himself remained a most influential and popular sage, publicly
thanked by some of the foremost people of his day for having
shaped their lives by his personality and his teachings, and
denounced by others – for instance Beatrice Webb – as a prime
source of corrupting immoralism.[6]

The case of moral philosophy is of course in some ways an
even more striking one than that of physical science, because in
it the extremes are further apart. The traditional function of
moral philosophy had been an exceptionally wide one, with an
exceptionally direct bearing on everyday life. Under Moore's
influence it became an exceptionally narrow one, even for a
branch of philosophy, minimizing its practical bearing, and also
isolating itself even from other neighbouring branches of
philosophy. Thus was produced a kind of purdah, which was
only gradually broken through, somewhat later, by cautious

149

fraternization with some areas in the philosophy of language. But the extremeness of the case does not change the essence of the trouble. In all such cases, isolation is fatal. As we have noticed, professional specialization always needs to be supplemented by an equally professional overview. A wider map, showing the relation between the various provinces of thought, is vital for any organized enquiry, and to draw such a map is the central task of any truly professional practitioner. Specialists who cannot do it are parasites on those who can. Physical scientists for their part are beginning to see this need, though a tradition of blinkers makes it hard for them to act on the insight. The notion of a responsible scientist has been gaining ground steadily over the last few decades, gradually replacing the idea of a blank, irresponsible 'freedom of science' which absolved specialists from ever having to think about the meaning or consequences of what they did. The practical bearing of physical science is again becoming a normal concern of scientists, as it was for Huxley, and along with it some of the metaphysical implications of various attitudes to science are coming within their sights again. But what about the practical bearing of moral philosophy?

ADMIRING CONTEMPLATION

On this point, notoriously, *Principia Ethica* speaks with forked tongue. The part that reached the public and shaped people's lives was the last chapter, on 'The Ideal', which contained a bold, impassioned, and unconventional exaltation of certain aesthetic and personal values over everything else in life – an exaltation every bit as dogmatic and as unexplained as Monod's later exaltation of scientific ones. As Maynard Keynes rightly said, this manifesto was certainly intended as a correction of utilitarianism, a counterbalance to Mill's and Bentham's emphasis on the active, outward, political aspects of morality. Because contemplation is – as we have earlier seen – a genuinely central element in human existence, I think Moore's emphasis on the inner life was admirable in itself, and deserved much more philosophic attention than it got. But his uncritical wholesaleness made it utterly overshoot this mark, seeming to demand a

150

fanatically exclusive exaltation of certain special kinds of individual fulfilment above all other ideals – social, intellectual, spiritual, or whatever else:

> By far the most valuable things, which we know or can imagine, are certain states of consciousness, which may be roughly described as the pleasures of human intercourse and the enjoyment of beautiful objects. . . . That it is only for the sake of these things – in order that as much of them as possible may at some time exist – that anyone can be justified in performing any public or private duty; that they are the *raison d'être* of virtue; that it is they – these complex wholes themselves, and not any constituent or characteristic of them – that form the rational ultimate end of human action and the sole criterion of social progress [this, Moore writes, is] the ultimate and fundamental truth of Moral Philosophy.[7]

Moreover, 'the pleasures of human intercourse', which might seem quite a wide category, are soon strangely narrowed to consist essentially in mutual admiring contemplation, and other elements also get alarmingly reductive treatment. What Moore is doing, in fact, is virtually to subordinate all other human aims to the experience of contemplation itself, and the strange features of his approach are due to his single-minded efforts to clear other possible candidates for primacy out of the way. He refuses to allow, say, that contemplation draws its value from that of the things outside human life that it contemplates. Unlike Plato and Aristotle (whose views on contemplation he certainly had in mind), he is resolutely and reductively humanistic. Aristotle thought of the world itself, in its intelligible and spiritual aspect, as being divine, intrinsically worthy of love and honour. Plato held the ideal Forms that were the source of the world's order to be also the source of all value and the proper objects of worship. But Moore, by contrast, was trying to assert the supremacy of human contemplation without allowing any substantial value to the non-human world at all except so far as it provides material for this human experience, and without invoking any kind of divinity either. He wants a transcendent value for an attitude which does not and cannot have any transcendent objects.

This project has enormous difficulties, but it is not a gratuitous one. Humanists who want to do justice to the richness of
the inner life, and especially those who exalt knowledge, may
need to take up exactly Moore's task, and, though they will
surely think he made some monstrous mistakes, they could do
much worse than use his proposals as a starting-point. If the
thing cannot be done better, then that is a general difficulty for
humanism. I think it is unlucky that, with the rapid narrowing of
philosophy, philosophers, including Moore himself, later
ignored this whole discussion, regarding it as merely a somewhat
embarrassing youthful excess.

I have discussed this project of Moore's a little more fully
elsewhere,[8] and Iris Murdoch has done it deeper justice in *The
Sovereignty of Good*. I cannot say more about it now. But it brings
up again the general topic of prophetic status, which is important for our theme. I suggested earlier (pp. 68–70) that what is
chiefly needed in dealing with prophets is a public well-briefed
enough and varied enough to stand up to them and complete
their work. This public has to ensure that we take from these
people what we need and what they can best supply, but without
being drawn into their errors, that we neither miss the essential
point of their work nor blindly follow their bias. Moore's
forceful, indeed bullying, approach in *Principia Ethica* caused his
academic public to accept submissively the destructive part of
his message. He had no difficulty in putting moral reasoning out
of fashion as unprofessional. But this brutal approach could not
be used for the much more subtle task of comparing values
which the last chapter demanded. Here, since moral reasoning
had been abandoned, he depended on fire and persuasion to
convey his own passionate conviction of the supreme value of art
and of contemplative love.

Time has passed; what do we think of this message today? It
belongs with an immense upsurge of excitement at that time
about the arts, especially the visual arts, whose splendours we
still acknowledge.[9] It also belongs with a less obvious but no less
real movement to humanize the framework of etiquette, to
make personal relations less formal and more spontaneous.
People engaged in both of these movements hailed Moore as a
founding father; he was the prophet of Bloomsbury, and this is
not now an inspiring title.

152

There is now the same time-distance between us and Lytton Strachey that there was between Strachey and the great Victorians he patronized, a distance at which one takes achievements for granted and needs to revolt against surviving mistakes. Yet, in reading Maynard Keynes's excellent account of the ethic that Moore's followers drew from him, we are probably likely to agree with Keynes that the positive values were all right, the trouble lay in the one-sidedness, in the aspects of life that Moore simply did not notice, and which nobody pointed out to him, because argument on the matter was suppressed. In particular, there was no correction of the excessively private and inward-looking slant that resulted from his own personality, along with the apparently secure state of society in which he had grown up. Moore himself does not seem to have been troubled by any conflicts that might have made him raise questions about the place of both art and thought in life. This has been peculiarly unfortunate because, as it happened, Wittgenstein too was in his quite different way an altogether private person, though for almost opposite reasons. Wittgenstein was troubled by so many conflicts that his own inner life, and other people's, tended to absorb him completely and, when he did attend to the outer, political world, he was inclined to respond to it with a Tolstoyan anarchism which had much the same practical effect as Moore's contented conformity. At this time, political philosophy was often treated as a separate and subordinate occupation, scarcely connected at all with real philosophy, and forming perhaps a branch of a non-reflective subject called 'history of thought'. The aesthetic and quietist ideals of *Principia Ethica*'s last chapter reinforced this kind of separation quite as strongly as did Russell's concentration on science.

Chapter Fifteen

_____

FACTS AND VALUES

_____

In this life we want nothing but Facts, sir, nothing but
Facts.

(Mr Gradgrind in Chapter 1 of *Hard Times*)

THE PANACEA

The rest of *Principia Ethica* – the part which furnished the
ground-rules for later professionalism – did not concern itself at
all with arguing for the value-judgment that exalted those
ideals, which Moore took to be already accepted and obvious,
but with proving the impossibility of using any arguments to
support any value-judgments whatever, and these were the
chapters in which he damned the earlier moral philosophers.
His attack showed – besides its great savagery – two other very
odd unexplained features. First, it concentrated exclusively on
logical rather than moral considerations. Moore did not say that
his predecessors' views were bad because they would lead people
to live badly, but that they were bad because they were confused,
and were so, moreover, always with the same confusion, namely,
the naturalistic fallacy. At this time of day, that name must still
stand because it is not worth while inventing another. But
certainly, as Bernard Williams remarks, since, so far as the thing
can be identified at all, it is neither naturalistic nor a fallacy, 'it is
hard to think of any other phrase in the history of philosophy
that is such a spectacular misnomer'.[1]

Moore's wholesaleness was surely the core both of his error
and of his appeal. His system, had it worked, would have been
splendidly simple and economical, and we can see why it seemed

154

to work. The half-truth from which he started was the tempting observation that all difficult moral arguments run into a dark patch somewhere. The error lay in concluding that there is therefore a single, incurably dark patch into which they all run, so that all that can be done is to placard its irremovable darkness. Moore's own terminology of failure to define 'good' was so strange, so remote from the language of his various victims, that it was easy for a writer of his buoyant, confident cast to carry his readers over the huge differences between the varying views he attacked, and to feel satisfied that they all fitted the same Procrustean bed. His successors, however, noticed its shakiness uneasily and substituted the idea of a logical gap between facts and values (or emotions, or attitudes) or between description and prescription. In each case, the appearance of uniformity was kept up by remaining very abstract. In each, the notion of the gap could be made plausible because, in moral as in other thinking, it is natural, when we reach a difficult point, to describe the previous, secure, accepted part of our thinking as representing 'the facts'. And it can be very important to distinguish this relatively secure area from the questionable one where choices have now to be made. Thus 'separating questions of fact from questions about value' can be a perfectly reasonable procedure. The mistake lies in supposing that no conceptual link can ever be found between them, in exalting a temporary separation, made for the sake of argument, into a permanent, impenetrable logical barrier.

Facts are data – material which, for purposes of a particular enquiry, does not need to be reconsidered. They are never completely 'raw data', 'brute facts',[2] because anything that we can think about at all has already been shaped by our concepts. And the data of any serious moral problem always incorporate quite complex pre-existing value-judgments and conceptual schemes. When, therefore, we reach these gaps or dark patches in our thinking, what we do is to work on the surrounding concepts, and to bring in others where necessary until (ideally) we construct a path across this particular dark area. The history of thought shows plainly how this has repeatedly been done. And although this work is very hard – though it is often done badly and is in a sense never finished – yet all the same, particular puzzles can be solved so completely that they are forgotten, and later generations see the solution simply as part of 'the facts'. The word fact, in its normal usage, is indeed not properly opposed to value, but to something more like conjecture or opinion, as Geoffrey Warnock reasonably points out:

> I believe that we all have, and should not let ourselves be bullied out of, the conviction that at least some questions as to what is good or bad for people, what is harmful or beneficial, are not in any serious sense matters of opinion. That it is a bad thing to be tortured or starved, humiliated or hurt, is not an opinion; it is a fact. That it is better for people to be loved and attended to, rather than hated or neglected, is again a plain fact, not a matter of opinion.[3]

YOUR FACTS AND MY FACTS

Interestingly, too, even 'facts' in the narrower sense in which they are not supposed to incorporate values tend to change their appearance where there are changes of value. We do not find it easy to see facts in a way which fails to fit our value-judgments. Thus, as European thought came to accept that slavery was wrong, its bad consequences came to be accepted as facts. But those who opposed this process took themselves to be equally factual. Thus Boswell:

> I will resolutely say that [Dr Johnson's] unfavourable notion of it [the slave trade] was owing to prejudice and imperfect or false information. . . . To abolish a status which in all ages God has sanctioned and man has continued, would not only be robbery to an innumerable class of our fellow-subjects, but it would be extreme cruelty to the African Savages, a portion of whom it saves from massacre, or intolerable bondage in their own country, and introduces into a much happier state of life; especially now when their passage to the West Indies and their treatment there is humanely regulated. To abolish this trade would be to 'shut the gates of mercy on mankind'.[4]

Again, it is worth while to notice this angle on certain well-known words of Russell's. They are not brought in here to belittle him. Everybody is inclined to say foolish things on this kind of topic, and the fact that Russell never minded making a fool of himself is on the whole a valuable trait in his character; it gave him the excellent habit of readily acknowledging his mistakes. But the point is to show what a strange and misleading effect, right across the spectrum of life, can flow from the notion of 'facts' as things totally detached from feelings and the will:

> I went out bicycling one afternoon, and suddenly, as I was riding along a country road, I realized that I no longer loved Alys. I had had no idea until this moment that my love was even lessening. The problem presented by this discovery was very grave.[5]

He treats it from then on as something irremediable – exactly as someone might discover that they have a flat tyre, although they had no idea till that moment that its pressure was even lessening, and can then be presented with its flatness as a simple datum, beyond their power to alter. It is extraordinarily transparent bad faith to treat one's own most complex and central motives like this. Certainly we can make sudden discoveries about those motives, but, when we do, they cannot be simple and final. They call for investigation and rethinking of the whole surrounding territory. And a great deal of this thinking will not be an attempt to discover any more facts, but a reflection on what one now wants to think and to feel, leading to questions about what one is now prepared to do, and to struggles to do it. It seems to me that Russell would not have described this experience in that way, nor begun to think of it in that way, without the unrealistic notion of simple, value-free facts that was built into his philosophy.

This mention of how the facts sometimes seem to vary with the values does not tip us into helpless scepticism. It simply calls attention to the unity of the moral enterprise, to the web of conceptual links between all its various facets. The process of change could, of course, be described just as well the other way round, in the form in which it often appeared to those who underwent it, as a recognition of the facts which entailed a rejection of slavery. What was happening was a single complex process with three conceptually linked aspects – a changing view of the facts, a change of feeling, and a change in action, arising

157

out of a changed sense of what action could be decently contemplated. It has been a real misfortune, not just for philosophy but for our civilization itself, that philosophers in the tradition we are discussing have tended to concentrate entirely on separating these factors and putting them in competition with each other, rather than on investigating the relations between them. In an age when the world itself changes so fast, it is vital to attend to this relation and to notice where it goes wrong. This is certainly difficult. But that is not a reason for saving ourselves the trouble by ruling that it cannot be done.[6]

NARROWING THE BOUNDS

To return to Moore: How was this simple, enormous diagnosis of the 'naturalistic fallacy' related to the substantial value-theory expressed in *Principia Ethica*'s last chapter?

Moore himself believed, with all the massive force of his pile-driving personality, that readers who avoided the irrelevancies induced by *this single fallacy* would find themselves left with the scheme of values displayed in his last chapter. Throughout, he recurred to visual metaphors; only look in the right direction and you cannot fail to see the colours before you. Alien approaches always seemed to him to be due to an unaccountable failure to look, a failure caused by an inner confusion which he was disturbed to find all around him. As Leonard Woolf says:

> When Moore said 'I *simply* don't understand *what* he means,' the emphasis on the 'simply' and the 'what' and the shake of his head over each word gave one a glimpse of the passionate distress which muddled thinking aroused in him.[7]

Keynes, similarly, has recorded the devastating effect Moore used to produce simply by saying, '*Do* you *really* think *that*?'[8] To those around him, Moore seemed quite simply to be gazing at a clearly revealed truth.

But this was not the situation for his academic successors. They did not necessarily see the moral scene in the least as Moore saw it. They had each their own view of morality, views which – as the world grew more and more confused from the time of the First World War – became increasingly various. The link between the two parts of the book was a loose one, depending largely on Moore's own character. What the academic successors chiefly saw in the book was something quite different, namely a way of keeping moral philosophy clear of confusing moral conflicts in the real world altogether. If the faults in bad ethics were always logical faults, then what was needed to combat them was simply training in the relevant areas of logic. And, if those logical faults were always due to just one newly discovered fallacy, then a full understanding of that fallacy could be the sole theme of professional training. This saved moral philosophers from the quite new danger that they might have to hand over their papers to the logic department and find themselves out of work altogether.

Of course I do not want to suggest that tribal and professional considerations of this kind were the only thing that led Moore's successors to accept the idea of the naturalistic fallacy. They were also moved by real and important moral considerations about the faults of existing doctrines, especially of utilitarianism, which we will look at shortly. But these were really moral objections – as they had a perfect right to be – and it was unfortunately central to Moore's method to treat them as purely formal ones. This greatly distorted the attack, concentrating it officially always on logical incompetence rather than on vice, folly, or danger. If this purely formal approach were really the only one open to philosophers – if they were always interested only in logical correctness – then they need not concern themselves at all about the moral implications of what was being argued. They should be perfectly satisfied with consistent iniquity. And indeed it began to be assumed that moral philosophers ought to be neutral in this way about substantial moral questions.

THE PROJECT OF MORAL NEUTRALITY

In the opening passage of his book *Ethics and Language*, C. L. Stevenson sounded the trumpet for this crusade:

> One would not expect a book on scientific method to do the work of science itself, and *one must not expect to find here any conclusions about what conduct is right or wrong.* The

purpose of an analytical study, whether of science or ethics, is always indirect. It hopes to send *others* to their tasks with clearer heads and less wasteful habits of investigation .... It does not require the analyst, as such, to participate in the enquiry that he analyses. In ethics, any direct enquiry of this kind might have its *dangers. It might deprive the analysis of its detachment, and distort a relatively neutral study into a plea for some special code of morals.* ... The present volume has the limited task of sharpening the tools which *others* employ.[9] (Emphases mine)

Thus moral philosophy could be done just as well by someone who did not take the slightest interest in actual moral problems as by someone concerned about them – indeed, perhaps better, since the temptation to partiality would be less. Officially, this move to neutrality is itself just a formal one, undertaken purely in the interests of clear thinking. But the reasons Stevenson gave for making it were moral reasons, reasons concerned with the dangers of taking sides. These are dangers of unfairness and oppressiveness, dangers of interfering with the reader's freedom of choice by undue influence. Now fairness and freedom are of course in themselves perfectly good moral values, but why, out of all the values that could be named, are these ones alone suddenly getting this preferential treatment? What makes Stevenson so partial to fairness and freedom? Why are unfairness and oppression not getting equal time and equal favour? More seriously, in cases where this particular kind of fairness and freedom conflict with other values – as they very often can – in what scales ought they to be weighed? The world is full of value-conflicts of this kind; they have always been the starting-point of moral philosophy. Emotivist ethics had only one way of dealing with them, namely, pleading professional exemption from the conflict. The most that Stevenson offered for these difficulties was a kind of therapy for the participants – an offer to make *them* clearer about what it was that they were trying to do. The philosopher himself was to remain neutral; in his professional capacity, he did not have moral problems. He remained a detached analyst, whose training evidently had not included any sessions on the couch. In considering how likely this is to be the slightest use, it is worth noticing the parallel that Stevenson draws with the case of science. His idea of the philosophic supervisor who 'sends others to their work with clearer heads', without himself bothering to study the subject they are working on, has proved less than satisfactory there.

This third-person approach is so strange that it may puzzle us how it can have remained for several decades, not just accepted, but treated as the core of moral philosophy. Considerations about professional status do seem to me to throw some light on this, because in general impartiality is indeed something often required of professionals – only you do have to get the right kind of impartiality. Doctors are supposed to devote themselves impartially to curing even their most odious patients, but they are still supposed to be on the side of health against disease. Barristers have to be ready to defend even abominable clients, but they still ought to be on the side of the law. I think that philosophers like Stevenson felt a kind of parallel in their situation to these initial demands for impartiality, and did not see how it could have any limits. Taking sides on moral questions seemed to them amateurish, something which, if they did it at all, they should only do in their spare time. From this angle, earlier moral philosophers – who certainly had taken sides strongly on such questions and supported their opinions by argument – appeared to be indeed the helpless amateurs that Moore had called them. They were convicted of being – as I remember hearing them called – 'pre-Copernican'.

THE APPARENT ABDICATION OF THE SAGES

Obviously, social considerations about professional roles like those just discussed cannot have been the main reason why moral philosophers accepted the transformation of their study. Something deeper is needed. We have to ask what was really going on here?

The first part of the answer to this is plain enough. There was going on a series of changes in the world so disturbing that we cannot wonder at scholars who took cover from it behind their professional barricades. People faced with a painful clash of cultures do tend to take refuge in relativism, subjectivism, and scepticism. The various forms of 'anti-naturalism' that stemmed from Moore mixed elements from all these forms of defence to brew strong solvents. These cleared many problems off the philosophers' plates altogether – for instance, Marxism, Freudianism, sex, war, religion, and the nature of change itself. By providing an all-purpose metaphysic, they also cut off the traditional entanglement of ethics with deep and central metaphysical issues such as free will, personal identity, and the mind–body problem – an age-old connection that had been just as important to empiricists like Hume and Mill as it was to Plato, Spinoza, or Kant. This situation is beginning to right itself. But there is surely still a space left near the centre of the philosophical map by this withdrawal, a space only gradually beginning to be filled again. Topics such as personal identity or consciousness or the nature of action become strangely thin and unreal when they are discussed without their moral dimension.

On the other hand, as we have seen, this withdrawal did not really exempt the philosophers from all moral commitments. Sceptical, reductive campaigns of this kind are always selective and partial. Even in the fiercest of them, some project survives, some chosen moral value is always being promoted. Nietzsche, for instance, waged his moral campaigns on behalf of freedom, honesty, and courage; these ideals were never in danger of having their prices lowered in his 'revaluation of all values', alongside chastity and prudence. I think that the anti-naturalist campaign too sprang partly from esteem for these same values, from the wish to assert the freedom of individual moral agents to make their own value-judgments boldly and honestly. This is the stance that Stevenson seems to be endorsing, and it has much in common with Sartre's contemporary exaltation of freedom as the only real value. But it seems to have been motivated too by another unacknowledged but substantial moral aim that would not have appealed at all to Nietzsche – namely, a distaste for the whole idea of blame and punishment. The exaltation of freedom had begun to mean, not only that free spirits must be honoured, but that all agents whatever must be free from the judgment of others. The fear of blaming or punishing unjustly was becoming so strong that blame and punishment themselves came to be seen as intrinsically unjust. For this revulsion there was of course good historical reason.

Throughout our history, appalling harm has been done in the name of blame and punishment, and the long-delayed recognition of this harm has been one of the real, profound moral insights of the later Enlightenment. It is a signpost that still guides our age. Moore's approach to morality was one that laid little stress on punishment and weakened the notion of blame to vanishing-point. This unmentioned negative fact about it was, I believe, one of its most attractive features to both its publics, and deserves a chapter to itself.

Chapter Sixteen

THE FLIGHT FROM BLAME

And they all with one consent began to make excuse.
(St Luke's Gospel, 14.18)

PUZZLES ABOUT WRONGNESS

Moore, of course, was not the pioneer here; the work had been begun by the classical utilitarians. John Stuart Mill and Jeremy Bentham had already turned their critical searchlight on confused and sinister ancient notions of punishment with tremendous effect. They had begun, too, to undermine the notion of blame by treating it as a mere secondary appendage of punishment. Thus Mill:

> We do not call anything wrong, unless we mean to imply that a person ought to be punished in some way or another for doing it; if not by law, by the opinion of his fellow-creatures; if not by opinion, by the reproaches of his own conscience.[1]

Thus the reproaches both of others and of one's own conscience began to be viewed primarily as a part of the punishment – as deterrents to further wrongdoing, rather than as judgments which might or might not actually be justified by the evidence. Moore carried this idea still further. Although elsewhere he attacked Mill sharply, in this matter and in many others he remained extremely close to the utilitarian thought in which he had been brought up. In the main part of his book, he was quite as extreme a consequentialist in morals as Mill or Bentham. (There are some isolated remarks on punishment in

164

the last chapter which seem to tell a different story, but they are at odds with the official doctrine of the book.[2]) He thought it obvious that actions were valueless in themselves and that only the states they produced could have value. He therefore followed the utilitarians in reducing all terms concerned with duties to a purely causal meaning, and he phrased that reduction even more strongly than Mill had. Thus he says, 'The assertion, "I am morally bound to perform this action" is *identical with* the assertion, "This action will produce the greatest possible amount of good for the universe"' (emphasis mine).[3] For Moore, as for Mill and Bentham, words like duty, right, and wrong are essentially predictive terms, simply noting the good or bad consequences to be expected. And Moore goes on to give an equally reductive account of general principles, writing, 'An ethical law has the character, not of a scientific law, but of a scientific prediction.'[4]

This approach implies an extraordinarily detached, purely descriptive attitude, possible only for remote spectators – perhaps for astronauts, able to watch what is happening on a distant planet but quite shut off from influencing it? Moore's definitions leave out the whole practical element in this moral language – the leverage, the deontic force, that gives such words their main meaning. In the same spirit, he goes on to emphasize how uncertain these predictions are. Things may easily not go as we expect, and in that case we shall simply turn out to have done wrong instead of right. Good intentions are of little account.[5] Morality is simply a device for producing, on average, rather better results than we would get without it. This has an implication which is important, though Moore does not mention it. If it is true, then blame, in its existing sense, can no longer be attached to doing wrong. That conceptual link must be finally broken.

THE FLIGHT FROM CONSTRAINT

We do not need to trouble ourselves at the moment with the many philosophical rows which have arisen about this consequentialist position, merely with understanding what has made it so attractive. I believe that the attraction arises from a profound horror of distorting people's lives by threatening them with blame. This horror is not just an irrelevant emotion, but a pervasive attitude, which shapes a whole range of thinking, and it poses certain very important questions, such as 'Can it be right that people should do their duty only because they are trying to avoid blame, not because they want to?' Or, again, 'Can we not somehow substitute a positive motive for the constraining sense of moral compulsion? Cannot ugly words like "ought" and "duty" somehow be transformed into "I desire"?' Very interestingly, Paul Levy in his life of Moore[6] gives a passage from a paper Moore read to the Apostles in 1900, where he quotes with enthusiasm a stanza that Wordsworth put in his *Ode to Duty* and later suppressed:

> Yet not the less would I throughout
> Still act according to the voice
> Of my own wish, and feel past doubt
> That my submissiveness was choice.
> Not seeking in the school of pride
> For 'precepts over-dignified',
> Denial and restraint I prize
> No farther than they breed
> A second will more wise.

Levy takes this to be a new value-doctrine, alternative to that of *Principia Ethica*'s sixth chapter. But it seems to me to be simply part of that doctrine, an attempt to name the force which was to move people so strongly as to make right conduct possible in the absence of all sense of compulsion.

Now all this is an extremely serious issue, one which has disturbed many major philosophers. When Plato argued in the *Republic* that it does in the last resort profit us to be just, he was facing just this kind of difficulty. He was trying to show that, at the deepest level, we do want to do right, so that moral compulsion, at that level, is not really external. This case can be made very impressive. But, in order to make it so, the level must be deep indeed. There must first be full recognition of the grim counter-arguments that surround us in everyday life; without that, the position is bound to become slick and evasive. In the *Republic*, Plato gives a central role to Glaucon and Adeimantus, who point out in black detail exactly how fully justice often fails to profit people in the real world, and how much of our outwardly just conduct in that world does flow merely from external compulsion.[7]

Principia Ethica, by contrast, pays no attention to such matters at all. In its fifth chapter (on 'Ethics in relation to conduct') Moore simply takes it for granted that the forward-looking motivation of desire for a good end will replace without loss the sense of compulsion that we now feel to act rightly. He casually remarks that this new motivation won't change our outward actions much, and we know from other evidence that he meant this. Moore was no social reformer, because he was not a political animal. But this conformism applied only to outward matters. What passionately exercised him as a moralist, and stirred his early disciples, were spontaneity and honesty within, an attention to deep values, instead of a reliance on guidance from convention. Accordingly, the main moral emphasis of this fifth chapter is on playing *down* the need for outward regularity, on the need to be flexible about established duties and ready for possible exceptions where the normal consequences are not to be expected. There is something remarkably and youthfully hopeful about his assumption that this would not alter practice much, that the predicted good consequences would usually point to the same actions as the existing rules. Like most consequentialists, Moore plainly had not noticed how people's expectations of consequences tend to change if their principles alter, and how much of what looks like causal prediction actually flows from previous moral views about the quality of acts. People tend to expect terrible consequences from acts that they see as wicked and not from ones they accept. This habit can be seen at work in Boswell's remarks about slavery, already quoted. It also appears in the belief that many primitive peoples apparently hold that incest will bring on plague and famine, as it does in the Oedipus story. These predictions are not explanations of why they think incest wrong. They are effects of thinking it so.

But a much more serious fault in Moore's approach lies in the neglect of bad motives, and of conflicts of motive generally. Moore assumes that the desire for future good, which is henceforth to do the whole work of recommending duty, will have no difficulty in acting on us. The inner scene will be clear of obstacles to it, once the clutter of previous notions about

167

compulsion has been swept away. He assumes that the whole notion of moral compulsion, of the authority of conscience, so central to thinkers like Kant and Butler,[8] is simply an obsolete error which has arisen out of confusion; it never had a real function. This was the kind of assumption that made Maynard Keynes later exclaim at Moore's psychological optimism:

> It is remarkable how oblivious [Moore] managed to be of the qualities of the life of action and also of the pattern of life as a whole. . . . The New Testament is a handbook for politicians compared with the unworldliness of Moore's chapter on The Ideal. . . . We [Moore's disciples] had no respect for traditional wisdom or the restraint of custom. We lacked reverence, as Lawrence observed and as Ludwig [Wittgenstein] also used to say, for everything and everyone. It did not occur to us to respect the extraordinary accomplishment of our predecessors in the ordering of life (as it now seems to me to have been) or the elaborate framework which they had devised to protect that order.[9]

Moore, in fact, not only expected perfect love to cast out fear, but wrote as if it would have no difficulty in doing so; as if – once people's ethical logic was purged of its fallacy – the vision of great goods to be gained by doing one's duty would alone be enough to make anybody do it. Blame, and the expectation of blame, would then not be needed.

THE FLIGHT FROM THOUGHT

What this did for the philosophers was to supply them with a reason for retreating from the business of moral judgment, which was seen as essentially one of allotting blame. (Praise seems to have been strangely forgotten.) Moore's position seemed to offer a welcome way out to humane people who were attracted in general by the reforming programme of utilitarianism, but who were still put off it by its emphasis on punishment, and who thought its theory of value vulgarly reductive. That Moore's own theory of value was just as reductive escaped notice, partly, no doubt, because its values were themselves less crude, partly too, no doubt, because it came at the end of his book. What was professionally noticed was the technique Moore provided for resisting the arguments used, both by utilitarians and by other philosophers, to establish their respective value-theories. The idea of a 'naturalistic fallacy' served, in fact, as an all-purpose blunderbuss for shooting down every kind of argument (apart from simple causal argument) which anyone might bring in support of any moral position. Since Moore himself used it against metaphysical ethics, its firing-range was evidently not restricted to targets which could, even in his wide sense, be called 'naturalistic'. In fact its animus was not so much anti-naturalistic as anti-thought, opposed to moral reasoning as such.

In the hands of trained intellectuals, anti-intellectual weapons like this have an odd effect. They supply a very easy way of putting other people down, and in particular they bear hardly on students. Coming up to university to study moral philosophy, these innocent individuals often expected, indeed hoped, to employ their minds on moral problems. Anti-naturalism required them, in effect, to stop thinking on these topics. It attacked equally all the available kinds of moral thinking, without supplying any new alternative to them. And its destructive zeal was particularly strongly directed against a theory which, for large-scale political purposes, was still one of the most frequent, reputable and natural sources of reforming arguments – namely, utilitarianism.[10]

Among philosophers today, this way of arguing is largely discredited because of its formal confusions. But the more we now discredit it, the more pressing I think it now becomes to understand how it came to command so much respect. We may ourselves be subject to influences no more cogent or relevant. In our age, the revulsion against 'making moral judgments' has a powerful hold both on theory and on practice. It runs right across the intellectual spectrum from B. F. Skinner[11] to Bernard Williams[12] – a distance which might otherwise seem hard to measure. The words 'judgmental' and 'moralistic' widely used as terms of abuse, testify to the strong link that has been forged in our century between the idea of moral judgment and the idea, not just of blame, but of unjustified blame. The precept 'judge not, that ye be not judged' has been inflated and given an absurdly wide meaning. The sense of awe which we quite properly attach to a very strong, final kind of judging – a kind which can perhaps belong only to God – has been strangely extended to cover also the weak and limited sense that is used in phrases like 'moral judgment'. The precept accordingly gets some such meaning as 'form no opinions, lest opinions be formed about you'. But this makes no sense because we do not even want people to form no opinions about us. We need the natural, sincere reactions of those around us if we are to locate ourselves morally or socially at all. They give us our bearings in the world. No child ever grows up without constantly experiencing both disapproval and approval, and the serious possibility that both will continue is essential for our lives. Sometimes we need to accept disapproval and to learn from it, sometimes to soften it by friendliness and argument, sometimes to persist in spite of it. But, if we did not know that it was there or understand its grounds, we could not begin to do any of these things.

So unfamiliar is this idea today that even readers who are inclined to accept it so far may want to stop it at the point of agreeing that we may each need to accept blame for ourselves, but still to deny that we can ever properly blame others. The internal difficulties of this idea are perhaps obvious; it is like a world where everybody gives presents but nobody will receive them. But, besides this, blame – the expression of disapproval – has an essential function in the interpretation of many important acts, both private and public. The question is often who is responsible – that is, who did something? Attempts to dissolve this question altogether have some odd consequences, as the following news item illustrates:

> Suicide has been officially abolished in the Irish Republic. A decision by the High Court in Dublin last April means that verdicts of suicide must not be brought in by coroners. . . . The law has always prevented coroners from apportioning blame; verdicts on road accident victims, for example, could not say who was to blame. . . . The High Court ruled that this prohibition extended to suicide, coroners could not blame victims for their own deaths either. . . . All verdicts are now open and record merely the medical causes of death. Dr Bofin said, 'What concerns me more than the suicide problem is that we cannot

bring in verdicts of accidental death either. . . . We cannot exonerate anybody.' Some coroners and juries are thought to be reluctant to bring in suicide verdicts for humanitarian reasons, not wishing to upset relatives.[13]

As the unfortunate coroner quoted points out, half the point of such enquiries is to exonerate the people who did not do these things, or who could not help doing them, and to clear them from confusions which link them with those who did. The whole idea of excusing people on special grounds ceases to work if all grounds and all ways of acting are made equal. Since the wish to admit legitimate excuses is often what leads people to attack the practice of blame in the first place, this is a very serious nuisance.

THE NEED TO DISCRIMINATE

Where do we stand on all this today? The proposal to abolish blame wholesale is certainly still with us, though it is starting to be damaged by protests from the unfortunate officials – not just coroners but probation officers, social workers, and many more – who are expected to put it into practice. If we are inclined to shrug off these protests by simply blaming the protesters themselves, the central difficulty again emerges that we are still making use of blame. Everybody who accepts this proposal makes some tacit exceptions to it. Typically, as is sensible enough, we still blame the powerful – rulers, officials, politicians, and the like. We also blame ourselves, and we blame those who blame others. This is not getting rid of the practice. The difficulty in doing so is not just a chance inconsistency in our thinking, for which we ourselves could be blamed. Praise and blame are unavoidable forms of moral light and shadow. Without them, the world would appear as a uniform grey. Depression sometimes does confront people with such a world, when they have ceased to care about anything that happens around them. But this can scarcely be seen as an ideal.

Thus the idea of a blame-free world seems not to make sense, and the onus of making sense of it rests on those who apparently demand it. Unless that is done, our aim must surely be (as Aristotle might have put it[14]) to blame the right people, in the right way, for the right things, on the right occasions, neither more nor less than is suitable. And, as philosophers, it is our business to explore the conceptual difficulties in understanding this task and also the psychological difficulties in carrying it out. It is because this work is so hard and so important that unrealistic proposals for ceasing to judge altogether are so misplaced. Of course monstrous excesses are committed under the pretext of blame. They are also committed under a huge variety of other pretexts, for instance that of love. But it makes no sense to blame the practice of blame itself for all these excesses.

The trouble is not that the abolishers lack moral concern. It is that this concern is so selective, concentrated wholly on one particular field of iniquity among the many which press on us. All other vices – greed, envy, pride, sloth, cowardice, destructiveness, meanness, dishonesty, even the main jungles of cruelty and injustice themselves, seem to be forgotten in the obsession with one particular area where these last two vices are indulged under the pretext of blame. As things are now, the practice of blame provides us with a rough taxonomy and ranking system for distinguishing and relating these and the many other vices which are a most important feature of our lives. The idea of abolishing it seems to depend on the value-judgment that the practice itself is a worse evil than the vices it exists to indict. That judgment, if squarely made, would itself be a contribution to this taxonomy, and it would take a lot of defending.

Is such a judgment actually made? It is not often explicitly stated, and the idea of it may seem a trifle fantastic. But it is often implied by the general shape of discussions, by the selection of problems, and by the kind of moral indignation that writers express. All this adds up to a tone and approach which are often baffling to readers until they pick up the clue of the judgment just mentioned.

THE MORALITY OF JONATHAN EDWARDS

An interesting case of this approach is Jonathan Bennett's condemnation of the eighteenth-century Puritan theologian Jonathan Edwards for endorsing the ancient Christian doctrine that the blessed in paradise need feel no pity for the pains of the justly damned.[15] 'I am afraid', says Bennett, 'that I shall be doing an injustice to Edwards's many virtues . . . for my concern is only

172

with the worst thing about him, namely, *his morality, which was worse than Himmler's*' (emphasis mine). Not 'worse in some ways' or 'worse in this respect', but just 'worse'. Himmler's saving grace was (Bennett tells us) that, in discussing the awkward tendency of officials in extermination camps to go sick from mere disgust at their work, he excused this weakness as a natural human reaction, perhaps even necessary if they were not to become 'heartless ruffians'. Bennett does not compare this remark with anything that Edwards may have said on the same subject – namely, about human pity for humans who are in one's power here on earth. He compares it with a remote, theoretical opinion which Edwards shared with many other theologians, about the speculative position of beings in a quite different situation – the blessed, that is, who have to have some way of living with the awkward fact that others have freely damned themselves, and are now beyond the power of anybody to help.

I entirely agree with Bennett in detesting the doctrine of eternal punishment, more especially if it is conceived as punishment inflicted rather than as self-destruction freely incurred. I also agree that Edwards's remarks about the feelings of the blessed (which he quotes) are odious. Nevertheless, what can it mean to write off 'his morality' on the basis of this single doctrine? How could his morality be only one limited thing about him? Edwards seems in fact to have been, not only a generally loved and blameless character, but a noted champion of the American Indians in his neighbourhood against their oppressors. What is the 'morality' which cannot be redeemed by these many virtues, and, again, what is Himmler's morality which soars above it? Himmler's remarks on the guards' weaknesses are an isolated soothing reference to an awkward phenomenon which was so glaring that it could not be ignored by the Nazi leadership. There was thus every reason in policy to make the best of it by citing any excuse that could be found. The word 'morality' is, I think, being used here in Williams's restricted sense – namely, to mean an attitude towards blame, punishment, and retribution. And this attitude is being given such special weight that it is taken as determining, *par excellence*, his whole 'morality'.

This use of such words does have some traditional roots. ('Morality consists in suspecting other people of not being legally married,' as Dubedat put it in *The Doctor's Dilemma*.[16]) But

173

it clashes with the very important wider sense – which Bennett also uses in this admirable article – of the whole system on which people organize, not just their doctrines, but their lives. In this sense, Edwards's morality is traditional Christian morality. And it is from this morality, as it happens, that the precept, 'Judge not, that ye be not judged,'[17] is drawn. The Sermon on the Mount, which is its source, has been mainly responsible for bringing into western thought the whole idea that retribution is not enough – that we must return good for evil, not just in acts but (what principally concerns Bennett) in thoughts and feelings as well. Notoriously, the weakness in this doctrine is that it is directed only to ourselves and does not apply to God, for whom retribution remains wholly proper. And the blessed are here assimilated to God. This is, to my mind as well as Bennett's, a fearful anomaly. But, if one evaluates 'a morality' in the ordinary sense, one must surely evaluate it as a whole, not by this particular corner.

THE IMPOSSIBILITY OF EVASION

All ages have their peculiar moral obsessions. It is my impression that, today, a self-righteous preoccupation with putting down self-righteousness holds that position, serving as a displacement activity, especially among intellectuals, to deflect us from the serious and increasingly difficult large questions about how we ought to live. It is not actually meant to affect practice, and, when it does do so, it leads to confusion. Outside the libraries, meanwhile, non-intellectuals, and all of us a good deal of the time, can still go on using ordinary, self-righteous disapproval of the more picturesque vices around us to fulfil this displacement function.

'Anti-naturalist' moral philosophy arose, I suggest, mainly out of this defensive attitude, and has owed much of its appeal to it. Though it has had certain incidental uses and virtues, the general effect of this kind of philosophy has been destructive. It is primarily a way of not doing something which not only needs doing but needs doing by philosophers – namely, taking up the intellectual floorboards and doing some hard plumbing on the intellectual schemes which are expressed in choice and action. Unsatisfactory though the results of this will always be, the work

174

is essential. The sense of professional modesty which made moral philosophers bow discreetly out of it has been as misplaced as it would be for someone who knows a bit about plumbing to stand back modestly when the pipes burst, or for someone who can speak a little Spanish to be silent in a frantic misunderstanding on a train because he cannot speak pure Castilian. Might we make things worse? Sure, we might in everything we do. But the emergency exists already, and at least we have one part of the equipment needed to understand it – namely, some acquaintance with the quirks of conceptual schemes, and some experience of their past working in parallel cases.

We cannot stop people thinking. Moral philosophy will be done in any case, well or badly, under that name or another, as people under strain try to adapt their concepts to changing circumstances. Somebody is going to make suggestions for new ways of treating problems. People who do that are not in any way committed – as seems so strangely to be thought – to claiming that they are the Pope, to issuing orders and behaving like a dominant parent. Instead, they are offering help in a cooperative enterprise which everybody feels to be necessary. They are joining in the attempt to answer questions that already arise. The current demand for medical ethics, and its growing extension to legal and other professional problems, shows how widely the need is felt. We will discuss possible responses to it in chapter 23. It does not always work well, but it must be done somehow. Moore, when he became a mature and admirable philosopher, engaged in the defence of common sense. As is well known, that does not mean accepting everything that people now say and think at its face value, but sorting out its surface confusions to reach the gold that underlies it. This process often involves rejecting theories and methods currently approved by scholars, because they do not fit our real needs. It is vital that we should not hesitate to do this when it is necessary.

It will be noticed that in this discussion I have flatly refused to accept Moore's claim that his move was a purely formal one, and have suggested instead what seems to me a much more plausible moral reason for it. Whether this particular suggestion (about the distrust of blame) is accepted or not, I want to be quite clear that there is always reason to reject purely formal explanations of any move of anything like this size – not only in moral philosophy, but also in the central areas of metaphysics, for instance over things like free will and causal necessity, personal identity and the relation between mind and body. Large formal changes on these matters are never just adjustments to the mechanics of reasoning. They are changes in the way we see and handle the world. They are suggestions about how it would be better to do this. Our attempt to find better and worse ways of regarding the world and of acting in it is not – as Russell thought – an irrelevant interference with our efforts to discover the truth about it. It is the whole enterprise within which those efforts are a part. We build within our moral and metaphysical assumptions. We can develop these assumptions by confronting them with all kinds of new experiences, and also by checking them against each other. But, in doing this, we do not have to make the moral ones always give place to the ones concerned with theoretical truth. For instance, if we have a strong preference for a particular way of life, it is perfectly in order for us to look for reasons to justify that bias, and to try to convert others to it, provided that we show honestly that that is what we are doing. This is the way in which Plato, Aristotle, and others have given reasons for exalting the life of the intellect, linking them to particular analyses of what a human being is and what kind of a thing the world is, and others – Nietzsche, for example – have given reasons for not doing so, linking them to different analyses. In choosing between world-views of this kind we are not forced to confine ourselves to looking for factual evidence. We can properly bring to this work all kinds of elements in our existing world-views. Dorothy Emmet has illuminatingly likened the moral scene to a prism emitting light of many different colours which are not at war with each other, but are all needed to complete the sum.[18] What constitutes bias is not acceptance of one's own existing scheme of values, because that scheme is always relevant. It is refusal to look at anyone else's.

176

Chapter Seventeen

THE CLASH OF SYSTEMS

Those ancient cities, which from being at first only
villages have become, in course of time, large towns, are
usually but ill laid out compared with the regularly
constructed towns which a professional architect has freely
planned on an open plain. . . . When one observes their
indiscriminate juxtaposition . . . and the consequent
crookedness and irregularity of the streets, one is
disposed to allege that chance rather than any human will
guided by reason must have led to such an arrangement.
. . . In the same way I thought that the sciences contained
in books (such of them at least as are made up of probable
reasonings, without demonstrations) composed as
they are of the opinions of many different individuals
massed together, are farther removed from the truth than
the simple inferences which a man of good sense using his
natural and unprejudiced judgment draws respecting the
matter of his experience.

(Descartes, *Discourse on Method*)[1]

THE PROBLEM OF ACCUMULATION

As I have suggested in chapter 12, at the end of the nineteenth
century a considerable emergency already existed in philosophy. It was certainly not caused (as Russell suggested in his
History) by excessive bias towards religion. Since the Enlightenment, that bias had been notably absent. Nor was it due – as he
further thought – to any dishonest wish to be edifying, or to an
addiction to system as such. It arose because the accepted

177

Cartesian paradigm could not deal with the sheer accumulation of different thought-systems, overlapping, interfering with each other, and competing for the single throne that it offered. Descartes himself, as the quotation at the head of this chapter shows, had in his day already been aware of this problem, and had designed his own approach in order to deal with it. In many ways, especially in science and above all in physics, that approach had been very successful, making possible an enormous development of organized thought. But this very success had led to still further and more puzzling problems, since the development branched out again into many distinctive and apparently separate ways of thinking, which sometimes seemed to compete for the same subject-matter. The Church no longer arbitrated between such systems, and, by the nineteenth century, they were not being weeded out by natural obsolescence either. Because of the steady increase in literacy, people were no longer forgetting and dismissing past ways of thinking as much as they had previously done. They were still using them, and were trying to fit them in with the new patterns of thought that were constantly arising.

This willingness to make use of past as well as present insights was not just an effect of nostalgia and reluctance to move forward. It was a reasonable attempt to accumulate what had been achieved instead of throwing it away. But the resulting accumulation was unluckily much harder to handle than it might have seemed. Different ways of thinking are not all made out of standard parts, prefabricated units, designed to fit together. They differ in structure. In order to weld them effectively together, the white heat of a considerable new insight is needed, and this white heat is rare. What usually happens instead is that bits are put together into a somewhat rough-and-ready arrangement, which answers some current needs but cannot command complete conviction or serve as a firm base for new developments. Or, as Nietzsche put it:

> With fifty daubs of paint on face and limbs sate ye there and amazed me, ye men of the present!
> Verily, ye could wear no better masks, ye men of the present, than your own faces. Who could know you?
> Covered in the writings and signs of the past, and with these signs over-painted with new signs – thus have ye well

concealed yourselves from all interpreters of signs!

All eras, all peoples, peer multi-coloured through your
veils; all customs and beliefs speak multi-coloured in your
gestures. . . . Ye seem to be compounded of colours and
of gummed fragments of paper.[2]

Nietzsche, because he is an individualist, can here bring out
well a tension which was already foreshadowed in Descartes's
remarks quoted at the head of this chapter – the tension
between the kind of thought-system needed by an individual and
the kind needed by a community. For a community, one might
think that what is needed is simply a handy assemblage of data –
a general storehouse of available facts and opinions, impersonal,
and arranged on whatever convenient plan makes it easy to refer
to. For an individual, however, what is needed above all is that
the arrangement should be one that makes sense, that really
suits the shape of the personality. If it does not, it forms no
organic part of the character that is to use it. It has then no roots
and cannot put forth any new branches. That was the thought
that made Descartes lay so much stress on the need for
individual good sense, and exalt it above co-operative work.

Yet naturally, once his methods began to be used, co-
operation was needed and the knowledge and opinions gained
became a corporate possession. And corporate cultural possessions of this kind do have to have their own kind of shape and
make their own kind of selection. They are not just inert,
indiscriminate storehouses of information. They too have a
character, a structure, and it has to be one which fits in with
and expresses to some extent the natures of the individuals.
Descartes was of course right to say that a mere shapeless
assemblage of information cannot do this. But he cannot
conceivably have been right to say that a shape must therefore
be imposed by a single individual, who would be an arbitrary
dictator. What both Descartes and Nietzsche, in their different
ways, overlooked was the range of much subtler and more
varied ways in which a group of people, co-operating together in
all the diverse forms of love and harmony, can combine to shape
their cities, their languages, their literatures, and their other
cultural possessions in a way that belongs to all of them, and is
immeasurably greater than anything that any one of them could
achieve alone, even though it does not express any one of them

individually and completely. But, in the nineteenth century, the difficulty was to make such a unity possible among elements so much more diverse than most cultures have ever had to deal with. It was a problem parallel to that of the late Roman Empire, but, since Rome wholly failed to solve it, that parallel was unfortunately not very useful to us.

THE BAUHAUS SOLUTION

This peculiar situation has an illuminating parallel with what happened at about the same time in the visual arts, especially architecture. During the nineteenth century, all kinds of architectural styles were miscellaneously revived. New techniques made it possible to imitate all of them to some extent, just as increased literacy put many diverse styles of thought more or less within the reach of new publics. Much of what was supplied was, in both fields, hasty and poor. In architecture, there was an uncontrolled carnival of mingled styles which disgusted many discerning people to the point where, by the end of the century, they called for a massacre of all existing styles, and a return to a stark, impersonal simplicity. The architects who answered this call supposed – just as Russell did – that their own work was unbiased, in some sense universal, pure, and self-evidently correct. They took their buildings to be 'scientific' in a sense in which no other architecture ever had been. The basis of these claims has now become mysterious, and the style of early twentieth-century architecture now strikes us as just one more style among a succession of others – an idiom belonging to a particular state of civilization and expressing its attitudes. But it has always claimed a much more special standing. It seems to have derived this claim from the force of contrast. The huge sense of escape from the welter of previous confusion produced a delusive air of finality, and a certain restfulness which brutally plain buildings provide for senses exhausted by variety still keeps this architecture in business.

SYSTEMS, SUPERSYSTEMS, AND ANTI-SYSTEMS

In the sphere of thought, things were slightly more complicated. Here the crisis had been spotted somewhat earlier. Already by the end of the eighteenth century, too many partial philosophical systems were visibly on offer for it to be plausible that any one of them could swallow up all the rest. Instead, they needed to be brought into some kind of intelligible relation. Hegel obliged by making a heroic attempt to do this, putting previous philosophies into a historical perspective. Instead of the earlier quest for timeless and final truths, he suggested that we should view ideas dynamically as stages in an endless dialectical process. Contradictions continually occur and are each in turn resolved into a higher synthesis, which will then be contradicted in its turn to make another and better synthesis possible. This process gradually purges away the faults in each suggestion, and accumulates all that deserves to survive.

Hegel's basic historical approach is surely a useful one. It not only helps us to understand the past history of ideas; it also reminds us that we ourselves cannot possibly have more than a part of the truth, that there will always be some point in what our opponents say. It has helped greatly in both these ways to sort out the confusions of the intellectual scene. Its wide acceptance throughout the nineteenth century is therefore not surprising. But there are limits to what it can possibly do.

In the first place, the dialectic itself is only a tool. It cannot itself supply the honesty and intelligence that are needed to use it rightly. It can be used as an idle game, or for all sorts of unsuitable purposes. One common misuse, which Kierkegaard complained of in *Either/Or*, was to excuse evasive indecision on points that really did need to be decided. Another was to excuse actual error and iniquity as constituting only one more necessary contradiction in the continuing process. It could also be exploited, as Nietzsche pointed out, simply to blur the platitudinousness of platitudes. In fact, even with good will, the dialectical formula cannot itself provide the power of judgment needed to find and crack the nub of any given problem. It tells us to look for some fruitful contradiction in it, but there are usually many such contradictions, and they point us different ways. If, however, we choose among them by crediting the dialectic itself with some more positive, specific direction which really does guide us, then it is no longer a neutral, general pattern holding equally between all kinds of thought. It now imposes a system of its own, a super-system qualified to show the point of all the other systems. But this cannot be the end of the game. It has now become just one more voice in the continuing debate, a historical entity like the others. On its own terms it too must then be due to be superseded in its turn by the next comer.

Clearly Hegelian thinking itself did aspire to occupy this more interesting position. It was not meant as a neutral formula, a mere framework to contain other ideas. It took sides on many crucial matters, most notably on the battle between idealism and materialism, between spirit and matter. The Hegelian historical process was explicitly a spiritual one, in which matter figured only as an incomplete expression of spirit – which, of course, was what Marx rejected. Politically, too, there was a substantial bias – a much greater emphasis on the subordination of individuals to the community that resolves their conflicts than on the need for these individuals to keep contradicting society in order to keep the dialectic going. And so forth. Hegelian Idealism, in fact, was not a final, comprehensive super-system, able to order the intellectual universe once and for all, and on its own principles it could not possibly have been one. It could not meet the demand that Descartes's ideas still posed.

Accordingly, the painful sense of disorder in the universe remained, and throughout the nineteenth century it imposed great strain. Many aspiring sages, such as Marx, Croce, the British Idealists, tried to complete Hegel's work by designing a better super-system, but none came out as the clear victor. Instead, things grew worse as these projects piled up one upon another. The sheer weight of technical jargon grew, as academics increasingly wrote both for one another and about one another's systems, rather than for or about anybody or anything else. Even in the *Communist Manifesto*, Marx and Engels are often so obsessed by the need to put down rival theorists that they seem entirely distracted from the business of arousing the masses. And this theory-building tendency is naturally still stronger in theorists who did not even try to be actively political. There are many prestigious philosophical books of the late nineteenth and early twentieth centuries, written nominally in English by philosophers such as Whitehead and Alexander, which are simply unreadable without a special dictionary – a dictionary that they usually do not provide. The British Idealists were better only in so far as they belonged to a larger tribe,

182

whose dictionary was to some extent already established. It is not surprising that people – not just the helpless public, but some very sophisticated thinkers as well – began to ask whether all this obscurity and infighting was really necessary.

THE ANARCHIST ANGLE

There were, then, demands for a fresh start. Schopenhauer and Kierkegaard were among the early protesters, but the real explosives-expert was Nietzsche, himself no outsider to the academic scene, but a professor of philology and by dedication both a psychologist and a philosopher. His favourite targets were humbug and pretentiousness of all kinds, and his work is confusing because he found these vices in such a huge range of places that it is often hard to see what he is actually recommending. But this many-pronged attack itself expresses one of his central ideas. Nietzsche is against thought-systems as such. He saw how obsession with a particular way of thinking can serve to justify a fatal laziness and dishonesty. He wanted people to react directly to different kinds of experience, making responses which would produce quite different kinds of thought. Like Russell, he attributed the prevalent passion for thought-systems mainly to hypocrisy. He thought that systems were chosen for their soothing and self-flattering qualities. But, beyond this, he often suggested an objection to systematizing as such. 'I mistrust all systematizers and avoid them. The will to a system is a lack of integrity.'[3] And again:

> *In the desert of science.* – To the man of science on his unassuming and laborious travels, which must often enough be journeys through the desert, there appear those glittering mirages called 'philosophical systems'; with bewitching deceptive power they show the solution of all enigmas and the freshest draught of the true water of life to be near at hand; his heart rejoices, and it seems to the weary traveller that his lips already touch the goal of all the perseverance and sorrows of the scientific life. . . . Other natures again, which have often before experienced this subjective solace, may well grow exceedingly ill-humoured and curse the salty taste which these apparitions leave

behind in the mouth and from which arises a raging thirst –
without one having been brought so much as a step
nearer to any kind of spring.[4]

Obviously, there is a difficulty about what Nietzsche is saying
here, because to think at all is to connect things, and everybody's
thought, including Nietzsche's own, has to have some sort of a
unity, a pattern shaped round certain basic ideas. The one-
sidedness that results is not confined to explicit, formal systems.
Biases are certainly troublesome, but they are part of the price
we pay for being able to see anything beyond our noses. Nobody
has yet found a better remedy for them than the one provided
by a determined effort to make ourselves aware of them, and to
allow for them as much as possible, both in ourselves and in
other people. The remedies Nietzsche was actually calling for
are often not now easy to pin down, sometimes because he has
successfully made his point and has managed to alter practice.
But in any case he was, quite reasonably, absorbed – as were
most other protesters, including Russell and no doubt also
Wittgenstein – by what seemed to them the urgent need of the
day, namely, to break the hold of Hegelian Idealism.

Chapter Eighteen

EMPIRICISM AND THE UNSPEAKABLE

A main source of our failure to understand is that we do not *command a clear view* of the use of our words. – Our grammar is lacking in this sort of perspicuity. A perspicuous representation produces just that understanding which consists in 'seeing connexions'. Hence the importance of finding and inventing *intermediate cases.*

(Wittgenstein, *Philosophical Investigations*, para. 122)[1]

RIVAL IMPERIALISMS

If we want to understand the fervour of the reformers, we need always to bear in mind how heavily the Hegelian influence loomed over them. Just as the earlier empiricists were always tacitly shooting at something they called 'the schoolmen' – that is, at the degenerate relics of medieval Aristotelianism, still lingering in the universities – so what the nineteenth-century rebels had in their sights, apart from Christianity, was nearly always German idealism. The power of Hegelian system-building in European countries, and indeed in Britain too until soon after the First World War, is something we now find it hard to conceive of. The special vice of this attitude – the quality which really did call for attack – was its exclusiveness, its imperialism, its conviction that a single faith could be found which would rightly drive out all others. Marxism, its main surviving representative, gives us some idea of this attitude, though it has itself today begun to fragment into competing and often very specialized forms. These systems were obviously dangerous because they had ambitions beyond their station. Not satisfied with the local order they could provide in their own areas, they were competing for the supreme position that Descartes had advertised – for the role of universal lawgiver.

Traditional empiricism might have seemed to provide a remedy against this malady. But in truth it did not, because it too was dominated by the Cartesian paradigm. Hume's scepticism – which so deeply impressed Russell – shows just the same hidebound obsession with excessive knowledge-claims as do the over-confident structures of the rationalists he was opposing. And his reduction of both people and things to a quite new and mysterious set of entities – unowned, wandering, atomic 'perceptions' – is as weird and esoteric a piece of metaphysics as anything on the Hegelian scene. This is not to say that it is insignificant. Hume's atomism pointed the way to what proved to be empiricism's main proposal for resolving the clash of thought-systems, namely a search, conceived on the model of physical theory, for the ultimate units of experience. Once these atoms were found, the empiricist programme was to treat all the different forms of thought as constructions out of them, many of which would then be seen to be extravagant and unnecessary. We have already mentioned this project, which found its final culmination in Wittgenstein's *Tractatus Logico-philosophicus*, and we must return to it later. But, in following this path, empiricism abandoned for the time its other role of serving as the champion of ordinary, everyday thinking, and did not come back to it until Moore and the later Wittgenstein turned their attention back to ordinary language.

What has gone wrong in all such cases – in Hume's as much as Hegel's – is that a philosophical insight, genuinely valuable in its own field, gets extended to others which do not suit it. Sometimes there are unexpected benefits even here. But sooner or later difficulties pile up, and it becomes clear that these tools are being used for work they cannot really do. At this point, the imperialistic enterprise ought to stop and make way for a deeper rethinking, a redesigning of the basic concepts for this job, or a clear statement that they are not to be used for it. If they are not, then it becomes necessary to acknowledge plainly the existence of other methods that can. Imperialistic thought-systems tend to say that beyond their limits lies nothing but outer darkness.

Exuberant or Hegelian imperialism stakes out this claim by implying that it is so rich that it can provide a mode of expression for everything that anyone might reasonably want to say. Ascetic imperialism in its Humean form does so by ruling that, as far as knowledge goes, we are all very poor, so poor that we do not actually possess the riches we believe we are using, but only the much smaller ration that scepticism tells us is legitimate. In its much more sophisticated *Tractatus* form, it says that we are very poor in regard to language, so poor that in some sense we can actually say very few of the things that we think we are saying. This is the attitude that got its definitive expression at the end of the *Tractatus*:

> The correct method in philosophy would really be the following; to say nothing except what can be said, i.e. propositions of natural science – i.e. something that has nothing to do with philosophy – and then, whenever someone else wanted to say something metaphysical, to demonstrate to him that he had failed to give a meaning to certain signs in his propositions. . . . What we cannot speak about, we must pass over in silence.[2]

DIFFERENT VARIETIES OF THE UNSPEAKABLE

This ascetic ordinance works, like the one Stevenson proposed for morals, in the third person, as a means of curing somebody else of a diseased tendency to think that they have got something to say. Stevenson in fact got this therapeutic model from Wittgenstein, but the effect of it varies immensely according to its tone. Its exponents may treat the unspeakable, as Wittgenstein himself always did, with real awe as an inexpressible mystery, hidden equally from us all but still far more important than what can be said.[3] Or they may treat it, like Ayer and Russell, with derision as pretentious nonsense. Or again they may appear as somewhat patronizing therapists, like Stevenson. Though the therapeutic model has the possibility of proper uses, on the whole it is a very dangerous one, because philosophical discussion absolutely demands equality of status.[4] All parties in it have to expect their own minds to be altered. This is true even when there is an explicit, agreed professional relationship; good teachers learn a great deal from their pupils, as indeed good psychotherapists also do from their patients. But, where there is no such relationship, to take up this attitude is simply monstrous. These last two approaches have therefore probably done more than anything else to get philosophy hated. Anyone who stands amazed – as most civilized people now do – at the fact that university departments of philosophy are today being steadily closed down in Britain might reflect that many of our current decision-makers, when young, made their first acquaintance with philosophy by hearing a superior voice drawl something like, 'But what could that possibly mean?' This kind of remark was not intended as a question, nor as an admission of ignorance, but as winning an argument and settling the whole issue. Merely not understanding what people said became for a time a safe passport to professional status. The habit was undoubtedly the last degenerate echo of Moore's exclamation, 'I *simply* don't understand *what* he means,' which so much delighted Leonard Woolf in the idyllic days of the movement.[5] It has now largely died out, but we are still living with its harvest.

What, however, was Wittgenstein really saying? Since he was a man with the highest possible opinion of St Augustine's *Confessions* and the works of Kierkegaard,[6] he clearly did not mean that what could not be said should literally not be mentioned, still less that it should be forgotten and neglected. He was struggling with an attempt to find a clear and limited role for science, and to give the rest of serious communication a proper place without counting it as science. Because his theory of meaning was tied to science, this seemed to him at that time to involve saying that it was not really meaningful speech at all. This is a very striking example of the epoch's tendency to treat science as co-extensive with light, and everything outside science as darkness. He wanted to count as 'meaning' only a special, formalized way of using words as completely reliable parts of the scientific machine that was to link us to the world, and he saw that they could not work in this same way when they were used for other purposes. Yet he wanted still to endorse those other purposes. The terribly difficult enterprise of combining these aims is the one that he later abandoned as mistaken.

It would be wild to try to say much more here about what Wittgenstein was really after. Any mention of his part in these developments of British empiricism must, however, at least point out that he was Austrian. He came to England originally to study under Russell, and stayed largely because he found the philosophical climate slightly less alien than it would have been anywhere else. He had brought with him an entirely different intellectual background, dominated on the one hand by technical questions about the meaning of physics, and on the other by Schopenhauer.[7] But more is involved than that, because it is not possible to disregard his personality. Dr M. O'C. Drury, when drafting a memoir of Wittgenstein, wrote:

> The number of introductions to and commentaries on Wittgenstein's philosophy is steadily increasing. Yet to one of his former pupils something that was central to his thinking is not being said.
>
> Kierkegaard told a bitter parable about the effect of his writings. He said he felt like a theatre manager who runs on the stage to warn the audience of a fire. But they take his appearance as all part of the farce they are enjoying, and the louder he shouts the more they applaud.
>
> Forty years ago, Wittgenstein's teaching came to me as a warning against certain intellectual and spiritual dangers by which I was strongly tempted. These dangers still surround us. It would be a tragedy if well-meaning commentators should make it appear that his writings were now easily assimilable into the very intellectual milieu they were largely a warning against.[8]

THE NEED TO SPEAK SOMEHOW

Drury puts his finger here on a grave problem about all serious attempts to criticize the world. It is the same problem that Tolstoy mentioned in *What Then Shall We Do?*, describing how he had come home and told his friends about the appalling scenes he had just witnessed in the slums of Moscow, and his friends responded by telling him what a noble fellow he was to investigate such things. Wittgenstein was intensely aware of this kind of difficulty about all explicit moralizing, of the sense of unreality that easily gathers around it, of the fatal tendency of thought to become detached from the world – a tendency that had specially disturbed other thinkers living under the stagnant, repressive, dying European empires of the late nineteenth century, where effective political action seemed impossible.[9] He responded to it as Tolstoy did but even more intensely, with undiscriminating disgust and denunciation at the inadequate way in which people talked about serious matters. The trouble with this wholly negative response is that, unless we have some immediately adequate action available, we have to work our way through a long series of inadequate responses if we are eventually to do anything about what is wrong. And pure disgust, whether expressed in denunciation or in silence, is not an adequate reaction either. It is tainted with common self-righteousness and aggression. In particular, Wittgenstein's quite genuine disgust at the workings of academic life has had little influence, even among his followers, because it was so wholesale and unconstructive that people could not see how to make any use of it.

I say these things here, not because I think for a moment that they settle the issues Wittgenstein and Kierkegaard raised, but because it is important to recognize this kind of motive behind the stand Wittgenstein took, especially at the end of the *Tractatus*, and to see that this attitude is not just a perverse one. If we ask what is wrong with a great deal of writing on general subjects such as ethics, and with the public response to it, Kierkegaard's parable is indeed in place. Yet we have to ask plainly, what *would* be the proper response? What is involved in admitting the reality of the fire and working to clear the theatre? Wittgenstein's frequent disgust was often honourable, but it led him to systematically avoid making positive suggestions, and the current publication of his numerous notebooks is not going to fill the gap that he deliberately left in his lifetime. A man who was able to tell F. R. Leavis to give up literary criticism[10] – a man who continually told other people to give up whatever they were doing and who, in his own life, gave up virtually everything except philosophy and made repeated attempts to give up that – is plainly something of a specialist in renouncing and denouncing. Yet the meaning of renunciation depends entirely on what the renouncer means to do instead. Since Wittgenstein did not write about this at all, the effect of the *Tractatus* position on moral philosophy was indistinguishable from Moore's. Wittgenstein was understood simply to be forbidding moral argument, and indeed he did explicitly do that, notably in his 'Lecture on Ethics'.[11]

I want to say that that is one of the points on which the linguistic revolution got stuck half-way, and that this was again due to not getting prophets into perspective. We have to take from them what they are capable of giving, not to follow their eccentricities and omissions. It was not necessary, it was extremely unlucky that in this matter Russell had no heir, that no one followed him who was equally attentive to the large problems of the world and who was not hindered from philosophizing effectively about them, as Russell was, by personal difficulties and a bad conceptual scheme. It is certainly true that, had someone come forward to do this, the narrowing of philosophy into more specialized forms would have made the work difficult. But there was nothing to make it in principle impossible.

Both Moore and Wittgenstein were, in their different ways, right to draw attention to the inner life, but there was no virtue in their isolating it from the life of action. For, whatever may be made of Kierkegaard's parable, it cannot fail to have a positive moral and political meaning. It calls for action, and for intelligent action at that, which means that moral and political questions must somehow be effectively discussed. And, if the Tolstoyan anarchism that attracted Wittgenstein paralyses such action, then Wittgensteinian thought has got into a blind alley. We would be acting in a way quite opposed to the man's own integrity if we let our personal respect for him obscure the fact that he has left us the task of getting out of this alley, and has not made it unnecessary.

The *Tractatus*, however, remained extremely obscure. And in view of this, it is not surprising that many of Wittgenstein's followers, especially in the Vienna Circle, saw his declarations simply as weapons to be used in a war waged on behalf of science against all kinds of non-scientific speculation. Since they expressed themselves freely, while Wittgenstein himself continued to wrestle inwardly with his problems, the message that spilled out was simply the reductive one – a message that seemed to put a veto on all expression of non-scientific thought.

CAN PLURALISM BE DISCRIMINATING?

People troubled by the plurality of thought-systems were thus offered a choice between bringing them all under one of the available faulty patterns, and giving up thinking altogether on

most subjects of serious import. Since neither of these alternatives is attractive, in recent years many people have naturally
taken a simpler way out that may be called slapdash pluralism, by
saying that all thought-systems are equally true, or, perhaps
better, equally 'valid' in their own terms or for their own
believers. This notion certainly has the merit of directing us not
to burn those believers at the stake, but it is no help at all when
we were not considering burning them, but were actually
needing to decide which kind of thought to use in a particular
difficulty – something which, in the mixed-up world that
Nietzsche described, happens increasingly often. What is actually needed here is some kind of more discriminating or intelligent pluralism, capable of saying, for instance, that Marxist or
Freudian concepts supply a good system of thought for certain
purposes but not for others, or that physics is fine for its own
purposes but not for those of psychology or biology or history or
poetry or religion. It needs then to go on to say something about
what these various purposes are. And that, I think, is the
direction in which the methods of Moore and the later Wittgenstein point us.

In order to make these moves, the people involved have to
stay flexible. They must not have embarked too much intellectual capital in existing versions of the concepts. This is always
hard, and it becomes much harder when disciples as well as the
inventors of the ideas are already committed to the project.
Disciples are less flexible, because they panic, having less
confidence in their ability to provide a new version if the old one
is altered. Thus the imperialistic ambitions of Marxism, originally vast enough, were strongly promoted by Engels when, after
Marx's death, he loyally devoted his old age to making dialectical materialism into an all-weather system, able to deal with any
intellectual emergency, especially in the physical sciences. We
have already seen the sad effects of this self-dedication on p. 86.

USING THE WHOLE TOOL-BOX

This kind of exclusive, monolithic imperialism was, I have been
suggesting, the true target of people like Nietzsche and Russell.
To keep clear of it, while still managing to get some order into

the intellectual scene, is still a central problem for us. We have somehow to steer a way between total anarchy and the methods of Procrustes. We shall not get very far with this project by simply denouncing all system as such. To understand things at all is to connect them, and that cannot be done without some simplification, some selection, some abstraction, some pattern-building, some one-sidedness. This, it seems, is how the human intellect works, and, if God has different ways of thinking, he has not imparted them to us. What is important is that we should recognize these limitations in a way that allows us to use, for each subject-matter, the way of thinking that suits it best. These ways of thinking vary in their uses just as different kinds of words do. Wittgenstein, when he abandoned the idea that words can have only one proper function, which is found in the propositions of natural science, pointed out their variability in a very illuminating comparison with tools:

> Think of the tools in a tool-box; there is a hammer,
> pliers, a saw, a screw-driver, a rule, a glue-pot, glue, nails
> and screws. – The functions of words are as diverse as the
> functions of these objects. (And in both cases there are
> similarities.). . . . It is like looking into the cabin of a
> locomotive. We see handles, all looking more or less alike.
> (Naturally, since they are all supposed to be handled.) But
> one is the handle of a crank which can be moved
> continuously (it regulates the opening of a valve); another
> is the handle of a switch, which has only two effective
> positions, it is either off or on; a third is the handle of a
> brake-lever, the harder one pulls on it the harder it brakes
> (and so forth).[12]

It was no chance that led Wittgenstein to mention the tool-kit here. Trained as an engineer, he understood very well that the use of analogies with machinery does not force us to accept the narrow, anti-human, standardizing approach for which they have often been used. He fully recognizes the extent to which the nature and purposes of the human user determine the structure of artefacts. If we want a unifying factor among all the things we call 'tools', he says, we must seek it in the work to which they contribute; to understand that work will involve grasping the way of life of which it forms a part. And the same thing is true of the various uses of language. Poetry is as different from physics as the glue-pot is from the hammer. But, if we want to understand either of them, what we shall need to do is to grasp the part that they play in our lives.

This does not of course mean that we always have to accept existing purposes, or existing forms of life. Nor does it mean that we cannot find relations between the different methods that we use. We often are able both to relate them and to reform them. Wittgenstein has been considerably misunderstood over this, because he was so anxious to reject the special kind of universal reforming enterprise on which he had himself been engaged that he often wrote as if it were wrong to try to change society – and language with it – at all. A more careful glance makes it clear that he did not mean to ossify current practice in this way,[13] nor, of course, did he mean to suggest that confused and lazy current habits of thought should be protected merely because they were current; he evidently could not have been doing philosophy at all if that had been his notion. Here Norman Malcolm's comment is useful:

> I think there was indeed something in the content of his philosophy that, improperly assimilated, had and still has an unfortunate effect on those influenced by it. I refer to his conception that words are not used with 'fixed' meanings [*Investigations*, para. 79], that concepts do not have 'sharp boundaries' [*ibid.*, paras 68 and 76]. This teaching, I believe, produced a tendency in his students to assume that precision and thoroughness were not needed in their own thinking. From this tendency nothing but slovenly philosophical work could result.[14]

What Wittgenstein was after was the use of relevant standards rather than irrelevant ones in making changes. His emphasis was on the perfectly sensible point that such changes must involve changes in the whole way of life; they cannot be imposed in isolation by intellectuals. In particular, we cannot reduce all thought to a single pattern, as he had hoped to do in the *Tractatus*.

That is the real point that finally emerges from the movement towards greater philosophical diffidence and modesty which took off about the turn of the century. Like other movements, it has not been straightforward or coherent. (Hermit-crabs in search of new shells are inclined to wander somewhat wildly in this way.) In both phases, the 'linguistic' movement has involved a good deal of exaggeration and overkill. On the return journey, there has indeed been an attempt to avoid imperialism by going to the other extreme of excessive and undiscriminating *laissez-faire* – an attempt to freeze out all change by exalting 'ordinary language' into a self-sufficient ideal, which is of course no more helpful than undiscriminating imperialism. There have been other false starts and unsuitable dramas, and (as I keep suggesting) the whole issue has been disastrously tangled with the general contemporary move towards greater academic specialization. All the same, it is a necessary movement, and it has made some vital progress. It will be worth while, at this point, to examine more closely the ways in which it was, and those in which it was not, a new departure in the tradition to which it officially belonged – namely, British, or rather English-speaking, empiricism.

Chapter Nineteen

WHAT EMPIRICISM IS

Let us then suppose the mind to be, as we say, white
paper, void of all characters, without any ideas; how comes
it to be furnished? Whence comes it by that vast store,
which the busy and boundless fancy of man has painted on
it with an almost endless variety? To this, I answer in one
word, from EXPERIENCE; in that all our knowledge is
founded, and from that it ultimately derives itself.
(Locke, *Essay Concerning Human Understanding*, Book II,
Ch. 1, Sec. 2)

ANCESTRAL VOICES

In English-speaking countries, this anti-imperialistic campaign
did not, on the whole, take its rise from Kierkegaard or
Nietzsche, because it had home-grown models more immediately at hand. British empiricism has always been more or less
sceptical, iconoclastic, pragmatic, vernacular, and disrespectful.
It has always opposed what it saw as needless complications of
theory in metaphysical systems, and has often dismissed them
with a good deal of confidence. Its approach has tended to be
that of James Mill, who is said to have remarked, after a glance
through the *Critique of Pure Reason*, 'Ah – I see what poor Kant
would be at.' This empiricist tradition has habitually avoided
technical terms, and has often derided them as vacuous. It
addressed itself mainly to non-specialists, often being quite rude
about the learned. It operated mainly outside the universities
and sometimes criticized them sharply, usually linking that
criticism with the notion that learned language was meaningless.

196

Hobbes, for instance, complained that the human privilege of speech

> is allayed by another; and that is, by the privilege of absurdity; to which no living creature is subject, but man only. And of men, those are most of all subject to it, that profess Philosophy. . . . If a man should talk to me of a *round quadrangle*; or *accidents of bread in cheese*; or *immaterial Substances*; or of a *Free Subject*, I should not say he were in an error, but that his words were without meaning, that is, Absurd. . . . And this is incident to none but those, that converse in questions of matters incomprehensible, as the Schoolmen; or in questions of abstruse philosophy. The common sort of men seldom speak Insignificantly, and are therefore by these other Egregious persons counted Idiots. . . . I say not this as disapproving the use of Universities; but because I must speak hereafter of their office in a Common-wealth, I must let you see on all occasions, by the way, what things would be amended in them; amongst which, the frequency of insignificant Speech is one.[1]

In fact, among the great British empiricists – Bacon, Hobbes, Locke, Berkeley, Hume, Mill – Hume was the only one who even applied for a university post. (He didn't get it.) Berkeley, though rather politer, takes a similar line:

> Upon the whole, I am inclined to think that the far greater part, if not all, of those difficulties which have hitherto amused philosophers [he means, have puzzled them] and blocked up the way to knowledge, are entirely owing to ourselves – that we have first raised a dust and then complained that we cannot see. . . . In vain do we consult the writings of learned men and trace the dark footsteps of antiquity – We need only draw the curtain of words, to behold the fairest tree of knowledge, whose fruit is excellent, and within the reach of our hands.[2]

And, in the same spirit, Locke offered the services of philosophy to those 'master-builders' in the commonwealth of learning, Newton, Boyle, and Huygens:

to be employed as an under-labourer in clearing the ground a little, and removing some of the rubbish that lies in the way of knowledge; which certainly had been very much more advanced in the world, if the endeavours of ingenious and industrious men had not been much cumbered with the learned and frivolous use of uncouth, affected or unintelligible terms . . . to that degree that *philosophy, which is nothing but the true knowledge of things, was thought unfit and uncapable to be brought into well-bred company and polite conversation.* Vague and insignificant forms of speech, and abuse of language, have so long passed for mysteries of science; and hard or misapplied words, with little or no meaning, have by prescription such a right to be mistaken for deep learning, that it will not be easy to persuade either those who speak or those who hear them, that they are but the covers of ignorance, and hindrance of true knowledge.[3] (Emphasis mine)

The suggestion I have emphasized may be startling, but it is no mistake. Locke's background was the Royal Society; in fact, he was one of that small informal group of private enquirers out of whose unofficial conversations that Society originally grew. In that circle, where large new questions were being handled by people from differing backgrounds, no fixed technical language could possibly be employed. Even if one had already existed, it could not have accommodated the new insights which were just beginning to emerge. There was no possible language for those discussions other than the common speech of the day. Only in it could they be reasonably sure of understanding each other. A main business of Locke's *Essay* was to relate their view of the physical world – notably their corpuscular theory of matter – intelligibly to the rest of the general world-picture which they and their contemporaries were using. In order to develop that world-picture effectively, they had to get rid of language that belonged to earlier thought-systems.

Though this was a somewhat special demand, the method chimed in perfectly with the spirit of the other great empiricists. It was an approach that had been characteristic of Descartes himself, who had also laid great stress on the need to avoid traditional technical terms. Indeed, the lasting popularity of

Descartes's ideas owes a great deal to this iconoclasm and insistence on clear expression. The drama of slum-clearance has always been exciting to readers. His rationalist successors, however, dropped this part of his legacy, and it was taken up seriously only by the British empiricists. Hume, in particular, echoed it forcibly in the gleeful last paragraph of his *Enquiry Concerning Human Understanding*. Here, having laid out his reductive plans, Hume observes with relish, in concluding:

> When we run over libraries, persuaded of these
> principles, what havoc must we make? If we take in our
> hand any volume; of divinity, or school metaphysic, for
> instance; let us ask, Does it contain any abstract reasoning
> concerning quantity or number? No. Does it contain any
> experimental reasoning concerning matters of fact? No.
> Commit it then to the flames, for it can contain nothing
> but sophistry and illusion.

Hume's rules allow meaning only to mathematics and to reports of sense experience; everything else is dismissed as nonsense. He does not tell us what he thought ought to be done with the volume containing the *Enquiry* itself, and with all the rest of empiricist philosophy. This was an early form of the reductive distortion that caused so much trouble later, the hasty adoption of a bizarrely restrictive view of meaning to shore up a shaky metaphysical position, without proper attention to the problem of what 'meaning' means.

For the time, however, this point received little attention, and British empiricist philosophy took its established stylistic course. All its great exponents wrote in clear, lively, forceful English, and dealt directly with topics of current concern. The political writings of Hobbes, Locke, and Mill arose straight out of the problems of the market-place and had great influence there. Berkeley's and Hume's work, though less directly political, had an important bearing on psychology and religion. And this avoidance of technical terms did not cheapen their work. These were no mere publicizers, but serious and original philosophers. Though they were all hostile to 'metaphysics' in the derogatory sense of extravagant system-building, they were all, in the wider neutral sense, considerable metaphysicians in their own right, who cleared up successfully many deep confusions in the world-views of their times, and put forward patterns of thought which have remained lastingly useful. Quite why philosophy in Britain should have run so consistently in this particular channel is not altogether clear. The steady bias – which goes back to medieval figures such as William of Occam – seems slightly surprising when one considers the wide variety of lines taken by our other literature. But this is the tradition that we inherit.

THE NATURE OF EMPIRICISM

In taking note of it, we might do well here to consider a question which this history brings sharply before us, namely, what empiricism actually is. Its name, like other names of schools or parties, has two aspects – the general spirit of the enterprise, and the particular doctrines that have become central for its exponents. The general spirit informing empiricism is simply an emphasis on experience as against theory, a call to attend to the shape of life as it actually hits us, rather than relying on a formalized account of it drawn from abstract schemes and imposed in advance by our reason. If this emphasis is seen merely as an emphasis, and is used as a corrective to the over-stressing of reason by rationalist thinkers, it is thoroughly legitimate and valuable. By carefully weighing the two emphases together, it ought to be possible for a fair-minded person to arrive at a balanced account of our knowledge, one which does justice to both elements. (This is the approach that Kant attempted.) But if the two sides are seen as warring alternatives – if each is put forward as telling the whole story – then empiricism, just as much as rationalism, has an impossible task. It is then committed to giving, alone and unaided, a complete account of the nature of knowledge, and moreover of the ultimate constitution of the universe that is to be known. And this account would have to be spun out of the materials of individual experience without the aid of rational systems. Hume, who devoted himself to this task, moved steadily away from simply using the realities of experience to correct particular over-abstract theories, and towards a concentration on constructing a rival metaphysic that could defeat the rationalist

200

ones. In this metaphysic, the essential point stressed was always universal contingency – the lack of all real connection between the atomic units out of which both the self and the universe were ultimately composed. 'All beings in the universe, considered in themselves, appear entirely loose and independent of each other,' wrote Hume, and the attempt to establish them as independent was a central theme of his *Treatise of Human Nature*.[4] The word 'empiricism' is often used today simply to stand for this belief in universal contingency.[5] Historically speaking, however, those who professed it have usually understood by it something much larger and more valuable than this particular belief – namely, a proper integration of thought into life, and an avoidance of certain particular unrealistic theories.

EMPIRICIST DIALECTIC

The tension between these two factors is an important element in much wider questions than these particular internal disputes in philosophy. For instance, the generous, receptive, background spirit of empiricism played a key part in the production of such admirable books as William James's *Varieties of Religious Experience*. By attending realistically to those varieties, James made possible a far more fertile and useful approach to the phenomena of religion than Russell's or even Hume's, and one that, to my mind, can far more suitably be called empiricist, because it shows a real respect for the actual range of experience. An even more striking example, however, is the work and influence of Darwin. Darwin's success had a great deal to do with the larger spirit of empiricism – with a ready acceptance of the richness of experience, and a refusal to distort it by a premature intrusion of theory. What distinguished Darwin from the innumerable scholars who were wrangling in his youth about the relations between different life-forms – and more especially from the Continental scholars – was his direct, undisputatious, fascinated absorption in the range of facts that the natural world laid before him. On the voyage of the *Beagle*, he was not looking for something that he could use to support a theory. He was absorbed in wonder at the immense range and variety of the life-forms that he saw. This delighted attention to variety was what

201

led him to notice with surprise the number and diversity of the species of finch on the Galapagos Islands. Proper reflection on that phenomenon, accompanied by a due degree of wonder, was a sufficient seed for his own theory, The soil in which that theory could grow was the mass of similar varied observations taken in by a mind that was always receptive and celebratory before it was analytic. On the other hand, when he did come to analyse and to build his theory, the narrower, more reductive and controversial side of empiricism also became very important. Though Darwin was so deeply concerned not to underestimate the existing richness and variety of life-forms, he still looked for a way of accounting for them that would be as clear and parsimonious as possible, that would invoke no mysterious underlying forces or tendencies. This quest for parsimony led him, as it had led other empiricists, towards an atomistic view, an account in which innumerable separate entities act each according to its own principles, and any appearance of common action or co-operation across the whole is delusive. The idea that what happens is in some sense 'pure chance' – is essentially contingent – does not appear to such thinkers as a hypothesis to be established, and often not as an obscure idea needing to be analysed, but as an unassailable presupposition guiding the whole enquiry. And it can sometimes appear as the only presupposition which ought to do so.

Darwin himself was by no means as confident about the omnipotence of this approach as those who claim to be his successors have been, and in fact he often suggested that other kinds of factor were involved in the evolutionary process as well. In his own mind, the general, positive, life-giving aspect of empiricism was dominant over the narrower, more exclusive, atomizing tendency; this is his characteristic greatness. But among those who followed him, the usual effects of controversy worked to produce just the opposite orientation. The claim to be a 'Darwinist' has increasingly been equated with a determined atomizing position, an *a priori* refusal to believe that there are any real connections in the world.

It is important to notice that this is not in itself a parsimonious view. It is not just negative. The belief that the world – or any special series of events within it – is actually made up of separate units having no real connection with one another is itself a positive belief, which needs its own supporting reasons as much as any other general belief does. And it is worth noting that it does not now have, as it did in the eighteenth century, the support of a specious analogy with current physics. The early corpuscular theories treated 'atoms' as separate, inert, impenetrable little pieces of matter like billiard-balls, essentially independent of one another, and requiring some kind of quite external force to fix them together so as to form larger bodies. The difficulty of seeing how such objects could ever be combined at all was a leading factor in causing this idea to be gradually abandoned in favour of the kind of notion of particles that is in use today. In that notion they have of course a complex internal structure which relates them necessarily to their surroundings. They are not in the least like billiard-balls, indeed, modern physics has abandoned the whole billiard-ball notion of solid matter. Many of these particles are not even conceived as able to exist in isolation at all. If, therefore, 'empiricism' is taken to mean a dogmatic belief that 'all beings in the universe, considered in themselves, appear entirely loose and independent of each other', it is as remote from modern science as it has always been from everyday experience. But of course this does not mean that the original insight that lay behind it has been wasted. There are indeed very many important particular cases where things which have been thought to be connected do turn out to be independent, or where wrong connections have been made, or where the extent of a connection has been exaggerated in the interests of theory. A suspicious attitude about this is in order, and it does not need to be supported by any arbitrary dogmatic belief. That attitude is part of the general empiricist tradition.

THE BASTILLE FALLS

But what, we must now ask, was to happen to that tradition in an age of increasing specialization? In his day, John Stuart Mill had no doubts about this. Though he wrote some good and serious specialized philosophy – notably in his *System of Logic* – he mainly worked on problems that concerned everybody, and so far as possible in a style to be read by everybody – everybody, at least, who was prepared to read seriously at all. Mill did not direct his work peculiarly at academics, and had no very high opinion of them. He certainly did often feel sharply the difficulties of dealing with a large, half-educated public. But on the whole his solution for this difficulty was to try to improve their education, not to move further away from them. In 1873, however, Mill died, and his seat in the market-place fell vacant, leaving a query over the whole status of vernacular philosophy. (In the USA, this crisis was delayed till rather later because vigorous writers such as William James and John Dewey continued the tradition – a fascinating story which I cannot attempt to follow further here.)

As we have seen, at this time British philosophy – now led from the expanding universities, and increasingly an academic business – was occupied chiefly with German metaphysics, particularly with that of Hegel. But, though this way of thinking had been in some degree domesticated by T. H. Green, it still remained something of an exotic, hothouse plant in Britain. It was not user-friendly. Its vocabulary, already much elaborated by German academics, had grown even harsher in translation. In substance, it called for many beliefs remote from common sense, as Russell noted when he welcomed back the tables and chairs, and Moore when he objected to being told that time was unreal.[6] Moreover, the Hegelian school was itself already riven by internal debates, which had made some of its general weaknesses obvious.

Altogether then, it is not surprising that British philosophers should have revolted against it, nor that Russell and Moore should have led them. Russell was just emerging from an oppressively narrow puritanical upbringing, and was working on logic, an area where Idealism was at its weakest. He was therefore ready, as soon as a hint of rebellion reached him, to use all the resources of his remarkable intellect for the smashing of idols. He was admirably equipped to 'philosophize with a hammer', as Nietzsche recommended. Moore on the other hand, much less quick and volatile, much less contentious, had a massive common sense which made him simply refuse to tolerate doctrines that lay too far away from the presuppositions of actual life to be seriously used. Though he was the younger, it was evidently he who led the way, and, from the beginning of the century on, their combined attacks sapped the foundations of the somewhat artificial imported system. With only that amount of delay which inevitably goes with the inertia of an academic mass carrying many careers – about a generation – it duly collapsed in the landslide that C. S. Lewis reported, somewhere around the late 1920s, probably on the death of Bradley. On the destructive side, the revolution was complete. But what sort of a revolution was it to be?

Chapter Twenty

STYLE AND SUBSTANCE

But in such lays as neither ebb nor flow,
Correctly cold, and regularly low,
That shunning faults one quiet tenor keep,
We cannot blame indeed – but we may sleep.
(Pope, Essay on Criticism, 239–43)

THE CHANGE IN SUBJECT-MATTER

In style, the new movement seemed at first to resemble earlier British empiricist revolts against extravagant metaphysic. From within, it could easily be seen as simply one more battle in the long war waged, since the days of William of Occam, on behalf of clarity and parsimony against the superstitious imposition of unnecessary entities imported from the Continent – one more demolition of useless metaphysical structures. Moore and Russell clearly did see it like this, and up to a point they were obviously right. In 1936 the opening sentence of *Language, Truth and Logic* still echoed this simple view of the matter, chanting that 'The traditional disputes of philosophers are for the most part as unwarranted as they are unfruitful.'

In spite of these apparent likenesses, however, there was the very serious difference that this time the revolution extended to subject-matter. Earlier empiricists had never proposed to pare down the range of subjects studied by philosophy. They had been quite as unashamedly wide in their philosophical interests as the rationalists they opposed. They were parsimonious about the *apparatus* of philosophical thought, not about the topics on which it could be used. They handled moral, political, and psychological concepts as readily as metaphysical and logical ones. But – as Russell declared at the end of his history – the latest revolutionaries meant to change all that. Philosophy was now to stop meeting the demand of people outside the universities for serious discussion of general topics. It was to confine itself to a few, carefully chosen problems where success could be expected – problems which should be closely related to science, and open to settlement by scientific methods. The style and language of the new movement were indeed to be vernacular, but not its subject-matter. Thus what was offered to the lay public – to everybody, that is, except professional philosophers – was a change from a somewhat difficult and jargon-laden discussion of the problems that concerned them to no discussion of those problems at all.

WHETHER TO EMIGRATE?

This largely remained, throughout most of the century, the melancholy choice offered to English-speaking people who were inclined to turn in irritation and despair from their local brand of philosophy to seek help from the Continental variety. (R. G. Collingwood, who did propound Hegelian ideas in clear and graceful English, was largely ignored by all parties.) On the Continental side, Phenomenology, Structuralism, Marxism, Existentialism, and the rest of the Hegelian heritage, in all their many varieties and avatars, do indeed treat of very important matters, and enjoy the benefit of an organic connection with the societies out of which they have arisen. But the price paid for this today is that they are all by now highly formalized, expressed in learned terms which are worn smooth by endless academic disputes, and therefore committed to handling these important matters from their own peculiar controversial standpoints. The vocabulary determines the kind of thing that can be said, and leaves no position from which those standpoints can themselves be criticized. The same thing is of course true of neo-Thomism, but it causes less surprise there because Thomism is the philosophy for which the adjective 'scholastic' was originally invented. Of course, it is not impossible to adapt these vocabularies for new uses. Scholars working in countries where Marxism is the only available philosophical language show great ingenuity in doing this, and so did many medieval thinkers under the Thomist dispensation. But the price is still being paid. The apparatus that stands between the individual thinker and the world grows slowly but steadily heavier, more elaborate, and harder to shift. The difficulty in expressing one's own thoughts in these languages is always increasing. In response to all this, there is now arising the intriguing situation that intellectuals in many Continental countries are beginning to reject their Hegelian heritage as outmoded, and turning to various forms of English-speaking linguistic philosophy. Native anti-Hegelian stocks are also available to them in such forms as positivism in France, and the Viennese investigations of language which furnished Wittgenstein's background.[1] Meanwhile the Anglo-Saxons continue to raid the Hegelian orchard for mysteries that they do not find at home, and it has also proved possible to get the worst of both worlds by turning British linguistic philosophy itself into a scholasticism, a project for which the technical terms invented by J. L. Austin have proved particularly useful.

The whole concept of 'empiricism' probably needs to be rethought in a way that will most likely break it up, as often happens, into a number of elements, each with their own uses. But, however that may work out, I think it is still true that, in principle, at its best and when it can avoid its own obstacles, the current form of linguistic philosophy which descends from British empiricism is indeed capable of being extremely useful in sorting out our present Tower of Babel, simply because it uses everyday language and directs attention strongly towards existing everyday thought as its starting point. Obviously the point is not that linguistic philosophers are any more free than anyone else of their own local prejudices and presuppositions. They are not. But their method positively demands that they should begin their work by examining local usage, whereas the method of Marxism or Thomism demands that its students should first learn a new language and adopt a new conceptual scheme, before they turn to look at the facts to which they are to apply them. And students who take courses in linguistic philosophy do often manage to pick up this skill, because it is often much better embodied in the teaching methods than it is in the writings. A general fact about academics, which can be cheering or depressing according to how you look at it, is that they can quite often be open-minded, inspiring, and interesting face to face, even when they write dreary and pointless articles. But of course it is the writings that reach the general public, and here improvement has been much slower, though it has certainly begun. For much of this century, the choice here has been a forced one between the two bad alternatives that were on offer at the beginning of it – the choice on which Russell and the young Moore parted from Lowes Dickinson, a choice between topic and methods. If one were directly asked whether it is more important that one's thinking should deal with important topics or that it should be clear and straightforward, one would surely refuse the choice and insist on both. Both things are equally necessary, and in general they go together. Yet in recent times many factors in the world have steadily tended to drive them apart.

When Moore and Russell introduced their change, their retreat from many interesting topics was emphasized by the particular character of the current opposition. Hegelian Idealism had its vices, but they did not include neglecting subjects of general interest. In ethics, in political theory, in aesthetics and the philosophy of history and literature and religion, that tradition had, and still has, a great deal to say, and not all of it is either nonsensical or Fascist. The British idealists, too, had in fact kept these parts of their work relatively free from jargon and bad metaphysics. Even McTaggart was not entirely esoteric. T. H. Green had written clearly and usefully about political theory; so had even Bosanquet. Bradley's *Ethical Studies* was an acute and helpful book, quite widely read. This more outgoing phase may indeed have been closing in by the time the new revolution was launched, and perhaps, if left undisturbed, British Idealism would have relapsed, into scholastic stupor. But the invaders did not ask whether that was true or not. They did not criticize this wider range of work at all. Their position was, not that it had been done badly, but that it ought never to have been done at all.

CLEANSING FIRES

In this respect then – in their choice of audience – the revolutionaries were much more like their opponents than they were like the ancestors under whose banner they officially marched. Indeed, like many revolutionaries, they were to some extent trying to change places with those opponents – to succeed them as the accepted leaders of technical, professional scholarship in their field. This new twist in the empiricist tradition had various odd results; notably, it produced a new style of writing. Long words and technical terms were indeed now avoided, just as Locke and Hume and Hobbes would have wished. But they were replaced by long strings of ordinary words used in special, recognized senses that were often hard for the uninitiated to pick up. Non-professional readers thus faced pages covered with quite short everyday words, arranged oddly in long sentences containing a great deal of repetition. Parts of these pages often seemed to make sense on their own, but it was hard to grasp their general bearing. By a custom that seems to have originated with Moore, the names of doctrines and schools that were being attacked or answered were often not mentioned, but were left to be inferred from arguments that seemed to be directly about the subject-matter. Moore's articles attacking Idealism very rarely mention that doctrine explicitly, seldom name its exponents, and systematically avoid using any of its characteristic terms. They say things like 'Certain philosophers seem to believe that . . . ' and then put the proposal in Moore's deliberately alien words. This method had of course great controversial use in showing how these doctrines could dissolve away when they lost their familiar dress. It was meant to paralyse the opponents, and plainly it often did do that. An older philosopher, Goldsworthy Lowes Dickinson, a friend of Moore's, has left an interesting description of what this process felt like. In a letter to Robert Trevelyan, written in 1898, before these developments can have gone very far, he says:

> I'm fagged to death – result of a metaphysical talk with Moore. What a brain that fellow has! It desiccates mine! Dries up my lakes and seas and leaves me in arid tracts of sand. Not that he is arid – anything but; he's merely the sun. . . . Oh dear! Surely I once had some rivers? I wish you were here to water me. All poets water. They are the rain; metaphysics are the sun; and between them they fertilize the soil.
> Yours, so far as there is anything of me,
> G. L. D.[2]

Dickinson gave up philosophy soon after this, not with a sense of glad liberation but with a sadness that proved to be lasting. The painful and destructive experience he went through is one that could, of course, in some circumstances be necessary and valuable. But anyone who thinks it always is so, and who therefore systematically subjects people to it, has some notion in their mind of what is to be gained by it, since suffering is not an end in itself. It is our main business in this book to try to understand the nature of that further end of thought. And the way in which this particular group of early twentieth-century philosophers perceived this general end is crucial, because it is still working among us. Did they merely want to get a certain drill right instead of wrong? Or were they looking to something further?

DWELLINGS FOR THE MIND

One aspect of the change should, I think, be recognizable by anyone familiar with twentieth-century art. Moore's revolution in style was a form of minimalism. The means of communication were being drastically pared down for the sake of clarity, of elegance, and of avoiding humbug. Extreme simplicity was enforced in the hope that it would convey only the essentials. The trouble with this plan has proved to be that it can only work where the earlier forms on which it makes a comment are still there as a background to make it intelligible. It is actually parasitic upon them, and very often its aims are still a part of theirs – a new selection from what was previously on offer. It may prove quite impossible to say merely what is essential without using this familiar background. Thus the music of Webern, and still more that of John Cage, only makes any kind of sense to people accustomed to a particular western tradition, and interested in a certain sort of comment on it. Others cannot possibly see the point of it – not because they are stupid, but because that point is a critical point, a comment on things that simply have not come before them or do not concern them. In this respect, the 'modern' development is like an in-joke among friends. The same thing is true of pictures that are black all over. It is also true of arguments aimed against the extravagances of religion, when they come to be read by people who simply have

211

not encountered those extravagances. Signs have to have their appropriate context, if they are to have their proper meaning. In just the same way, Moore's manner of writing philosophy had the unintended effect of making it quite impossible for anyone who did not know a good deal about the doctrines that were being attacked to understand what he was saying at all. In a somewhat paradoxical way, even when he was defending common sense against the attacks of the learned, he did so for an almost wholly learned audience.

In this matter Moore parted from Russell, who always held himself accountable for giving genuinely intelligible explanations, and Wittgenstein went further still in leaving things unexplained. Here, however, difference of cultural tradition made things much worse. The discussion of the mystical at the end of the *Tractatus* owes much to Schopenhauer, and some other remarks in it are probably replies to his views.[3] Being used to circles where these views were constantly discussed, Wittgenstein supposed his references to be obvious. English-speaking interpreters of the *Tractatus*, however, at first missed these points entirely, because they mostly belonged to an academic tribe that would have thought it downright unscholarly and superstitious to read Schopenhauer. The same simple-minded chauvinism also produced a more general incomprehension of Wittgenstein's style of philosophizing in separate propositions or apophthegms, rather than in continuous prose. In German, readers knew how to handle this approach because it was familiar from writers such as Schopenhauer, Lichtenberg, and Nietzsche. It was, moreover, just one mark among many of the thorough continuity that still remained between German philosophizing and German literature. German readers expected to bring their imaginations with them to an argument, using them to distinguish between different styles of thinking and to supply new backgrounds when necessary for new kinds of thought.

Though this flexibility can obviously be misused, I suspect that it is essential to serious philosophizing, and it seems clear that Wittgenstein, for one, never abandoned it, and that it underlay the disgust he frequently expressed for the task of reading current philosophical journals. For instance in a letter thanking Malcolm for sending him some detective magazines he wrote:

If I read your mags I often wonder how anyone can read
Mind with all its impotence and bankruptcy when they
could read Street and Smith mags. Well, everyone to his
taste. . . . If philosophy has anything to do with wisdom
there's not a grain of that in *Mind*, and quite often a
grain in the detective stories.[4]

This was not just a piece of paranoiac eccentricity. It marked a
serious criticism, which might have been useful if it had been
explained more fully, and also followed out more consistently.
For, on the other hand, his own writing tended to suffer from
both sorts of obscurity, since it did often concentrate fairly
narrowly on existing scholarly controversies, and was also
broken up into separate propositions which needed some work
to interpret.

All these stylistic problems naturally tended to enhance
Wittgenstein's prophetic status, adding a kind of mystified awe
to the deference proper to the force of his genius. He seemed
disturbingly universal, a voice from Mount Sinai, against which
there could be no appeal. Janik and Toulmin's book,
Wittgenstein's Vienna, has now luckily done something to dispel
this cloud of misleadingly numinous ignorance. But the alien
element arising from the fact that Wittgenstein was Austrian
only added one more twist to the impression of alienation
already produced by Moore's deliberately distanced style. The
sense of detachment from all local roots – of owning a universal
steamroller licensed to override all particular attachments – was
again something characteristic of the age, marking every
movement which described itself at this time as 'modern'. Tom
Wolfe, in explaining how the devotees of Bauhaus architecture
confidently imported it to America without any attention to
local conditions, puts the point well:

They gave no indication that the International Style –
and their label caught on immediately – had originated in
any social setting, any *terra firma*, whatsoever. They
presented it as an inexorable trend, meteorological in
nature, like a change in the weather or a tidal wave. The
International was nothing less than the first great universal
style since the Mediaeval and Classical revivals, and the
first truly modern style since the Renaissance. And if

213

American architects wanted to ride the tidal wave, rather than be wiped out by it, they had first to comprehend one thing; the client no longer counted for anything except the funding. . . . How much explaining does a tidal wave have to do?[5]

Thus in architecture, as in philosophy, form was to be imposed from above on the customers by the dictates of a vision, not to grow in response to local and personal needs inside a common culture, a country that the practitioners inhabited along with their clients. In architecture, too, the public that the practitioners mainly addressed was now to consist chiefly of their colleagues – other architects, readers of the architectural journals – and the impact of their theories on these colleagues was to count for much more than the effect of the houses on those who were to live in them. The ideas, along with the vision behind them, were absolute and self-justifying.

THE RELEVANCE OF ARCHITECTURE

Of course, the comparison between philosophy and building must not be pushed too far; it is only a comparison. Nevertheless (as already mentioned) it has been a strong and seminal one in western thought ever since Descartes, and it did play a specially important role in shaping the early thought of Wittgenstein. His close friends in Vienna did not only talk about Schopenhauer. They talked a great deal about architecture, and several of them were architects. Their ideas took their rise from those of Adolf Loos, which were close to those of the Bauhaus. These intensely purist schemes so deeply impressed Wittgenstein that for a time he turned architect himself and designed a house for his sister, insisting on taking it over from his friend Paul Engelmann[6] by sheer force of his fascination with the subject, and working at it with obsessive and inexhaustible thoroughness. This house was built with the utter starkness and plainness that the theories demanded. Judging from accounts and photographs,[7] its proportions seem impressive and many of its shapes elegant. Nevertheless, it was certainly the kind of house that (as Tom Wolfe reasonably points out) hardly ever actually got built except for peculiarly kind and well-heeled relatives of the architect, simply because nobody else would have wanted to live in it. It was an end in itself, not a house meant for people at all. In spite of a nominally functionalist approach, the relation between creator and user had become fatally loosened in such architecture. That it was also somewhat loosened in the corresponding kind of philosophy may perhaps be seen from the letter that Wittgenstein wrote to Russell after the First World War, proposing to send him the manuscript of his now finished *Tractatus*. Wittgenstein says that he believes that this piece of work has solved their problems finally, but that it will not be possible for Russell to understand it without a previous explanation, and he adds in brackets, '(This of course means that *nobody* will understand it, although I believe it's all as clear as crystal.)'[8] What kind of crystal clarity is it that is clear to nobody except its author? Clarity is here evidently conceived in relation to some ideal audience, not as a feature of communication with any actual one. Since clarity was a central idea for the exponents of this kind of philosophy, the oddities of this idea are rather serious. Even very well-equipped and highly motivated readers have often found the *Tractatus* obscure, and nobody could hope to understand it who did not know something about its controversial background. The sense in which Wittgenstein found it so clear seems to have been one concerned with its internal coherence as a system. Living, as it were, at that time inside the *Tractatus* world, he saw it as perfectly organized and logical. But people outside that world could not see it so, and as time went on he himself ceased to do so, because he had moved to an outside viewpoint and had begun to recognize how far that tight little system was from doing the large, untidy task that was set for it – the task of explaining meaning, of showing how language as a whole related to the world:

> The more narrowly we examine actual language, the sharper becomes the conflict between it and our requirements. (For the crystalline purity of logic was, of course, not a result of investigation; *it was a requirement*.) The conflict becomes intolerable; the requirement is now in danger of becoming empty. – We have got onto slippery ice where there is no friction and so in a certain sense the conditions are ideal, but also, just because of that, we are unable to walk. We want to walk, so we need friction. Back to the rough ground![9]

One more note, rather a sad one, is needed here about the part this new movement has played in the long development of British empiricism. Because of these varying kinds of obscurity, and also because of accounts that did leak through of things like logical positivism, the linguistic movement began to grow rather unpopular, and the ancestors then took an unexpected revenge. As a legacy of their effect on public opinion, readers in Britain were already prepared – far more prepared than they would have been in any comparably educated country – to dismiss as nonsense any philosophy that could not be easily understood. They had been trained to be chronically suspicious of obscurity, fully convinced of the need to make havoc in libraries. The local sages had always preached a somewhat unselective anti-intellectualism whose oddity had never till now been pointed out and grasped, and its price only now began to be paid. Linguistic philosophy was dismissed as not only obscure but perverse and misguided. Language, it was felt, was not philosophy's proper business, since to talk about words was to fail to talk about real things. But words are real enough, and often very influential. It is indeed sometimes necessary to talk about them.

Chapter Twenty-One

LANGUAGE FOR SOLITARIES

This is the speculative absurdity of considering ourselves
as single and independent, as having nothing in our nature
which has respect to our fellow-creatures.

(Bishop Butler, Sermon 1, section 10)

THE MEANING OF MEANING, ESPECIALLY IN SCIENCE

Why had words begun to matter so much? There were, as I have
already suggested, two main reasons, which were now beginning
to draw together. One was the ancient, Socratic need to define
particular words for the sake of understanding what one was
actually saying. The other was the new need to attend directly to
the whole concept of meaning, a need that inevitably arose out
of the determined Cartesian pursuit of knowledge. As different
forms of learning developed, the need for more terms to be
defined, in the old Socratic style, naturally grew. But also, more
and more, when people asked whether or how they *knew* some
proposition, they found that they had to ask first what that
proposition meant, or indeed whether it meant anything. For, as
the sciences developed, the possibility that it might not do so
became more pressing. Hobbes's idea that words were sometimes used without a meaning had been vigorously pressed by
both Berkeley and Hume to explain the existence of whole
realms of theory which they thought were empty. But this
approach was not needed only for such destructive purposes.
Berkeley made two very important suggestions about ways in
which words which did not in the strict sense have a meaning
might all the same have a use. The first was that words could

217

sometimes be used merely to produce emotions.[1] The second, still more interesting, was that certain terms in science (for instance 'atom' or 'gravitation') might have a use if they were understood to work merely as predictors of future human experiences, even though they apparently could not have meaning because they did not actually refer to any object that people could perceive.[2] This is what came to be called an operationalist or instrumentalist view of their working, rather than a realist one. Berkeley suggested it because he did not see how these items, which were never revealed in experience, could actually be being spoken about. Yet he did not at all wish to suggest that such speaking ought to stop.

In the nineteenth century, this idea was urgently needed for puzzles about possible meaninglessness which arose, not over remote philosophical speculations, but at the heart of those very sciences which Descartes had regarded as the clearest and most certain – mathematics and physics. In what sense did the propositions of these sciences now have meaning? In physics, there were no more easily imaginable billiard-ball atoms. The talk was increasingly of objects quite unlike any that could possibly be supposed to figure in human experience. In mathematics, there had always been a doubt about what kind of thing the numbers, points, lines, and so forth that were being talked about actually were, but this doubt got a much sharper edge when non-Euclidean geometries began to portray spaces that were demonstrably not those of human experience. There was great difficulty in seeing how these ways of talking and thinking could have meaning at all, at least if the essential way for a word to have meaning is to act as the name of something. On this pattern, each word, and more generally each sign that was genuinely significant, needed to have its own proper object. Berkeley's speculations suggested that that object might possibly be something rather different from what it appeared – for instance, it might be some possible future experience of our own – but they did not suggest any wider idea of what could constitute meaning.

At this point, however, British empiricism impinged on European philosophy of science, since the physicist Ernst Mach took up Berkeley's ideas vigorously, and started a line of largely operationalist speculation – the line out of which, later, Wittgenstein's enquiries arose. Those engaged on these speculations were, on the whole, interested simply in their effect on physics itself. Wittgenstein, however, thought he saw something much larger – namely, a way in which these ideas might serve to resolve the whole Cartesian predicament.

THE SOLITARY VOYAGER

How was that possible? To see this, we need to look once more at what that predicament involved. The Cartesian picture showed human beings as passing their lives in a manner depressingly familiar to this century – as solitary astronauts, each shut in a hermetically sealed cabin and communicating only through an array of screens and controls placed before them. Hegelian Idealism had softened this stark picture by providing controls which were supposed to connect the astronaut, as a spirit, directly with other spirits and with the single great Spirit of which they were all part, through wires proved to exist by *a priori* rational principles. Empiricism, however, denied the existence of these wires and the force of these principles. It held that this mass of apparently helpful controls was really idle and useless, connected with nothing and moving nothing, so that panels should be stripped down, leaving only two arrays which could actually provide effective input. (There must of course be controls for producing action as well, but they do not now concern us.) The most obvious source of input was a set of screens showing sense-data. But those data could not be held to be directly connected up with real objects outside the cabin, since the astronaut had never been outside, and perhaps could not even speculate meaningfully about whether anything outside existed. What he had to do, then, was to relate his sense-data rightly to each other, with a view to predicting them and to finding patterns among them. In doing that, he was licensed to use his thought to collect data together into objects – to make 'logical constructions'. Among these constructed objects would be his own body, other human bodies around it, and even possibly other minds occupying those bodies. All these things, however, must be understood to be merely the products of his own intellectual work.

LANGUAGES, IDEAL AND OTHERWISE

The prisoner's business was therefore to carry on these constructive activities rightly, for which his prime tool was plainly
language, the means by which his constructed objects were
named and described. Since empiricists did not want to make
this process rest on rational principles, the structures provided
by language itself were specially important. Accordingly, an
array of words, placed perhaps beneath the screens showing the
sense-data, must be his other main piece of equipment. In so far
as he could relate the members of these two sets rightly and
regularly together – could make each word correspond to its
relevant batch of sense-data according to the proper rules – the
words would have meaning. Science would then become possible, and the whole business of legitimate human communication could safely rest on it. But language in its present form
could not be used to do this delicate work. Ordinary speech was
not a calculus, it was not the language of science, and was not
even regularly related to it. A quite new, ideal language must
perhaps be invented for this work – a project earlier conceived
by Leibniz. As P. M. S. Hacker puts it, both Frege and Russell

> had independently embarked upon the great logical
> programme of reducing arithmetic to logic. In the course of
> so doing, they developed powerful artificial languages of
> symbolic logic, and highly sophisticated systems of
> philosophical logic. The invention of an ideal notation
> was not only justified by reference to the systems and
> rigour required to fulfil the reductivist aims, but also as a
> quite general tool to solve logical and philosophical
> problems which hitherto had been intractable. *Thought
> was enslaved, Frege remarked, by the tyranny of words. Ordinary
> language is riddled by unavoidable confusions which can only
> be brought to light in an ideal notation.*[3] (Emphasis mine)

Or, as the young Wittgenstein put it in the *Tractatus*:

> Language disguises thought. So much so, that from the
> outward form of the clothing it is impossible to infer the
> form of the thought beneath.[4]

There are two ways, however, in which this distorting
tendency of language could be viewed. One might see it as

merely a passing defect, to be remedied by better understanding and greater care, or as an incurable feature of existing language, which could only be guarded against by not trying to make words do work for which they were unfit. Russell chose the first way. The enormous emphasis which he put throughout his life on the need to speak and write more clearly seemed to him continuous with the project of the new ideal language. He saw the building of a special scientific terminology as simply a part of this more general effort to clarify speech. The important notion that philosophy was *analysis*[5] meant for him equally the attempt, at an ordinary level, to break up complex ideas into their various parts, and the much more ambitious project of finding the ultimate logical constituents underlying them, the atoms out of which they were all finally built. He saw the first process as leading on smoothly to the second, which would supply the needed correspondence between words and the elements of experience.

Wittgenstein, however, had no such hope. Coming later to the project, he saw that the various efforts already being made to design special scientific languages held out no prospect of being neatly related to a chastened and clarified form of ordinary language. They were not moving in that direction at all. Ordinary language was not just a rather confused and embryonic form of scientific language; it was something quite different, with properties of its own. Even in the *Tractatus*, he declared that these properties must be respected. 'All the propositions of our everyday language, just as they stand, are in perfect logical order.'[6] But (he concluded) these properties play no part in securing the needed correspondence between language and the ultimate elements of experience. Instead, this correspondence takes place at a much deeper level between the structure of atomic facts and that of ideal atomic propositions – both of them entities as far from our ordinary experience as the particles of physics. They are the elements of the facts and propositions that we handle. But only in the propositions of natural science are those elements brought together in a way that is clear and reliable.

In comparing these two kinds or functions of language, Wittgenstein at this time thought it necessary to choose only one of them as actually 'saying something', and he found it obvious that this must be the language of science. Because urgent problems about that language were what had brought him into this enquiry, and because indeed he had taken little interest at that time in any other kind of philosophical problems, Wittgenstein simply limited the realm of 'what can be said' to the propositions of science. What cannot be said was, as he remarked, far more important than what can – but it was still unspeakable. It could only be shown. As he wrote at the end of the *Tractatus*:

> 6.522. There are, indeed, things that cannot be put into words. They *make themselves manifest*. They are what is mystical. . . .
> 7. What we cannot speak about, we must pass over in silence.

SCREENS AND CHANNELS

At this point, if not before, thoughtful astronauts must surely reflect that their position seems to be getting steadily worse, not better. They were told in the first place that they were shut off from the outside world – if indeed there was such a world – by a screen of their own perceptions. But now even that screen of perceptions turns out to be partly hidden from them by a further screen of ill-designed language. The array of words has not stayed quietly on its own level, but has been interfering systematically with the constructive work it was supposed to further. 'We have only to draw the curtain of words', Berkeley had said, 'to behold the fairest tree of knowledge.'[7] But our thoughts are composed of words, so how can we ever draw that curtain? It now seems that we can only do this by replacing it with another, by constructing and learning a new, alternative language, which is bound to be very difficult and technical. Moreover, this language is not yet actually available, because logicians are still disputing about its principles. Is it possible instead to stay with Berkeley, and somehow to regard the sense-data themselves as the world that we have to know, thus remaining in direct contact with it? The trouble with this idea is that knowledge is more than just direct contact, it calls for understanding. If we try this approach, our next move will probably have to be, as Berkeley's was, to ask how we shoud put the sense-data together and use them to understand the world.

Berkeley answered that we should treat these data as the words of God, who is telling us through them what we need to know, without needing to stick any gross material object – any 'stupid, thoughtless Somewhat'[8] – on behind the data to justify them. But this again leaves us with problems about language; how are we to understand God's words and translate them into our own? Whatever we may think of Berkeley's answer, it does not take us away from this linguistic range of difficulties.

There is, too, a further extremely odd point about both these barriers separating us from the world. They are both composed of exactly those things which, on a more natural view, do not constitute barriers at all, but are actually the channels that connect us to it. We might normally compare our sense-perceptions to a window through which we look out upon it, not a screen concealing it. Similarly our words are surely the open channels through which we communicate with others, not a wall that divides us from them. In spite of the many gaps and difficulties that dog our communication, we do manage to talk, and – as the deaf and the dumb can sadly testify – our speech is on the whole an enormous asset to us. And this effective communication is certainly not confined to science. Wittgenstein, who in his early days had exclaimed in despair that 'This beating against the limits of our language is perfectly, absolutely hopeless!', cried out later, in astonishment at this attitude, 'Language is not a cage!'[9] That realization led him to his later view that, by and large, meaning is not correspondence but *use* – 'the meaning of a word is its use in the language'.[10] Words work in the most varied ways in conjunction with each other and with the whole mass of our actions to bring about whatever we aim at in our forms of life. They cannot possibly be reduced to a single function.

THE TROUBLE WITH HOMUNCULI

It is easy to see that something has gone wrong with a model that turns out as unrealistic as this, but much harder to see just how to change it. The key is to concentrate our attention on the self, the actual prisoner or astronaut – the strange being who is supposed to be sitting inside the cabin and working the controls. What kind of creature is this taken to be? As with all images that contain such a homunculus, it has to be a tiny replica of the complete human being. It therefore tends to contain in itself, on a small scale, just the same problems that it was invented to illuminate, and so to obscure them rather than to help solve them. Thus, for instance, when people tried to understand how sight worked by considering the retinal image, they thought of this image as a small picture being scanned by a small spectator within. Great puzzles then arose about the fact that the image seemed to be the wrong way up; how was the tiny spectator supposed to deal with that? Progress only became possible when it was realized that the image is a stage in the complex process of sight, not itself one more thing to be seen. There is no hidden inner spectator. What we see when we look around us is not just the retinal image; we ourselves look directly at the world. The retinal image is a part of the equipment that makes it possible for us to do this; it is not itself a substitute object.

This same approach is surely the one needed if we are told that what we are looking at is only a range of sense-data, and that we are only constructing or inferring from it the trees and people that we think we see. The notion of our 'sense-data' as separate objects, things to be seen, heard, or felt on their own, is a confused one.[11] The images and noises that occur during perception are real as parts or aspects of the perceiving process, but they are not separate objects forming a screen between that person and the world. Certainly we can misperceive things. But when we do that we are not perceiving a strange extra entity called a sense-datum; we are just doing our perceptual job badly. And here again we can turn from the bogus objects to the bogus subject that has been invented to fit them. What is this strange shrunken creature within who is supposed, not just to see and hear the data, but to do such an amazing job of constructing and inferring material things out of them? Any sort of being that could manage to do this would have to be one that had grown up, as we all at present do, out in the world, as a being originally adapted to perceive that world directly. It could not have lived always hidden in a cabin, any more than a real astronaut does. In seeing the images, it would have to be able to think at once, as we nearly always do now on looking at a picture, 'ah – that's a house', or 'that's a child', recognizing the objects, not constructing or inferring them.

The whole process of perception only works as part of the

larger process of conscious thought and action, performed by the whole person, a point that Gilbert Ryle put admirably in his book *The Concept of Mind*[12] when he compared the Cartesian picture to a ghost in a machine, and insisted that what really exists is indeed this whole person. If we ask what are the objects that this person perceives, the answer is normally, not separate images, but things and, above all, people. From the deepest roots of our existence up, we are social beings directly inhabiting the world, members of a community and of a species whose faculties have all evolved to fit them for a wide physical and social context, not solitary astronauts. Solitude, and the thoughts appropriate to solitude, are indeed a part of our experience, but they are a derivative one, getting their meaning only gradually against the background of a thoroughly plural existence. Human babies (if so vulgar a point may be mentioned) cannot survive at all unless other people constantly look after them. Other bodies and other minds are given as parts of our world from the start, and our faculties are adapted to respond to them directly. There is no possible position from which a human being could need to construct or infer their existence. Accordingly, the astronaut picture does not have the authority that a careful, exact, minimal depiction of reality would have. It is not parsimonious. The enclosing cabin which it has added around the perceiving subject is a monstrous and gratuitous fancy, needing to be cut away with Occam's razor or whatever other instrument may be found handy. The burden of argument does not rest on people who propose to get rid of this extra entity, but on those who invented it and propose to keep it.

Chapter Twenty-Two

ESCAPING FROM
SOLITUDE

Is this mine own countree?

(Coleridge, *The Ancient Mariner*)

MOORE ON COMMON SENSE

In a number of his articles, Moore set about amputating the unnecessary, isolating shell, in which Descartes had enclosed the self, with great zest and some success. But he always became entangled before the end with pieces of it that he had not fully managed to throw away. Probably his most successful onslaught is the one in 'The defence of common sense'.[1]

Here he starts by putting it to his readers that both he and they know with certainty a long list of truisms, for instance that their own bodies exist and have long existed on the earth, that this earth has itself long existed, along with many other bodies on it, that some of these bodies are human and belong to other, equally conscious beings who have and have had experiences of their own. What follows from all this? Moore's manner might suggest at first that he merely expects to stun his readers into admitting their belief in these truisms by a burst of honesty, in the style that might have been used by Dr Johnson. But this is not all. Moore does indeed mean to shift the mood of the argument in this direction by his contagious honesty and courage, to show up the element of chronic humbug in scepticism, but he knows that an argument is needed as well. He understands that people may rightly hold on to strange and paradoxical conclusions which they have reached by reasoning, since some strange and paradoxical conclusions are indeed true.

226

(For instance, the world really is round and there really are people on the other side of it.) It is still necessary, however, that these conclusions should make sense. Moore, therefore, goes on to ask what anyone who claims to doubt these truisms means by their doubt. As he points out, it is hard to see what a doubt can mean if it is impossible to express it except in terms which imply that it has already been settled:

No philosopher has ever been able to hold such views consistently. One way in which they have betrayed this inconsistency, is by alluding to the existence of other philosophers. Another way is by alluding to the existence of the human race, and in particular by using 'we' in the sense in which I have already constantly used it, in which any philosopher who asserts that 'we' do so and so, e.g. that 'we sometimes believe propositions that are not true', is asserting not only that he himself has done the thing in question, but that *very many other human beings, who have had bodies and lived on the earth*, have done the same.[2] (Emphasis Moore's)

As he goes on to point out, this fact is particularly glaring when these philosophers discuss 'common-sense beliefs' which they want to reject.

When such a philosopher says – 'No human being has ever known of the existence of other human beings', he is saying, 'There have been many other human beings besides myself, and none of them (including myself) has ever *known* of the existence of other human beings.' If he says: 'These beliefs are beliefs of Common-Sense, but they are not matters of *knowledge*' he is saying 'There have been many other human beings, besides myself, who have shared these beliefs, but neither I nor any of the rest has ever known them to be true.'[3]

In short, this argument, like all other arguments, is necessarily conducted in the language of a many-personed world. And this has not happened just by chance, through an oversight which greater care might rectify, but because there is not and could not be any other sort of language. The whole point of language is to make possible communication between distinct people, just

227

as the point of a bridge is to join two distinct banks. By opening our mouths to speak at all, we concede Moore's truisms. Even if we merely say inwardly, 'I think, therefore I am,' we have in effect also said, 'I speak; therefore you are too – all of you, including the whole multitude of you that has been needed to invent language.'

How conclusive is Moore's argument? Here, as with other answers to sceptical contentions, a strangely unreal approach is often taken, by which 'the sceptic' is treated with awe as a mythical, essentially impregnable, wily being who is determined to keep up the game for ever and who always has one more shot in his locker. If he is resolute enough (people say), if he is really hard-nosed, he will refuse to admit the relevance of the fact that he uses language, and then where will you be? Or perhaps he will retreat into a more ingenious kind of solipsism, or offer to go away and invent a private, non-interlocutory language.[4] Anyway, who can be sure that he has not got some sort of further trick up his sleeve? The extraordinary thing about this line is that it treats the argument as if it were a game played between contending parties with conflicting aims and interests, instead of – what, as we have earlier noticed, it always ought to be – a genuine attempt by each single person to think out the issue. Moore's point is not just a blow intended to knock down an opponent. It is a genuine question to each of us, namely: If you doubt the existence of other minds, what do you mean by this doubt? What do you think is true instead? Since the very language in which you express this doubt implies a thoroughgoing, confident belief in the existence of those minds, what further question do you actually want to put? Moore is rightly shifting the question from 'Are you sure that you know this?' to 'What do you mean by this?'

THE MEANING OF MEANINGLESSNESS

Questions can only make sense in a context where they can arise, and this must be a context containing clear alternatives. It makes perfectly good sense for me to doubt whether I have locked the door, or added up my bill correctly, because I know what I think might have happened if I have not. But what is the alternative to the existence of the whole physical world, or of all other minds?

Dreams will not supply it, for they exist only within the world and by reflecting parts of it. The only other faint attempt that has been made to supply one is Descartes's idea of the Great Deceiver who imposes it all, and this, besides being demented, fails to work, because the Deceiver himself evidently is some kind of other mind. This incredibly general kind of doubt is not just unreasonable, it is unreal; it does not make sense. This point is important because many people have attacked Cartesian doubt on the weaker ground that it is merely unreasonable in the sense of uncalled-for, unhelpful, or imprudent. Locke, for instance, wrote that

> We shall not have much reason to complain of the narrowness of our minds, if we will but employ them about what may be of use to us; for of that they are very capable. . . . It will be no excuse for an idle and untoward servant, who would not attend his business by candlelight, to complain that he had not broad sunlight. The candle that is set up in us shines bright enough for all our purposes. . . . If we will disbelieve everything because we cannot certainly know all things, we shall do much-what as wisely as he who would not use his legs, but sit still and perish, because he had not wings to fly.[5]

This way of talking concedes the existence of broad sunlight, or of wings that can fly, and only claims that as a matter of brute fact they happen not to be available to us. It is not obvious why, if that were all, ambitious thinkers who are keen to fly or to reach the sunlight need be deterred from trying to gain these advantages. And indeed the fact that, since Locke wrote, human beings *have* in a peculiar and limited sense learnt to fly shows the uncertain limits of such ambitions. But suppose the ambition had been to produce a round square, or dark light, or a true falsehood, or even a perpetual-motion machine? Or again, suppose somebody asks for subscriptions in order to found a society of solipsists, and does so on the ground that solipsism is true? Proposers of these schemes would need something more than a mere general claim that supposedly impossible things sometimes turn out to be possible after all. They would need to show a clear, specific sense in which these words could have

229

meaning, a sense which would also carry a specification of what was wanted and the reasons for wanting it. As it happens, I do possess a round square – namely, a little steel cylinder, measuring one inch each way. If this was all that was needed, it could easily be supplied. Similarly, there could be all manner of poetic ways in which one might describe something as dark light or a true falsehood, and the inventors of perpetual-motion machines can beaver on at redefining their aim, as well as at actually fulfilling it. Correspondingly, what is needed in the case of Moore's truisms is a clear sense in which they can be denied. It is not enough merely to pronounce the words of denial, any more than it is enough to pronounce the words 'round square'. It is necessary also to make sense of them, to show how they could be applied. And because the truisms are so sweeping, this involves a great range of concepts. It calls on us to show how the denial can fit into the general landscape of our thought, and what changes would be needed to accommodate it there. In particular, its effect on the notion that we have of ourselves, a notion which is the centre of this inner landscape, must be properly filled in and made plausible.

That is the burden that lies on anyone who wants to propound and defend the Cartesian picture, once questions begin to be asked about it. The burden is, of course, one of explanation rather than of proof. In principle, it is perfectly possible, once the question is put, to show that some particular image or way of thinking does have a point, and so to justify its use. But this justification will only hold for the kind of use that has actually been pointed out; it will not be an all-purpose license. This is the situation about many popular images that have been far too widely used; for instance, the notion of inevitable progress, whether in biological evolution or in human history, the notion of competition in economics, and the machine analogy in psychology. The Cartesian picture of a solitary knower isolated in his cabin is, on the face of things, very likely to form one of this group, simply because it is so extravagant – it goes so far beyond what its inventor's purposes required. Those purposes centred on some special doubts about the relation between the various sciences, and about the kind of thinking that could best be used in them. There was no special intention of constructing a general model for the human condition, still less of proving that that condition was one of incurable solitude. If anybody now wants to use it for this purpose, they have to give their own explanation of what their reasons are, which would be quite different from those that relate it to the quest for knowledge. Individualistic moral systems, such as Existentialism and Social Darwinism, which do make that emphasis, cannot properly draw support from Cartesian views about the nature of knowledge, even though, historically speaking, they have certainly grown out of those views. And as far as the quest for knowledge itself goes, the Cartesian model has visibly reached the limits of its use and begun to be a real hindrance.

CLEARING UP THE CONCEPT OF KNOWLEDGE

That is the moral that emerges from Moore's 'Defence of common sense'. As I mentioned, it does not emerge quite clearly. This is largely because, in that article, Moore still used the notion of *knowledge* in the traditional way, without paying any special attention to its meaning. He did not explicitly centre his discussion on the nature of the knowing or doubting subject, but simply claimed that he and others *know* these truisms. Since this kind of claim had long been understood as a claim by an imprisoned astronaut to have somehow smuggled in information about something outside his cell, it was not clear why Moore seemed to think that he had overcome the difficulty of this. And he made this confusion worse both by worrying at considerable length about the position of sense-data, which he ought to have been jettisoning, and by the wording of his claim that he and others had '*frequently* known' the truisms. This sounds as if knowing were a special kind of process or performance, like a gaolbreak, whose nature was already well understood, and he was reporting that the prisoners did actually go through it successfully at times – perhaps twice a year? The traditional sceptic then naturally asks for the process to be demonstrated, and for its success to be proved, perhaps by producing external objects gathered during the gaolbreak by methods distinct from ordinary experience. And of course this cannot be done.

But the real enquiry is quite different. As Wittgenstein puts it, 'We are asking ourselves: What do we do with a statement "I *know*. . ."'? For it is not a question of mental processes or mental

231

states.'[6] People who say 'I know' or 'She knows' are not making a report about some special state or performance by themselves or someone else, as they would be by saying 'I'm hot' or 'She's slipping.' They are making claims, as much as they would by saying something like 'The bridge is safe now,' or 'I can show you the way.' These are not primarily remarks about the speaker, but something much more like offers to take responsibility. Any questions that arise about them will most naturally be questions directly about the outside objects involved – for instance about the bridge, or the particular route to be taken. Accordingly, the question often raised by Descartes and others, 'How do you know that you know?', has perhaps as little sense as 'How do you know that you offer?' or 'How do you know that you thank?' The meaning of the word 'know', like that of other words, is its use. This word is not the name of a peculiar mental state or process because, like very many other words, it is not a name at all. Its work is not the work of referring or correspond- ing to some set object, but of helping people to distinguish between the more reliable and the less reliable parts of the world around them. In doing this, speakers offer their own guaran- tees, which are of course understood, like all other human guarantees, to be fallible. Though it is our business as citizens and language-users to offer these guarantees carefully and responsibly, and therefore only to offer them when we do have reason to feel certain, it is not our business to be omniscient. The appearance of permanent, lifelong confidence which seems to attach to some uses of words like 'know' is a superficial one, and does not even attach to all their uses. As Wittgenstein remarks, 'One always forgets the expression, "I thought I knew." '[7] The context of human life supplies the normal background for this claim, as it does for all others. And the perfectly sensible quest for better evidence and more careful reasoning in the sciences does not in the least require that we should step outside that context and become gods.

THE STATUS OF TRUISMS

This is a central case where to treat of meaning widely as use, rather than narrowly as reference or correspondence, saves us from a whole mass of unnecessary confusion. There is no reason to expect a word like 'know' to be the name of a peculiar kind of process, nor to suppose that this word can be given an unrealistic sense which interferes with its previous function, merely to meet the demands of a theory. But until this general point about the way in which words have meaning has been grasped, Moore's truisms are puzzling. What is supposed to be their status? Can Moore be saying that there really is a particular set of propositions – perhaps even a particular number of them, say a hundred? – which are infallibly known, by contrast to all others, which cannot be so known? If so, there would be a real difficulty about the fact that they seem at times to change. For instance, people used once to think it a truism that the world was flat, and that it was impossible for people to go to the moon, and that events could be genuinely simultaneous with one another. Accordingly, slapdash relativism, emphasizing such cases, sometimes seems to destroy Moore's point. Yet open-minded readers still feel its force. There really does seem to be something dishonest and confused about pretending to doubt things which in fact we do not see how to doubt. And it surely is not honest to evade this difficulty by pretending to treat seriously a position like full-scale solipsism, or belief in Descartes's Great Deceiver, when we know very well that, if anyone actually defended these positions, we would rush them round to get psychiatric help as quickly as possible. All this is disturbing because the appeal of the sceptical stance has always centred on its apparent honesty. Moore, however, seems to be showing it here as dishonest, and indeed, when we think about it, this alarming fact is seen to have a wider application. As suggested earlier, in the actual world, rampant humbug quite as often takes the form of pretending not to know things that one does know as of pretending to know things one does not know, and is equally discreditable in both forms. The sceptic as folk-hero is no sort of reliable guide. So what are we to do?

Shaking the kaleidoscope slightly, Wittgenstein gives the matter a much more hopeful twist. The point, he says, is not that these particular propositions have a special intrinsic quality, making them alone permanently and absolutely certain. It is that, for every individual and every society, some set of propositions at any time must occupy this base position. That set provides the background against which other things are questioned; it forms the underlying world-picture. Its various elements are not themselves in principle incapable of being questioned. But they cannot be questioned unless some other set gains a special force and solidity, and supplies a ground adequate to make questions arise about them. He gives the useful analogy of a river-bed:

> (95). The propositions describing this world-picture might be part of a kind of mythology. And their role is like that of rules of a game; and the game can be learnt purely practically, without learning any explicit rules.
> (96). It might be imagined that some propositions, of the form of empirical propositions, were hardened and functioned as channels for such empirical propositions as were not hardened but fluid; and that this relation altered with time, in that fluid propositions hardened, and hard ones became fluid.
> (97). The mythology may change back into a state of flux, the river-bed of thoughts may shift. But I distinguish between the movement of waters on the river-bed and the shift of the bed itself; though there is not a sharp division of the one from the other.
> (98). But if someone were to say, 'So logic too is an empirical science' he would be wrong. Yet this is right; the same proposition may get treated at one time as something to test by experience, and at another as a rule of testing.
> (99). And the bank of that river consists partly of hard rock, subject to no alteration or only to an imperceptible one, partly of sand, which now in one place now in another gets washed away, or deposited.[8]

How well does this image do its work? It is designed to do justice to both of two conflicting demands, the first of which has in recent times been stressed out of all proportion to the second. The first is the need to remember that we might be wrong. The second is the need to be honest about the extent to which we actually believe that we are, on some central points, right, and to register our claim that we are so. In stressing the first more than the second, theorists have always had some special purpose. They have concentrated their scepticism either on particular beliefs which they really doubted, or on a social need for tolerance, or else, more generally, on attacking the disproportionate confidence now placed in 'science' by comparison with other forms of knowledge. In order to do these things, however, they have inevitably always still been taking for granted an immense range of other propositions which they had no reason to doubt, and have also been strongly affirming certain truths, in which they insist that it is necessary to believe. But nothing at all can be strongly affirmed unless a whole mass of truisms is taken for granted as a background for it. For instance, it is not possible to stress the variety of cultures and the need to take seriously the beliefs of unfamiliar ones, without taking every one of Moore's truisms for granted, because, unless they were all true, those other cultures could never even have existed. If we did not commit ourselves to a great mass of such beliefs – and commit ourselves in the sense of positively endorsing them, not just being willing to gamble – we could not think or act at all. The peculiar way of talking that seems to treat all beliefs as equally valid in their own cultures is an artificial, anthropological approach; it is essentially a way of talking about *other people*. The world, however, does not consist only of other people. Each of us is somewhere inside it, not a superhuman anthropologist observing it from outside. For each of us, the question of just where we stand in that world is a crucial one.

The need to bring these two half-truths together effectively seems to me a central one both for our thought and our life today. Wittgenstein's river-bed image is designed to help us there, and it surely does so. More sharply and simply, Neurath made a similar point when he suggested that a sensible person at sea in a leaky boat will be willing to sit on some unexamined parts of that boat whilst repairing the others. A purist who, by contrast, refused to start any repair work until all the timbers beneath him had been guaranteed sound would become a martyr to principles whose value is a trifle obscure.

SUMMARY: THE IMPORTANCE OF LANGUAGE

This brief survey cannot of course possibly do justice to the very important work that has been done in this century in relation to our ideas about meaning. It is designed just to resist certain common errors on the subject, and to show its relation to our main theme. (1) The first error is the idea that all this talk about language has been a mere gratuitous piece of mandarin frivolity, devised by philosophers who simply wanted to avoid looking at real life. As against this, I have tried to show why it was crucial for our culture to think hard about language and meaning, in order to avoid damaging confusion.

The next three errors are related, arising out of a partial understanding of what was going on in linguistic philosophy. First among these comes (2) the notion that a proper, disciplined use of words is not possible except in science. The whole language of everyday life, and especially that of morality, is then dismissed as incapable of system, sometimes indeed as 'nonsense'. This idea is obviously relevant to the general split between thought and feeling, which is a central theme of this book, so I have taken some pains to argue against this view of language in so far as it affects moral questions, mainly in chapter 12. Since then, I have been trying to show how the peculiar view of meaning implied by that way of dividing language flows from some quite general and glaring faults in the Cartesian picture both of knowledge and of personal identity. I have suggested that things go much better if we abandon that picture, and (in general) consider meaning, along the lines proposed by the later Wittgenstein, as the use of words within a particular form of life.

The last two errors are complementary ones, one or other of which is liable to arise once we do take up that Wittgensteinian standpoint. We might then either (3) treat a single form of life (namely our own) as final arbiter, not just of current meanings, but of all legitimate thought and action; or (4) stress the plurality of such forms to the point of insisting that none can say anything intelligible about another, nor indeed about itself – that every thought or action is equally valid and acceptable within the circle that finds it so. Both these conclusions have in fact been quite widely drawn from one-sided reading of Wittgenstein. Both seem to be obvious and glaring half-truths, and the attempt to treat them as alternatives is surely one more of those vacuous academic tournaments we discussed earlier. The notion that a 'form of life' could be a sealed, exclusive circle containing a set of ideas that are wholly fixed and harmonious with each other is unreal. Everybody lives in many such overlapping circles, and conflict and development is always going on within all of them.

The circles do not supply the infallible authority for which we pine to resolve our dilemmas. They only provide a setting, a context, a usable tradition, a set of conceptual tools. We are much better off with these things than without them, as Neurath's analogy of the boat rightly stresses. We quickly find this out if we are isolated among strangers who do not share or understand our concepts. So we should regard the circles as our own homes, with gratitude and respect, not with the simple resentment which romantic individualism inculcates towards 'society'. Yet – and indeed all the more for that reason – we still have both the right and the duty to criticize their laws, and to take part, along with the other inhabitants, in changing them where we think they need it.

For all sorts of reasons, this view of meaning and the view of personal identity that goes with it seem to me much more realistic and workable than their predecessors. For our present purpose, however, one particular reason stands out, namely, that they give us back the space we need for our moral thinking. Had Russell's view proved to be the only possible one, the whole business of serious thought would have had to be routed through science, and ethics would then have consisted only of facts, established by specialists in the social sciences. Had the *Tractatus* view prevailed, the social sciences too would apparently have been reckoned as part of 'what cannot be said' along with the rest of ethics. ('If a man could write a book on ethics which really was a book on ethics, this book would, with an explosion, destroy all the other books in the world.'[9]) Now though there is indeed always a mass of bad and pernicious thinking and writing going on on these subjects, we would not actually gain by silencing all talk about them, nor by excluding that talk from serious and systematic criticism. The remedy for the bad talk is not to stop talking, but to talk better. The whole idea that sensible, organized talk ought to belong only to the brain and not to the heart was a mistaken one, as Wittgenstein later saw. There is no such frontier; our language, like our thought, is a continuum. There is therefore no reason why moral philosophy should not go on, as it used to do, by dealing with the conceptual difficulties that arise out of the practical problems of the day – out of our form of life. Today, this is again happening. To some extent, it had already begun to happen even before official philosophical permission was given for it, because some current conceptual problems, especially in medical ethics, were becoming so knotty that other professionals, growing desperate, had started to call in philosophers. But any sense that this offended against philosophical principles has now largely dissolved as those supposed principles have become discredited. Moral philosophers are back in the world, which is certainly the right place for them, and this should make it possible for them to help set right many of the things I have complained of in the course of this book. If they are to do so, however, their methods in some ways need to change. And that is a matter we had better discuss in the next chapter.

Chapter Twenty-Three

PHILOSOPHIZING OUT
IN THE WORLD

What is the use of studying philosophy if all that it does
for you is to enable you to talk with some plausibility about
some abstruse questions of logic etc., and if it does not
improve your thinking about the important questions of
everyday life?

(Wittgenstein, letter to Norman Malcolm)[1]

THOUGHT AND THINGS

Philosophy seems, then, to have been paroled from the ivory
tower. How can we best use it once it is loose? How shall we avoid
the various kinds of trouble that led to its being locked up in the
first place?

This seems to be part of the wider question, how are we to
apply our thinking to reality? How can we close the gap which
constantly tends to open between theory and practice, between
our minds and the world? Human intelligence is not automatically self-directing. One of the most striking things about it is
how unevenly it gets applied. In every culture, intense loving
attention to certain chosen problems contrasts with a startling
neglect of others, some of which are far more pressing, not only
for justice, or for happiness, but for mere survival. Large,
obvious, central questions can be entirely ignored. This is
natural, because they are very frightening. To move towards
them when we have not been thinking about them before is
especially hard. Our thought therefore tends strongly to stay in
its established tracks, and also to shift those tracks themselves

239

gradually and imperceptibly away from these problems. All human patterns of thought contain defence mechanisms designed to do this, mechanisms which very much need our attention. They are not necessarily illicit. We do have to have some defence against the vastness and alarmingness of the surrounding world, some sunscreen against its glare. But we also need to have some inkling how we are providing that defence, some awareness, however dim, of the part our own motivations play in the matter.

In this book, we have been watching a number of these defence mechanisms at work. As citizens, the one that most of us chiefly rely on is sheer inattention, but we usually supplement this by some quarrelsomeness. Our tribal loyalties enable us, in the first place, to distract ourselves from large issues by feuding over small ones, and in the second, if that fails, to blame our opponents for what goes wrong in the world, to use what energy we do give to these matters partly in feuding against these opponents, and to feel excused for our inaction by regarding them as all-powerful. When we turn from this general background to ask about the special forms that these defences take for intellectuals – which has been a central theme of this book – we find, naturally enough, that this same method is widely used there too. An obsession with controversy continually distorts our approach to our enquiries. It has a tendency to split us up into ever smaller groups with less and less understanding of each other's projects. This is not, as is often supposed, a necessary effect of enquiry itself, nor an advantage to it. It is a pathological by-product of our attitude to it. Though I have already said something about it in chapter 7, I want to say a word more in ending, because I think the matter is extraordinarily neglected.

Our tribal loyalties serve to over-simplify our dilemmas. Most of the time they work to keep us fairly near to where we started. But, if we start to disagree with members of our existing tribe, the easiest way to deal with the painful stress of opposition is to sign up for a ready-made opposing group. This ensures that our intellect never has more than two alternatives to consider, and that it usually knows in advance which of them to reject. However bad both these alternatives may be, we find it fearfully hard to reject both of them and apply our minds directly to the problem. Even very highly trained intelligence can be dominated in this way by tribal feeling, and the training can be used merely to obscure the process. If we do not become much more aware than we now are of these restricting forces, we become their helpless victims and our thought does not engage with the world at all.

INTELLIGENCE IS NOT ENOUGH

As I have insisted throughout this book, this attention to motive and context is not a distraction from the real work of philosophy, but an essential part of it. The meaning of words depends on how they are used and intended.[2] We cannot split off feeling from intellect and look for our salvation from intellect alone, though that policy of division is of course often recommended today. Many people, for instance, suggest that what is wrong with the human race is simply a shortage of intelligence, a shortage which can perhaps be cured by raising IQ through genetic engineering. This is an odd suggestion. Never mind the technical and scientific problems of IQ-raising, it is clear that we don't use a tenth of the intelligence we have got already. If we had more, we would certainly squander it in the same ways as we do now. Very high intelligence can be seen running to waste all round us, both inside and outside our institutions. Outside them it runs to waste in suicide and depression, in quarrelling, alcoholism, neurosis, and organized crime, in various ways of killing time without much enjoyment, and most recently down special sinks designed for it, called computer games. Inside the institutions, it lavishes itself on intrigues and obsessions of the most various kinds, on internal feuds and deceptions, and on finding ways to block measures introduced by other people.

These remarks are not intended as just one more denunciation of mankind, but simply as a reminder. We know already that these things are true. My present point is just that they make clear that it is sense we lack, rather than intellectual power. And, when we are wondering how to apply intellectual power to the world, some of this sense is what we chiefly need. That does not mean that we don't need philosophy. In finding and formulating the rules that underlie sense, the inarticulate patterns by which it works, in noting their clashes and inadequacies and looking for ways of dealing with them, we are bound to be doing philosophy whether we recognize it or not. Philosophy is the formalization of an ancient art which used to be called the search for wisdom, but we have got too prissy to use such words today.

DISPUTES AND COMPROMISES

One obvious trouble about controversies is the way in which they tend to assimilate opposing arguments to one another, so that lifelong opponents can end up as almost indistinguishable from each other. This happens partly because of the simple temptation for them to copy each other's methods on a tit-for-tat basis. More deeply, however, it happens because it is hard to state disputes plainly unless both sides use the same terms, and this tends to make them share the same presuppositions. Errors which both sides share therefore become very hard to notice. The religious wars and persecutions that followed the Reformation make an instructive example here. For a long time, Catholics and Protestants shared the view that only one of their creeds could survive. This meant that one had to destroy the other, and they differed only on which it should be. For rulers therefore, the question was simply 'Which towns are to be put to the sword? Which believers must be burnt?' Certain people, however, such as Montaigne and Locke, saw a possibility of approaching the problem differently, so that this kind of question would not arise. They proposed finding a way to view this disagreement as a normal one, containable within the scope of a decent human life. Their work made it possible gradually for toleration to be developed without the fearful sense of betrayal which it had at first seemed to involve.

This is surely the kind of achievement which should be our model when we look for the synthesis that is to resolve any fierce dialectical clash. Because this particular solution – the invention of toleration – is now so familiar, its boldness and originality may need to be stressed. The quest for compromise does not mean a willingness to settle for some confused half-way position between existing errors. What was needed at the Reformation was not a proposal that both sides should get together to burn Episcopalians. Nor was it Luther's bright idea that Protestants should burn Anabaptists as well as Catholics. It was a radical reshaping of the whole conceptual scheme that had legitimized the burning. It had to be designed to make room in the world for the values of both sides. The project called both for great intellectual exertion and for a lot of courage. When both sides are embattled, there is nothing in the least safe or easy about a serious effort to find a compromise.

In bringing up this example, I am of course not saying that this particular solution is yet complete or satisfactory. Of course liberalism has its own problems. Dialectic is endless, and each generation has its own work to do. It is just an instance of the way in which errors common to both sides can make a conflict seem irresoluble. And of course, the hotter the opposition grows, the harder it becomes for anyone to see the part of the truth that belongs to the other side. That makes it impossible for anybody to reach the synthesis, which is supposed to be the point and justification of the whole dialectic.

If opposition is really to become fertile, as it is supposed to do, we need much more stress on the need for reconciliation, much sterner discipline about the habit of competitive feuding, than has ever yet been present in our tradition, either in intellectual debate or (still more obviously) in politics. It is interesting to wonder whether the aggressive pattern of dialectic is actually a necessary one at all. Would *any* intelligent being have to use it, or might there be creatures somewhere which simply explored topics as a team of geographers might map a piece of country, co-operatively rather than in competition? And is there anything wrong when human thought does operate in this way? Would there be anything wrong if the ecological metaphor I mentioned in chapter 3 – the notion of asking how best to cultivate a garden or a piece of countryside – were to come to seem more natural to us in our thinking than the image of warfare, or the picture of knocking down other people's buildings in order to put up our own? Would it do any harm to move at least some distance towards the image of exploring and mapping a terrain? If our natural motivation really does force us to reason wastefully by constant jousting, then this seems to be a nuisance that should have more attention than it has had so far.

THE EXALTATION OF DIALECTIC

Whether there is such a natural compulsion or not, however, the tradition of our particular society has certainly piled on the competitive element. Intellectual debate as we know it grew up among the Greeks as an offshoot of a strongly developed tradition of word-battles in the political arena, and above all in the lawcourts. It has always kept the marks of that origin. Though the weapons were only words, among the Greeks these battles could be lethal. Life or death for the client, or indeed for the speaker himself, often hung on them. At the least, political careers were at stake, banishment and confiscation of goods were common, scurrilous personal abuse was normal – circumstances which don't make for scrupulous dialectical fairness. And, even when only victory in the argument itself was at stake, the background was still the intensely competitive spirit which informed Greek politics as it did Greek games.

Do people really have to do their reasoning like this, in terms of winning and losing? The anthropologist Colin Turnbull has recorded the astonishment shown by the pygmies to whom he described the school games on which he had been brought up – notably football.[3] The pygmies couldn't understand how anyone could deliberately devise pastimes in which, inevitably, somebody had to lose. Now it will rightly be pointed out that the pygmies haven't written Plato's *Republic* or invented particle physics. My present question, however, is about the price we pay for that sort of achievement, especially in the realm of moral and political thinking. Can anything be done to make it a little bit less extortionate?

INTERNALIZING THE DEBATE

In his day, Plato already saw that we need to try, and gave strong warnings about it. In his dialogues, Socrates provides impressive arguments for always making the debate internal, in a way that would prevent outside rivalries from distorting it. We need, says Socrates, to grasp both sides of the argument as our own, to feel the force of both, and to direct the whole of it towards the truth, regardless of which side gets the victory.[4] The trouble is that, in spite of this, time and again on the next page we find that same Socrates grabbing his advantage like a shyster lawyer, and putting down opponents by tricks that would shame a second-year student. The temptations of the competitive intellect, backed by the forensic tradition, are simply too strong.

What should we do about this? The lawsuit model is obviously bad if we merely identify as one of the contending litigants, because it does not require us to be fair or comprehensive. To use that model properly, we need perhaps to internalize the whole lawcourt, to include both litigants, and judge and jury as well, within our own minds. Where two people really are contending, their only chance of reaching a satisfactory synthesis lies in their both doing this. The same sort of treatment, too, seems to be needed for another very influential model which Socrates used at his trial, that of the gadfly, which we touched on briefly in chapter 9. He explained that the reason why he was maddening everybody by his destructive arguments, and was accused of corrupting the youth, was that the gods had sent him to save his fellow-citizens from idleness and complacency. He was therefore like a gadfly sent to pester a horse which was 'strong and noble, but a trifle lazy', and give it some healthy exercise.

Now it has never been sufficiently noticed that this arrangement only works if it is a symbiosis. Horse and gadfly need each other and must suit each other. If the horse is already ill, jumpy, and neurotic, or if the gadfly merely stings other gadflies, the system fails. To interpret the fable: The business of intellectuals cannot be merely to annoy people and to undermine their confidence. These delightful occupations have to be selective, and to be balanced by more positive efforts from both sides. Philosophers and other academics who refuse to make positive suggestions themselves are relying on other people's. For useful gadfly behaviour, the critics need to share their central standards with their victims, as Socrates certainly did with the Athenians. This does not necessarily make them any less annoying. They may still get arrested and end up with the hemlock. But it is possible in principle for them to be heard as the echo of a voice already sounding within those whom they criticize. Conscience, which was murmuring already in a confused, rudimentary way, resonates with the outside critics and can now be heard.

This is surely the model on which all rational persuasion between people must actually work. The picture that emotivist ethics painted, in which they push each other about mechanically and externally by emotive forces, like stones in an avalanche, is quite unreal. Of course human persuasion does sometimes work like that, and there are also plenty of ways of pushing people about like stones without bothering to persuade them at all. But, if reasoning does come into the matter, then both sides are trying, however confusedly, to internalize their debate. They are not locked away, each inside its own impenetrable viewpoint. If they do become so locked, then things cease to be normal, and it is then that we may begin to talk of a dispute as a war. Marx used the language of class war in order to single out one particular conflict as a case where it was no use for the parties to hope to understand each other. This was his point in making the dialectic an external and material one, essentially a mere physical process like an avalanche. The same idea seems to lie behind the term 'cold war', used as a description of the east-west conflict today. Both these phrases are loaded, fatalistic devices, specially designed to make disputes look incurable. They serve to extend the notion of communicative isolation – an isolation which does indeed go very far in actual warfare – to cover situations where there is not in fact any real fighting to produce this block. They suggest that a conflict of interests, if it is severe enough, can absolutely stop communication and absolve both sides from the responsibility, which is normally basic to human life, of looking for ideas in common so as to get on speaking terms again. And they claim that these are cases of this kind of communicative breakdown.

ACCEPTING SYMBIOSIS

This sort of contention does not seem to me convincing even in these extreme cases. But our business just now is with much less extreme divisions, ones which are scarcely likely to be called wars in any but the idlest of rhetoric. We are talking about the relation between opponents in controversy, about academic and political debates, and about more general disagreements over current social and political problems. In these conflicts, the relation between the two sides must normally be a symbiosis. This should be plain in the case of academic specializations, since they all study the same world. It also seems obvious in the case of political parties and groups, since these exist to represent people who are actually living together symbiotically in the same country. They cannot work effectively by locking themselves into separate, mutually impenetrable, spheres of discourse, speaking different languages, because their supporters are people who talk to each other. Moreover, they all need to get themselves understood by people who do not support them yet. Their policies, too, are normally formed in response to one another, as Protestantism was formed in response to Catholicism. If one such party or group is suddenly removed, others can find themselves in trouble. Moreover, people can quite often be seen moving from one group or party to another in the course of their lives without any agonizing conversion, in a way which shows that ideas from both were present within them all the time. And when this change is violent – when, as sometimes happens, middle-aged converts lash their former comrades with special venom – the bitterness often seems to flow from a still unresolved inner conflict, rather than from a mere external house-moving. As for academic specialities, people would often like to move between them, and they sometimes succeed in doing so to very good effect. But institutional obstacles often make this move extremely hard.

THE PROBLEMS OF PUBLIC PHILOSOPHIZING

If all this had not been true, there could hardly be any point in unleashing philosophy again on the world. If all debates really were external – if everybody had only one opinion and never felt any doubts about it – we should need nothing more than lawyers and (for emotivist purposes) skilled public relations consultants, emotional engineers. But, as people do not seem to be made on this simple plan, perhaps the diagnosis of internal dialectic *is* true, and true not just in sophisticated western democracies, but in any country at any time where feuds do not run so high as to make rational debate quite impossible. When feuds do do that, clearly mutual understanding cannot get a grip at all. But the human race is not incessantly caught in that kind of acute, mind-paralysing warfare, and to pretend that it is is to let propaganda for our local, wildly competitive, ethic distort the facts. The evidence, both from history and anthropology, shows us *Homo sapiens* as indeed often engaged in mild chronic feuding, with sporadic acute phases. But this does not normally insulate people mentally. They are in general still capable of gradually taking on board new customs and ideas, of becoming reconciled to particular sets of opponents, and generally of settling down to situations which they once thought they would die sooner than put up with. Of course, this shift of ideas is largely unconscious and inarticulate, a change of habits, of myths, of images, and of expectations rather than of beliefs. But in the end, articulate beliefs are needed as well, and once they are present, they too will have to be altered in order to play their part in the drama. There is then no escape from doing some philosophy – from trying to restate the basic connections of things. The alternative to doing it deliberately and attentively is to let it do itself at random and unwatched. The shifts of ideas will happen one way or another in any case, and, in a rapidly changing world, there will be more of them. How, then, had we better deal with them?

The most obvious and straightforward method is for philosophers to rush out into the world, sign up for a political party or group, and simply use their dialectical training to argue for it in public. If they do this, however, they will function purely as lawyers or public relations consultants, and they contribute nothing to our problem. Their special contribution as philosophers ought to be something rather different, namely to help rethink the terms of the debate. People who do this are often in trouble from both sides, as Hobbes was in the Civil War, and can very seldom afford to find themselves a secure political home by identifying with a party. Nor does it help if they evade the stresses of party warfare by retreating to generalities, using their training and prestige to repackage familiar, popular ideas so that they can be swallowed whole without any troublesome rethinking. This easy approach is, of course, the one that has done most to discredit popular philosophizing. Kant, a strong campaigner against it, put the point fiercely:

> It is not merely that such a procedure can never lay claim to the extremely rare merit of a true philosophical popularity, since we require no skill to make ourselves intelligible to the multitude once we renounce all profundity of thought. What it turns out is a disgusting hotch-potch of second-hand observations and semi-rational principles, on which the empty-headed regale themselves, because this is something that can be used in the chit-chat of everyday life.

248

Men of insight, on the other hand, feel confused by it, and avert their eyes with a dissatisfaction which, however, they are unable to cure. Yet philosophers, who can perfectly well see through this deception, get little hearing when they summon us for a time from this would-be popularity in order that they may win the right to be genuinely popular only after definite insight has been attained.[5]

Kant's words have not been wasted. This kind of thunderous denunciation is so sharply present to the minds of philosophers today that they largely overlook his clear instruction to bring philosophical ideas back to the market-place *in the end*. People forget Kant's own role in history as a hugely influential political theorist, a main architect of the notions of freedom that we live by today. They see him chiefly as one of a formidable team of policemen, patrolling the borders of proper specialization. It is not surprising, then, if these philosophers, when they are asked to talk about the real world, immediately wonder how they can possibly avoid becoming mere popularizers like *X* and *Y* and *Z*, and search desperately for ways of avoiding Kant's frown. Nor is it surprising if the first way which occurs to them, and one to which they cling like drowning sailors, is to make their discussion as difficult as possible.

It is, of course, usually quite easy to make it difficult. For a start, if they have actually been asked to help with it at all, it is probably quite difficult in the first place. If the general populace calls in philosophers, it commonly does so on the same principles as relatives who are unwilling to fetch doctors unless the patient is already actually dying. The unlucky philosophical practitioner then confronts an almost hopeless case, very often a frightful choice of evils, an almost insoluble dilemma where physical obstacles tangle with conflicts of standards – hard cases of possible euthanasia or abortion, or, on a larger scale, world hunger or the arms race. If the people who brought the philosopher in expect him or her to be a new kind of doctor with a special magic, able to wipe out the whole problem, they are going to be disappointed, and they had better be told so at once. As things are in our culture just now, they probably don't know quite what to expect, because there has been something of an interruption in the tradition of public philosophizing. This makes the job of asking them to be patient during discussions of things which don't at first seem to be directly concerned with the painful case before them even a little harder than it was for Kant.

LOOKING FOR A CENTRE

It will take some time for philosophers to earn this patience. But they will be helped here by the sheer difficulty of finding any other way to tackle these problems, and by the fact that there clearly isn't any other kind of specialist ready to deal with them – something deeply puzzling to people who expect to find some scientific speciality on tap to answer every question. But the philosophers will still have to work very hard. There is no substitute here for the careful practice of an extremely difficult informal art – the art of finding the centre of a problem. When we look back, this is surely what we see as the achievement of the people whose thought has been most helpful in the past – of people, to take the moral side of the matter only, like Socrates, Rousseau, Kant, or Nietzsche.

Philosophers who do take on the job of saying something useful about a particular dilemma will usually have to start by distinguishing a number of different questions that are tangled up together in it. And they will have to do this in a way that makes further progress possible, not dishonestly, so as to let these distinctions become a pretext for evasion – a use to which this honourable and necessary technique can of course too easily be put. When this has been done, some of the questions involved will usually turn out to be factual ones, but this does not mean that they cease to concern the philosopher. It will then be necessary to run over the evidence about these facts so as to say roughly what the trouble is, what the actual situation seems in general to be. (The idea that this empirical survey defiles the purity of philosophy is a confused one.) Out of this survey, the general shape of a central conceptual problem should gradually become clear. And here the philosopher will usually need to point out that the way in which the dilemma has so far been seen is much too narrow. There will commonly be a whole background way of thinking which is going wrong and needs attention.

For instance, questions such as euthanasia and abortion are often made unmanageable by being treated in arbitrary isolation, as if they were the only moral issues in sight. They cannot be effectively thought about apart from wider issues. To name just one, they lead us into questions about the emphasis on brute, unreasoning competition that arises from arguing always in terms of absolute, competing 'rights', rights whch are not brought into intelligible relations within any wider system. They also bring in question the general unrealistic attitude to the inevitability of death which has long prevailed in our society, and which is only now beginning to be made more realistic because the hospice movement has, for the first time, brought the opinions of terminal patients and their nurses into the controversy. But, besides this lack of a proper background, much-litigated questions like these are bedevilled by the disputants' refusal to admit that they are dealing with a genuine conflict, a real choice of evils. Out of the welter of previous argumentation, argumentative people have constantly picked in advance some set of concepts which favours their own attitude, and refused to extend it so as to make recognition of opposing arguments possible. This is one of many ways of refusing to see what the trouble is all about. We absolutely have to resist it by turning from the prefabricated dispute to the larger problem behind it.

TRAPS AND ENTANGLEMENTS

Many things, however, make it hard for philosophers today to take this wider view. Disputatiousness itself, as active inside the ivory tower as outside it, and indeed so habitual a part of academic life that it may seem strange to complain of it, generates many obstacles. One of these is the mere disinterested love of paradoxes, the tendency to keep them as pets for their own sake, and because they are a fertile source of arguments. Philosophers addicted to this may react to something like the euthanasia problem with delight, by simply adding half a dozen new twists to make it still more insoluble. They may indeed not see that anything else could possibly be called for; the idea of actually helping to find a solution to it may seem to them downright unprofessional. There is also the technique of taking

251

a small slice out of the side of the problem and providing it with an entirely negative solution. This habit flows from a convention which already does a lot of harm inside the ivory tower itself, namely the rule that, in prestige, the negative always wins. Scholars who reject something are always one up on scholars who accept it, and it pays to raise very small issues, because this makes it easier to avoid accidentally appearing to have accepted something after all.

Notice, for example, the well-known article called 'Euthanasia: some fallacies', in which Dr Hammer attacked the arguments used by Professor Tongs. Tongs had rashly cited an example involving mercy-killing in the course of a paper attacking somebody else about something quite different. In the approved style, Hammer began his attack with a disclaimer, stressing that neither he nor Tongs was saying anything about the wider issue of euthanasia itself; his intention was simply to find fault with Tongs's reasoning. This he did for thirty pages, without, so far as he could see, committing himself to saying anything at all about the actual problem. Here, however, he proved mistaken, as Mr Shovel pointed out in an article of equal length called 'Euthanasia: a reply to Hammer'. Shovel showed that some of Hammer's own arguments were invalid, unless they had the support of certain substantial views about euthanasia, for which of course he had produced no argument. (It is worth just noting that nobody, from the Angel Gabriel downwards, has ever produced an article about which this kind of criticism could not be made.) However, in the general shortage of helpful material about life and death, these articles are regularly placed on the reading-lists of first-year students. They also get, for stimulus on this subject, Professor Poker's famous article 'Is murder wrong?' The populace, says Poker, seems to think that it is, but it is not altogether easy to find out what are their grounds for doing so. Are people perhaps afraid of getting murdered themselves? Are they, in their muddled way, attempting to increase the general happiness? Are they perhaps moved by some confused notion about rationality? Poker has no trouble in setting up these various straw men in indefensible forms. His language is neatly adapted to stun his simple-minded readers into feeling that they must somehow either manage to accept one – and only one – of these bad arguments, or withdraw their objections to murder. They become very confused. But the one thing that emerges clearly for their immediate purpose is that, during the rest of their university course, it will be much safer to agree with Poker, and to learn to adopt his methods, than to expose themselves by asking what he means or by trying to defend their principles against him.

Am I being unfair to Poker? Is he perhaps a valuable Socratic gadfly? He might be. This is an open question. We can look at what is going on and see how well he has suited his particular kind of sting to the horse before him, and how the total symbiosis is working out. But we are not forced to assume that all stinging is valuable, merely because Socrates had a sting. That sting had Socrates, and Poker's hasn't. And Socrates did not set examinations.

In these brief suggestions I have been trying to locate some of the central difficulties that arise when, starting from a contemporary academic position, we try to apply philosophical thought again to those problems in the world where it is most needed. I have suggested that what chiefly wastes our efforts here is not lack of intelligence or even of application, but the distorting effect of bad intellectual habits which have a strong emotional basis. I have concentrated on just one of these, the addiction to dispute. Though this has of course some admirable uses, it can serve too easily as a defence mechanism, an alternative to direct work on the central problems rather than a tool for it. Perhaps indeed it serves as displacement behaviour, irrelevant but intense activity relieving the strain of unresolved conflicts. Other psychological dangers of related kinds will certainly arise, which is one reason why I have been insisting throughout that the motives for philosophizing are not irrelevant to its substance, but are something that should have active and constant attention. What we cannot do, however, is to erect a negative defence against all these dangers – to prevent all sophisticated thinkers from attending to all important questions. This has been thoroughly tried in this century, and it does not emerge as a sane option. If thinking is our professional concern, then wisdom and wonder are our business; information-storage, though often useful, is just an incidental convenience. So we will do better to pursue wisdom and wonder, however haltingly and weakly, than to rival Wells's moon-monsters with the contents of our computer-assisted memory-banks. That, too, is how the story of *The Crock of Gold* ended:

> And they took the Philosopher from his prison, even the Intellect of Man they took from the hands of the doctors and lawyers, from the sly priests, from the professors whose mouths are gorged with sawdust, and the merchants who sell blades of grass, the awful people of the Fomor ... and then they returned again, dancing and singing, to the country of the gods.

SUGGESTIONS FOR
FURTHER READING

Non-philosophers may find it useful if, besides the rather wide
spread of books already mentioned in the notes, I first name
here a few representative, recent, non-ivory-tower-based philosophical discussions of current problems, and then give some
hints on books which put the useful features of linguistic
philosophy in accessible form, and especially on the difficult but
rewarding art of reading Wittgenstein.

First, then, Sissela Bok has written two books, both about
forms of oppression practised on the relatively helpless in our
complex society through the manipulation of information by
those in positions of authority. In striking contrast to abortion
and euthanasia, this range of problems had before had virtually
no philosophic attention, and often was not recognized as
serious at all by those responsible. The books are *Lying, Moral
Choice in Public and Private Life* (New York, Pantheon Books,
1978) and *Secrets: Concealment and Revelation* (Oxford, Oxford
University Press, 1986).

Tom Nagel's book *Mortal Questions* (Cambridge, Cambridge
University Press, 1979) deals admirably in many short papers
with conceptual difficulties that arise about a wide range of
serious real-life questions – not just with their moral aspects, but
with all kinds of tangles in our thinking about them.

Peter Singer's *Animal Liberation* (London, Jonathan Cape, 1975)
and Stephen Clark's *The Moral Status of Animals* (Oxford, Clarendon Press, 1977) and *The Nature of the Beast* (Oxford, Oxford
University Press, 1982) have brought clearly forward many
urgent problems about our society's treatment of non-human
animals, another topic which had before been almost wholly
neglected by academics.

John Passmore, in *Man's Responsibility for Nature* (London, Duckworth, 1974), has tackled the still wider and more pressing problem of our moral relation to the whole non-human world, a context of thought which had been obscured by over-confident humanistic ideas for several centuries, but which now even the most euphoric of us can see is going to need attention.

Anthony Kenny, in *The Ivory Tower, Essays in Philosophy and Public Policy* (Oxford, Basil Blackwell, 1985), has discussed in clear, shrewd, short papers some knotty issues concerning war and peace, the nature of responsibility, and the general relation of thought to action in the world.

As regards linguistic philosophy itself, despite the general fashion which confined its practitioners to short articles for their peers, several really useful non-technical books did emerge.

Gilbert Ryle's *Concept of Mind* (London, Hutchinson, 1949) effectively outlined a post-Cartesian notion of a whole person who was not just a loosely joined mind and body. This job was well done in spite of an occasional confusing and unnecessary bias towards behaviourism.

J. L. Austin's *How to Do Things With Words* (Oxford, Oxford University Press, 1962) spelled out clearly the notion of language as a set of versatile tools rather than a set of tokens or tickets corresponding to the set of objects in the world, and his *Sense and Sensibilia* (Oxford, Oxford University Press, 1962) elegantly exploded the notion of sense-data as a set of substitute objects to which the ordinary world must be reduced.

John Wisdom in *Philosophy and Psycho-Analysis* (Oxford, Basil Blackwell, 1953) dealt with many deep and central questions in a particularly human, vigorous, and imaginative style. His *Other Minds* (Oxford, Basil Blackwell, 1952) concentrated this fire effectively on the solipsistic notion of the secluded self, but is rather harder to read. John Wisdom, like Wittgenstein, often alternates beautiful clarity with intense obscurity. In starting to read both of them, the best remedy at first is intelligent skipping.

The ideas in these books are in general accord with those of Wittgenstein, and can be used in some degree as an introduction to him. For reading his own works, the first thing needed is to grasp what questions he was trying to answer. That issue, which has been hastily sketched in this book, is thoroughly dealt with in *Insight and Illusion* by P. M. S. Hacker (Oxford, Clarendon Press, 1972). Hacker gives useful references for tracing it further, but enquirers should be warned that competitive Wittgenstein-interpreting is now a huge industry, into which they may not want to get drawn. Stanley Cavell, in *Must We Mean What We Say?* (Cambridge, Cambridge University Press, 1976) and *The Claim of Reason: Wittgenstein, Skepticism, Morality and Tragedy* (Oxford, Oxford University Press, 1979), seems often to indicate the best way out of this labyrinth. Other useful books are *Wittgenstein* (Harmondsworth, Penguin, 1973) and *The Legacy of Wittgenstein* (Oxford, Basil Blackwell, 1984), both by Anthony Kenny, *Wittgenstein* by David Pears (Collins, Fontana Modern Masters, 1971), and *Wittgenstein* by Sir A. J. Ayer (London, Weidenfeld & Nicolson, 1985) – less sympathetic but, as usual, very clear.

But there is no substitute for reading the man himself. People who cannot stand books made up of separate short paragraphs can find clear, forcible, continuous prose in his 'Lecture on Ethics' (*Philosophical Review* 74, 1965), which expounds his early, sceptical view of a sharp division between the speakable and the unspeakable. *The Blue and Brown Books* (Oxford, Basil Blackwell, 1964) are also written in continuous prose; they contain ideas already outlining his later thinking. But the core of the later thought is in the *Philosophical Investigations*, which is the only book that he did largely prepare for publication before he died. (Perfectionism prevented him from publishing anything but the *Tractatus* in his lifetime.) Much of it is clear enough. Apart from the sheer originality of the ideas, the main difficulty is that one section often follows another without a clear dividing mark. That the sections are meant to be distinct, and to build up a composite picture rather than a systematic argument, is explained in the preface.

On Certainty was also a notebook written out more or less as a whole, as was the *Philosophical Remarks*. Apart from these, the various other volumes that now bear his name consist simply of detached observations culled from his notebooks by editors and grouped according to their ideas, not his.

NOTES

1 MOON-MONSTERS AND FREE PEOPLE

1 For the quite special absurdity of this mindless accumulation in non-scientific subjects, see Stefan Collini's article 'Research in the humanities', *Times Literary Supplement* 3 April 1987.
2 A point strongly stressed by Sir George Porter in a protest against the policy in his Anniversary Presidential Address to the Royal Society, supplement to *Royal Society News* 4 (6) (1987).
3 A. Einstein, *Ideas and Opinions* (London, Souvenir Press, 1954), p. 80.
4 John D. Barrow and Frank J. Tipler, *The Anthropic Cosmological Principle* (Oxford, Oxford University Press, 1986), p. 706.
5 Charles Dickens, *Our Mutual Friend*, book II, ch. 2.
6 H. G. Wells, *The First Men in the Moon*, ch. 24.

2 WISDOM AND CONTEMPLATION

1 Aristotle, *Nicomachean Ethics*, book 10, 1177ab.
2 Aristotle, *Metaphysics*, book 13, 1072b.
3 Plato, *Republic*, book 6, 508.
4 Plato, *Symposium*, 212b.
5 Edward O. Wilson, *Biophilia* (Cambridge, Mass., Harvard University Press, 1984), p. 58.
6 Nicholas Maxwell, *From Knowledge to Wisdom: a Revolution in the Aims and Methods of Science* (Oxford, Basil Blackwell, 1984), p. 2.

3 THE CITY OF ORGANIZED THOUGHT AND ITS TOWN-PLANNERS

1 C. H. Waddington, *The Scientific Attitude* (West Drayton, Middx., Penguin Books, 1941), pp. 53, 61.
2 ibid., p. 170.
3 ibid., p. 63.
4 ibid., p. 125.

5 L. Wittgenstein, *Philosophical Investigations*, trans. G. E. M. Anscombe (Oxford, Basil Blackwell, 1958), para. 18.
6 ibid., para. 123; see also the first two paragraphs of the preface.
7 Steven Weinberg, *The First Three Minutes* (London, André Deutsch, 1977), p. 155.
8 Jacques Monod, *Chance and Necessity*, trans. Austryn Wainhouse (Glasgow, Collins/Fount Paperbacks, 1977).

4 SCEPTICISM AND PERSONAL IDENTITY

1 R. G. Collingwood, *Autobiography* (Oxford, Oxford University Press, 1939), p. 48.
2 Jacques Monod, *Chance and Necessity*, trans. Austryn Wainhouse (Glasgow, Collins/Fount Paperbacks, 1977), pp. 159–66.
3 I have discussed the reality and unreality of various questions raised about moral clashes between different cultures in 'On trying out one's new sword' in my book *Heart and Mind: the Varieties of Moral Experience* (Brighton, Harvester Press/Methuen Paperback, 1981).
4 Maurice Wilkins, 'The nobility of the scientific enterprise', *Interdisciplinary Science Reviews* 10 (1) (1985).
5 Sir George Porter, Anniversary Presidential Address to the Royal Society, supplement to *Royal Society News* 4 (6) (1987).
6 St Matthew's Gospel, 13.46.
7 St Mark's Gospel, 8.36.
8 Plato, *Republic*, book 2, 357a–67b, and book 9, 579–end.

5 PERSONAL AND IMPERSONAL

1 James Stephens, *The Crock of Gold* (London, Pan Books, 1953), p. 31.

6 AUTONOMY AND ISOLATIONISM

1 F. M. Cornford, *Microcosmographia Academica, Advice to a Young Academic Politician* (Cambridge, Bowes & Bowes, 1949), p. 11.
2 See an extremely helpful discussion of the nature of professions by Renford Bambrough, 'Power, authority and wisdom', *Southwest Philosophy Review* 4 (1) (1988).

7 RIGOUR AND THE NATURAL HISTORY OF CONTROVERSY

1 John Milton, *Areopagitica and Other Prose Works* (London, Dent & Dutton/Everyman, 1927), p. 30.
2 See chapter 3, pp. 26–7.
3 Aristotle, *Nicomachean Ethics*, book 1, ch. 3.

8 THE SECLUSION OF SCIENCE

1 Sir Ernest Chain, 'Social responsibility and the scientist', *New Scientist*, 22 October 1970, p. 166.
2 A. Einstein, 'The laws of science and the laws of ethics', in H. Feigl and M. Brodbeck (eds), *Readings in the Philosophy of Science* (New York, Appleton Century Crofts, 1953), p. 779.
  I owe these two passages to Nicholas Maxwell, who cites them together on p. 131 of *From Knowledge to Wisdom: a Revolution in the Aims and Methods of Science* (Oxford, Basil Blackwell, 1984), but without commenting on their hidden differences.
3 Chain, op. cit., p. 169.
4 ibid., p. 167.
5 For this remarkable story, see Otto Nathan and Heinz Norden (eds), *Einstein on Peace* (New York, Schocken Books, 1968), p. 3 and (for Planck) p. 11; sources given on p. 638. The manifesto, of which many people were later clearly ashamed, raised a stir at the time but seems to have had little attention from historians. The biologist Georg Friedrich Nicolai, who organized the protest, tells the story in his book *The Biology of War* trans. C. A. and J. Grande (New York, Century Co., 1918).
6 Quoted by Jacques Monod, *Chance and Necessity*, trans. Austryn Wainhouse (Glasgow, Collins/Fount Paperbacks, 1977), p. 45, from Friedrich Engels, *Herr Eugen Dühring's Revolution in Science (Anti-Dühring)* (London, Lawrence, 1935), pp. 154–5.

9 CAN PHILOSOPHY BE NEUTRAL?

1 C. S. Lewis, *The Screwtape Letters* (London, Geoffrey Bles, 1942).
2 On the difficulties that infest this notion of philosophy as an esoteric skill, see Renford Bambrough, 'Power, authority and wisdom', *Southwest Philosophy Review* 4 (1) (1988), and also his 'Question time' in S. G. Shanker (ed.), *Philosophy Today* (London, Croom Helm, 1986), p. 58. On the range of work available for philosophy, see John Wilson, *What Philosophy Can Do* (London, Macmillan, 1986).
3 Ludwig Wittgenstein, *Philosophical Investigations*, trans. G. E. M. Anscombe (Oxford, Basil Blackwell, 1958), para. 123.
4 The point is well discussed by Brian Klug, 'On doing, teaching and studying philosophy', *Studies in Higher Education* 4 (2) (1979).
5 Plato, *Apology of Socrates*, 30a.
6 ibid., 39d.
7 Ved Mehta, *The Fly and the Fly-Bottle: Encounters with English Intellectuals* (London, Weidenfeld & Nicolson, 1961), p. 47.
8 Wittgenstein, op. cit., para. 38.
9 The word 'game', freely used in this sort of context, has itself

given a good deal of trouble, which I have discussed in 'The game game', *Philosophy* 49 (1974), reprinted in my book *Heart and Mind: The Varieties of Moral Experience* (Brighton, Harvester Press/Methuen Paperback, 1981).

10 C. S. Lewis, 'Fern-seed and elephants', in his *Christian Reflections* (Glasgow, Collins/Fount Paperbacks, 1981), p. 203.

10 THE WORK OF PURIFICATION

1 René Descartes, *Discourse on Method*, part 2, trans. John Veitch (London, Dent & Dutton/Everyman, 1937), p. 12.

2 ibid., part 4, p. 26.

3 Bertrand Russell, *History of Western Philosophy* (London, Allen & Unwin, 1946).

4 The quotations that follow are all from this passage (ibid., pp. 788–9) except where otherwise stated.

5 W. V. O. Quine, 'Philosophical progress in language theory', *Metaphilosophy* 1 (1) (1970).

11 THE PROBLEM OF THE UNKNOWN

1 Gilbert Ryle, *The Concept of Mind* (London, Hutchinson, 1949), p. 26.

2 Bertrand Russell, *History of Western Philosophy* (London, Allen & Unwin, 1946), pp. 14–15.

3 ibid., p. 515. The passage is cited by John Wisdom in an acute review of the book in his *Philosophy and Psycho-analysis* (Oxford, Basil Blackwell, 1953), p. 196.

4 See Immanuel Kant, *Critique of Pure Reason*, preface to 2nd edn, margin reference BXXV, trans. Kemp Smith (London, Macmillan, 1933), p. 26, and the last two sections of 'On the extreme limit of all practical philosophy', *Foundations of the Metaphysic of Morals*, trans. L. W. Beck (New York, Bobbs-Merrill, 1969), p. 74.

5 Gilbert Ryle, op. cit. See especially his discussion of 'Knowing how and knowing that' in ch. 2.

6 Ludwig Wittgenstein, *Philosophical Investigations*, trans. G. E. M. Anscombe (Oxford, Basil Blackwell, 1958), para. 123.

7 ibid., preface and para. 123.

8 Renford Bambrough, 'Question time', in S. G. Shanker (ed.), *Philosophy in Britain Today* (London, Croom Helm, 1986), p. 59.

9 Ronald Clark, *Life of Bertrand Russell* (London, Cape, 1975), p. 347.

10 ibid., pp. 350–1.

11 Nietzsche states the point vehemently in *On the Genealogy of Morals*, sects 5–7, and in *Beyond Good and Evil*, sect. 229.

12 For instance, Stuart Hampshire in *Thought and Action* (London,

Chatto & Windus, 1965), pp. 119, 216–22, and 245–50, and
G. E. Moore in his paper on 'The nature of moral philosophy',
in his *Philosophical Papers* (London, Allen & Unwin, 1959),
p. 316. I have discussed this extremely odd doctrine in 'The
objection to systematic humbug', *Philosophy* 53 (1978), reprinted
in my book *Heart and Mind: the Varieties of Moral Experience*
(Brighton, Harvester Press/Methuen Paperback, 1981).
13 Ernest Gellner, *Words and Things* (London, Gollancz, 1959).
For a reply to this attack, see Michael Dummett's powerful
paper 'Oxford philosophy' in his book *Truth and Other Enigmas*
(London, Duckworth, 1978), p. 431. Accusations similar to
Gellner's, but from within the castle, can be found in Eugene
Freeman (ed.), *The Abdication of Philosophy* (La Salle, Ill., Open
Court Publishing Co., 1976).

12 THE QUESTION OF CERTAINTY AND THE REAL PHILOSOPHICAL REVOLUTION

1 Ronald Clark, *Life of Bertrand Russell* (London, Cape, 1975),
p. 167.
2 Bertrand Russell, *Autobiography* (London, Allen & Unwin,
1967), vol. 1, p. 134.
3 Ronald Clark, op. cit., p. 238. Ottoline herself, who probably
knew him as well as anybody did, says the same thing strongly
in her diary, ibid., p. 188.
4 ibid., p. 176.
5 Katharine Tait, personal communication. Her book *My Father
Bertrand Russell* (London, Gollancz, 1976) gives very good
insights into the background of the movement, especially into the
deep general confidence in sweeping theories – especially
behaviourist psychological theories – which reigned in Russell's
circle, and its effect on those around him.
6 The very possibility that some knowledge might be valueless is
hard to fit into our current way of thinking today. I have
discussed it in a paper called 'Why knowledge matters', in David
Sperlinger (ed.), *Animals in Research: New Perspectives in Animal
Experimentation* (Chichester, John Wiley, 1981). Jane Heal has
similarly stressed the need to remember that some knowledge
is trivial in 'The disinterested search for truth', *Proceedings of the
Aristotelian Society* 88 (New Series) (1987–8).
7 The *Discourse on Method* tells this story.
8 See chapter 22.
9 Wittgenstein discusses this possibility very interestingly in his
'Lecture on Ethics', *Philosophical Review* 74 (1965), 8–11.
10 In his utopia: J. D. Bernal, *The World, the Flesh and the Devil*
(Bloomington, Indiana University Press, 1969, original 1929),
pp. 46–9, 63, 80–1.

NOTES

11 Freeman Dyson, 'Time without end: physics and biology in an expanding universe', *Review of Modern Physics* 51 (3), 453.
12 I have discussed some of these quasi-religious, scientifically clothed dreams of future glory in my book, *Evolution as a Religion* (London, Methuen, 1986).
13 St Augustine, *Confessions*, opening passage.

13 WHAT FOUNDATIONS ARE

1 René Descartes, *Discourse on Method*, beginning of part 3, trans. John Veitch (London, Dent & Dutton/Everyman, 1937), p. 19.
2 ibid., opening of Meditation 2, p. 85.
3 Bertrand Russell, *Autobiography* (London, Allen & Unwin, 1967), vol. 1, p. 67.
4 All this is a central theme of Wittgenstein's book *On Certainty* (Oxford, Basil Blackwell, 1974), and is also shrewdly discussed by John Wisdom in 'Philosophical perplexity' in his *Philosophy and Psycho-analysis* (Oxford, Basil Blackwell, 1953), p. 36.
5 Again, a point strongly argued in *On Certainty*, op. cit.
6 See Katharine Tait, *My Father Bertrand Russell* (London, Gollancz, 1976), pp. 58–66, especially Dora Russell's comment on parents not properly trained in these theories – 'Those people who are not prepared to equip themselves in the necessary way must either abandon parenthood or have recourse to the expert' (p. 59).
7 A matter dealt with by Wittgenstein in the opening sections of *Philosophical Investigations*, trans. G. E. M. Anscombe (Oxford, Basil Blackwell, 1958), especially paras 23 and 27.
8 ibid., para. 23. See also J. L. Austin, *How To Do Things With Words* (Oxford, Clarendon Press, 1962), a very helpful book, though one with an inconvenient habit of straying on to the sports or hobbies shelves of public libraries.
9 *Philosophical Investigations*, op. cit., para. 43.

14 MOORE AND THE WITHDRAWAL OF MORAL PHILOSOPHY

1 G. E. Moore, *Principia Ethica* (Cambridge, Cambridge University Press, 1903), preface, p. ix.
2 ibid., pp. 14–15.
3 Bernard Williams, *Ethics and the Limits of Philosophy* (London, Fontana Masterguides, 1985), p. 16.
4 Both these couplets are apparently isolated epigrams, and I have followed *The Oxford Dictionary of Quotations* in attributing the second to J. C. Squire.
5 See an admirable discussion by Sheridan Gilley and Ann

Loades, 'Thomas Henry Huxley: the war between science and religion', *Journal of Religion* 61 (3) (1981).

6 The most impressive, as well as the most interesting, testimonial is surely that of Maynard Keynes – 'My early beliefs' in his *Two Memoirs* (London, Rupert Hart-Davies, 1949). Leonard Woolf gives another very impressive one in *Sowing* (London, Hogarth Press, 1961), pp. 131–49 and 154–7, rejecting Keynes's criticisms but displaying Moore's character with so much loving penetration that a balanced judgment emerges. Strong testimonials from Clive Bell, Lytton Strachey, Bertrand Russell, and many other much less expected people are quoted by Paul Levy in the opening pages of his book *Moore: G. E. Moore and the Cambridge Apostles* (New York, Holt, Rinehart, & Winston, 1979). Levy also cites a letter of Beatrice Webb's as follows:

> *Principia Ethica* – a book they all talk of as 'The Truth'! I never can see anything in it, except a metaphysical justification for doing what you like and what other people disapprove of! So far as I can understand the philosophy it is a denial of the scientific method and of religion – as a rule that is the net result on the minds of young men – it seems to disintegrate their intellects and characters.

(Quoted from Norman Mackenzie (ed.), *The Letters of Sidney and Beatrice Webb*, vol. 2 (Cambridge and London, 1978).)

7 Moore, op. cit., pp. 188–9.
8 In 'G. E. Moore on the Ideal' in my *Heart and Mind: the Varieties of Moral Experience* (Brighton, Harvester Press/Methuen Paperback, 1981). See also some very good discussions of it in Iris Murdoch, *The Sovereignty of Good* (London, Routledge & Kegan Paul, 1970).
9 See Clive Bell's panegyric on *Principia Ethica* in his book *Art* (New York, Capricorn Books, 1958), p. 80, and the similar attitudes expressed in Roger Fry's *Vision and Design* (London, Chatto & Windus, 1920). Fry, who was older than Moore, is likely to have been a source rather than a disciple.

15 FACTS AND VALUES

1 Bernard Williams, *Ethics and the Limits of Philosophy* (London, Fontana Masterguides, 1985), p. 121. The logical weaknesses of the whole 'naturalistic fallacy' approach and the best ways to avoid them are discussed with beautiful clarity in Julius Kovesi's shrewd little book, *Moral Notions* (London, Routledge & Kegan Paul, 1967).
2 See G. E. M. Anscombe, 'Brute facts', *Analysis* 19 (1958).
3 Geoffrey Warnock, *Contemporary Moral Philosophy* (London, Macmillan Papermac, 1967), p. 60.

4 James Boswell, *Life of Johnson* (London, Dent & Dutton, 1906, Everyman Edition), vol. 2, p. 148.
5 Bertrand Russell, *Autobiography* (London, Allen & Unwin, 1967), vol. 1, p. 147.
6 On facts and values in general, see my *Beast and Man* (Hassocks, Harvester Press, 1979), ch. 9, and 'On the absence of a gap between facts and values', *Proceedings of the Aristotelian Society* 54 (suppl.) (1980).
7 Leonard Woolf, *Sowing* (London, Hogarth Press, 1961), pp. 135–6.
8 Maynard Keynes, *Two Memoirs* (London, Rupert Hart-Davies, 1949), p. 85.
9 C. L. Stevenson, *Ethics and Language* (New Haven, Yale University Press, 1944).

16 THE FLIGHT FROM BLAME

1 J. S. Mill, *Utilitarianism* (London, Dent & Dutton, 1910, Everyman Edition), ch. 5, p. 45.
2 G. E. Moore, *Principia Ethica* (Cambridge, Cambridge University Press, 1903), pp. 214–16, 221.
3 ibid., p. 147.
4 ibid., p. 155.
5 ibid., pp. 174–6, 182.
6 Paul Levy, *Moore: G. E. Moore and the Cambridge Apostles* (New York, Holt, Rinehart, & Winston, 1979), p. 218.
7 See especially their intervention at the beginning of Plato's *Republic*, book 2, sections 357–67.
8 See the preface to Butler's *Sermons*, sections 24–9, and the whole of sermon 3.
9 From 'My early beliefs' in Maynard Keynes, *Two Memoirs* (London, Rupert Hart-Davies, 1949), pp. 93–4, 99–100.
10 The peculiarly ill-judged attacks on Mill are in G. E. Moore, *Principia Ethica*, ch. 3, pp. 64–72, 77, and 102. They are interspersed with some shrewd and admirable general criticisms of hedonism. Because Moore had a real sympathy with hedonism, these criticisms, along with the last chapter, are to my mind the best parts of the book.
11 It is a prime theme of Skinner's manifesto, *Beyond Freedom and Dignity* (London, Cape, 1972).
12 See Bernard Williams, *Ethics and the Limits of Philosophy* (London, Fontana Masterguides, 1985), pp. 177, 194. I have discussed Williams's views on the relation between the idea of blame and that of morality in my original article 'The flight from blame', *Philosophy* 62 (241) (1987), section 9, but have omitted this section in the present version.
13 Report in the *Guardian*, some time in early November 1985.
14 This indeed is what he does discuss in his admirable

investigation of excuses. See Aristotle, *Nicomachean Ethics*, book 3, chs 1–5.

15 Jonathan Bennett, 'The conscience of Huckleberry Finn', *Philosophy* 49 (188) (1974).

16 I have discussed these sardonic uses of the word, and their relation to its other uses, in 'Is "moral" a dirty word?' in my book *Heart and Mind: the Varieties of Moral Experience* (Brighton, Harvester Press/Methuen Paperback, 1981).

17 St Matthew's Gospel, 7.1.

18 Dorothy Emmet, *The Moral Prism* (London, Macmillan, 1979).

17 THE CLASH OF SYSTEMS

1 René Descartes, *Discourse on Method* (London, Dent & Dutton, 1916, Everyman Edition), opening section of part 2, p. 10.

2 F. W. Nietzsche, *Thus Spake Zarathustra*, trans. A. Tille and M. M. Bozman (London, Dent & Dutton/Everyman, 1933), part 2, 'Of the land of culture', p. 109.

3 F. W. Nietzsche, *Twilight of the Idols, or How to Philosophize with a Hammer*, trans. J. Hollingdale (Harmondsworth, Penguin, 1968), 'Maxims and arrows' no. 26, p. 25.

4 Aphorism 31 of F. W. Nietzsche, *Assorted Opinions and Maxims* (1879), cited by J. Hollingdale in Appendix A to *Twilight of the Idols*, op. cit., p. 188.

18 EMPIRICISM AND THE UNSPEAKABLE

1 Ludwig Wittgenstein, *Philosophical Investigations*, trans. G. E. M. Anscombe (Oxford, Basil Blackwell, 1958), para. 122. John Wisdom has developed this point very helpfully in 'Philosophical perplexity' and 'Metaphysics and verification', both in his *Philosophy and Psycho-analysis* (Oxford, Basil Blackwell, 1953).

2 Ludwig Wittgenstein, *Tractatus Logico-philosophicus*, trans. D. F. Pears and B. F. McGuinness (London, Routledge & Kegan Paul, 1971), 6.522 and 6.54.

3 Thus, in sending the newly completed *Tractatus* to a friend, he wrote, 'My work consists of two parts – of the one which is here (the *Tractatus*) and of everything which I have *not* written, and precisely the second part is the important one.' (Letter to Ludwig von Ficker, 1919, quoted in the editor's appendix to Paul Engelmann, *Letters from Ludwig Wittgenstein, with a Memoir*, ed. B. F. McGuinness, trans. L. Furtmüller (Oxford, Basil Blackwell, 1967), pp. 143–4.)

4 Therapeutics is at its most attractive in the work of John Wisdom, who uses it in several papers in *Philosophy and Psycho-*

analysis, op. cit., and often manages to avoid the patronizing tone
that makes it damnable.

5 Quoted in chapter 14, p. 146.
6 See G. H. von Wright's biographical sketch in Norman
  Malcolm's *Ludwig Wittgenstein: a Memoir* (London, Oxford
  University Press, 1958), p. 21, and M. O'C. Drury, 'Some notes
  on conversations with Wittgenstein', in Rush Rhees (ed.),
  Ludwig Wittgenstein: Personal Recollections (Oxford, Basil Blackwell,
  1981), p. 104.
7 See A. Janik and S. Toulmin, *Wittgenstein's Vienna* (London,
  Weidenfeld & Nicolson, 1973), especially the introduction.
8 *Ludwig Wittgenstein: a Memoir*, op. cit., preface, p. ix.
9 See *Wittgenstein's Vienna*, chs 1 and 9.
10 *Ludwig Wittgenstein: Personal Recollections*, op. cit., p. 72.
11 Ludwig Wittgenstein, 'Lecture on Ethics', *Philosophical Review*
   74 (1965). Note especially Wittgenstein's flat refusal even to
   consider the question raised by Rush Rhees, about the possibility
   of justifying Brutus's stabbing of Caesar – a question which
   quite plainly does admit of useful and intelligible discussion – on
   p. 22.
12 *Philosophical Investigations*, op. cit., paras 11 and 12.
13 See for instance Ludwig Wittgenstein, *On Certainty*, trans.
   D. Paul and E. Anscombe (Oxford, Basil Blackwell, 1974),
   paras 65 and 256.
14 *Ludwig Wittgenstein: a Memoir*, op. cit., p. 63.

19 WHAT EMPIRICISM IS

1 Thomas Hobbes, *Leviathan* (London, Dent &
  Dutton/Everyman, 1931), part 1, chs 1, 5, and 8, pp. 4, 20,
  and 40.
2 Bishop Berkeley, *Principles of Human Knowledge*, end of preface.
3 John Locke, *Essay Concerning Human Understanding*, Epistle to
  the Reader, concluding section.
4 David Hume, *Treatise of Human Nature*, book 3, part 1, section
  1. I have discussed the huge difficulties that this approach
  raises for biology in my book *Beast and Man* (London, Methuen
  Paperback, 1982), pp. 275–6.
5 See the essays collected in R. F. Holland's attractive book
  Against Empiricism (Oxford, Basil Blackwell, 1980) for some
  good criticisms of various effects of this belief.
6 Moore attacked this view effectively in his paper 'The
  conception of reality' in his *Philosophical Studies* (London,
  Routledge & Kegan Paul, 1922), p. 197, and, what is more
  impressive, he seems already to have been able to dispute it in
  conversation when, as a second-year undergraduate not even
  reading philosophy, he first met McTaggart: see his
  autobiography in P. A. Schilpp (ed.), *The Philosophy of G. E. Moore*

(Evanston and Chicago, Northwestern University Press, 1942).
This is a typical example of the kind of independence of mind
that made him so effective.

20 STYLE AND SUBSTANCE

1 See Allan Janik and Stephen Toulmin, *Wittgenstein's Vienna*
(London, Weidenfeld & Nicolson, 1973), introduction and
chapter 5.
2 Paul Levy, *Moore: G. E. Moore and the Cambridge Apostles* (New
York, Holt, Rinehart, & Winston, 1979), pp. 198–9.
3 See P. M. S. Hacker, *Insight and Illusion* (Oxford, Clarendon
Press, 1972), pp. 58–9, 64ff., 70ff.; also P. Gardiner,
Schopenhauer (Harmondsworth, Penguin, 1963), pp. 275–82, and
Wittgenstein's Vienna, op. cit., chapter 5, 'Language, ethics and
representation'.
4 Norman Malcolm, *Ludwig Wittgenstein: a Memoir* (London,
Oxford University Press, 1958), p. 36.
5 Tom Wolfe, 'From Bauhaus to our house', *Harpers*, June and
July 1981.
6 Paul Engelmann's *Letters from Ludwig Wittgenstein, with a
Memoir*, ed. B. F. McGuinness, trans. L. Furtmüller (Oxford,
Basil Blackwell, 1967) casts a valuable light on this background.
7 Some editions of *Wittgenstein's Vienna*, op. cit., give a
photograph of it opposite p. 97; others apparently do not. For
the story of its building, see the memoir by his other sister
Hermine Wittgenstein, 'My brother Ludwig', in Rush Rhees
(ed.), *Ludwig Wittgenstein: Personal Recollections* (Oxford, Basil
Blackwell, 1981), pp. 6–9.
8 Bertrand Russell, *Autobiography* (London, Allen & Unwin,
1967), vol. 2, p. 116.
9 Ludwig Wittgenstein, *Philosophical Investigations*, trans. G. E. M.
Anscombe (Oxford, Basil Blackwell, 1963), para. 107.

21 LANGUAGE FOR SOLITARIES

1 Bishop Berkeley, *Principles of Human Knowledge*, para. 20.
2 ibid., paras 58 and 110–17.
3 P. M. S. Hacker, *Insight and Illusion: Wittgenstein on Philosophy
and the Metaphysics of Experience* (Oxford, Clarendon Press,
1972), p. 5.
4 Ludwig Wittgenstein, *Tractatus Logico-philosophicus*, trans.
D. F. Pears and B. F. McGuinness (London, Routledge &
Kegan Paul, 1971), 4.002.
5 For the various possible meanings of this term, see
C. H. Langford, 'Moore's notion of analysis', in P. A. Schilpp
(ed.), *The Philosophy of G. E. Moore* (Evanston and Chicago,

Northwestern University Press, 1942), p. 319, with Moore's reply, p. 660. See also helpful articles by John Wisdom, 'Is analysis a useful method in philosophy?' in his *Philosophy and Psycho-analysis* (Oxford, Basil Blackwell, 1953), and Stefan Körner, 'On some methods and results of philosophical analysis', in S. G. Shanker (ed.), *Philosophy in Britain Today* (London, Croom Helm, 1986).
6 *Tractatus*, op. cit., 5.5563.
7 Bishop Berkeley, *Principles of Human Knowledge*, introduction, para. 25.
8 ibid., para. 75.
9 Ludwig Wittgenstein, 'Lecture on Ethics', *Philosophical Review* 74 (1965), 3.
10 Ludwig Wittgenstein, *Philosophical Investigations*, trans. G. E. M. Anscombe (Oxford, Basil Blackwell, 1963), para. 43.
11 J. L. Austin did a splendid demolition job on sense-data in *Sense and Sensibilia* (Oxford, Clarendon Press, 1962) from which they have never recovered.
12 Gilbert Ryle, *The Concept of Mind* (London, Hutchinson's University Library, 1949).

22 ESCAPING FROM SOLITUDE

1 G. E. Moore, 'The defence of common sense', in his *Philosophical Papers* (London, Allen & Unwin, 1959), p. 32.
2 ibid., pp. 40–1.
3 ibid., pp. 42–3.
4 That the idea of such a private language is incoherent is a central point of Wittgenstein's. *Philosophical Investigations*, trans. G. E. M. Anscombe (Oxford, Basil Blackwell, 1963).
5 John Locke, *Essay Concerning Human Understanding*, book 1, chapter 1, section 5.
6 Ludwig Wittgenstein, *On Certainty*, trans. D. Paul and E. Anscombe (Oxford, Basil Blackwell, 1974), para. 230.
7 ibid., para. 12.
8 ibid., paras 95–9.
9 Ludwig Wittgenstein, 'Lecture on Ethics', *Philosophical Review* 74 (1965), 7.

23 PHILOSOPHIZING OUT IN THE WORLD

1 Norman Malcolm, *Ludwig Wittgenstein: a Memoir* (London, Oxford University Press, 1958), p. 39.
2 This was the point that always occupied R. G. Collingwood; see for instance his *Autobiography* (Oxford, Oxford University

Press, 1939), chapters 5 and 6, and the opening sections of his *An Essay on Metaphysics* (Oxford, Clarendon Press, 1940).

3 See Colin M. Turnbull, *The Human Cycle* (London, Jonathan Cape, 1984), p. 105.

4 See, for instance, Plato, *Gorgias*, sections 457–8, *Theaetetus*, sections 172–6, *Republic*, sections 498–500.

5 I. Kant, *Groundwork of the Metaphysic of Morals*, trans. H. Paton under the title of *The Moral Law* (London, Hutchinson, 1948), p. 74.

INDEX

action, 13, 21, 157–8, 191
analysis, philosophical, 23, 59, 110, 221, *see also* linguistic movement
anecdotal evidence, 53–4
Anthropic Principle, 9, 128, 133
anti-naturalism, in ethics, 162, 174
Archimedes, 135
architecture, modern, 25, 214; as image for structures of thought, *see* metaphors
Aristotle, 12, 49, 67, 151, 176, 185
art, 82, 152–3, 211
atomic facts, 221; *see also* facts
atomism, logical, 139, 221; metaphysical, 186, 202, 221; physical, 218.
Augustine, St, 115, 133, 188
Austin, J. L., 101, 208, 256
autonomy, 57–8, 74–82, 88
Ayer, Sir Alfred, 111, 138, 139, 147, 187

Bambrough, Renford, 118
Bauhaus, 180, 213, 214; *see also* architecture
behaviourism, 4, 48, 119, 140
Bennett, Jonathan, 172
Bentham, Jeremy, 150, 164, 165
Berkeley, Bishop George, 138, 197, 199, 217–18, 222–3
Bernal, J. D., 25, 85, 133
biology, 72, 84, 87, 192

blame, 162–74
Bloomsbury, 127, 152
Boswell, James, 156, 167
Bradley, F. H., 103, 205, 209
Boyle, Robert, 197
Butler, Bishop Joseph, 145, 168

Cartesianism, 36–7, 107, 124–31, 134–8, 140–2, 177–9, 186, 217–19, 225, 229–33
certainty, 36–7, 116–17, 126–31, 134–6, 142
Chain, Professor Ernest, 74, 79, 80
Cherry-Garrard, Apsley, 15–16
city of organized thought, 23, 28, 29, 52, 62; *see also* architecture
clarity, as dominant philosophic ideal, 97, 102, 206, 211, 215, 220–1
Cogito 135
Collingwood, R. G. 19, 33, 207
common sense, 144, 175, 186, 204, 212, 226–8, 241; *see also* everyday thinking
conceptual schemes, 48, 124, 155, 175
contemplation, 12–13, 41, 134, 150–2
controversies, 63–6, 70, 107, 240–4, 246
Cornford, F. M., 55
Cromwell, Oliver, 66, 68
curiosity, 39–40, 42–5, 105

271

Socrates, 71, 96–9, 104, 139,
    244–5, 250, 253
solipsism, 126, 228–9, 233
solitude, metaphysical, 219, 225
specialization, 4, 43, 48–9, 56, 88,
    94, 105, 121, 148, 203, 246–9
Spinoza, 12, 49, 107, 137, 162
Stevenson, C. L., 159–162, 187
subjectivism, 34, 37–8, 52, 161
symbolism, 48, 133
symbiosis in controversy, 245–8
systems, *see* thought-systems

teaching, 7, 10, 61, 63; of
    philosophy, 94–102, 249–53, *see
    also* therapeutic model
theology, 10, 24, 81, 140, 172
therapeutic model of teaching, 97,
    187–8, 256
Thomism, 122, 207–8
thought-systems, 49, 56, 86,
    122–5, 130, 177, 180–4, 198, 215
Tolstoy, Leo, 189, 190, 191
tools, 193–4 *see also* metaphors
Tractatus Logico-philosophicus, 27,
    138, 141, 186–7, 190, 191–4, 212,
    215, 220–1, 237
transcendent value, 151, *see also*
    value
truisms, 226–35
truth, 36, 65, 75, 110, 136, 141,
    176, 235, 244, *see also* half-truths
truthfulness, 110
Turnbull, Colin, 244

understanding, 8, 28, 40–5, 64,
    128, 222; refusal to do so used as
    ploy in argument, 188

values, 14–17, 24, 28–9, 75, 111,
    152, 165, 242; and love, 38–40; *see
    also* facts
verification, 86, 139
Voltaire, 121

Waddington, C. H., 24–8, 80, 85
Warnock, Geoffrey, 156
Weinberg, Steven, 28, 43
Wells, H. G., 3, 10, 254
Whitehead, Alfred North, 147,
    182
wholeness, 4, 39, 94, 106, 224
Wilkins, Sir Maurice, 39
Williams, Bernard, 146, 154, 169,
    173
Wilson, Edward O., 15, 17, 18,
    43, 68
wisdom, 12, 17–18, 20–2, 45,
    76–9, 93, 96, 118, 168, 213, 253
Wisdom, John, 256
Wittgenstein, Ludwig, 26–7, 37,
    68–9, 95, 100–1, 108–9, 117–18,
    123, 128, 130, 138, 145, 153,
    168, 184, 186, 194, 208, 223–31,
    237
Wolfe, Tom, 213, 214
wonder, 41, 57, 202, 253
Woolf, Leonard, 158, 188